1988

writing
to
be
read

HAYDEN ENGLISH LANGUAGE SERIES

Robert W. Boynton—Consulting Editor

Principal of the Senior High School
Germantown Friends School

AN INTRODUCTION TO MODERN ENGLISH GRAMMAR
J. Malmstrom

LANGUAGE IN SOCIETY
J. Malmstrom

THE DICTIONARY AND THE LANGUAGE
R. Lodwig and E. Barrett

WRITING TO BE READ
K. Macrorie

KEN MACRORIE

Professor of English
Western Michigan University

writing
to
be
read

HAYDEN BOOK COMPANY, INC., NEW YORK

The author would like to thank the proprietors for permission to quote from copyrighted works, as follows:

PHILIP BOOTH: "First Lesson" from *Letter from a Distant Land* by Philip Booth. Copyright © 1957 by Philip Booth. Reprinted by permission of The Viking Press, Inc.

RAY BRADBURY: from "Seeds of Three Stories," written for *On Writing, By Writers*, William W. West, Editor; copyright 1966 by Ginn and Company. Reprinted by permission of the publisher.

SAMUEL BUTLER: from *The Complete Works of Samuel Butler* and *The Notebooks of Samuel Butler*, published by Jonathan Cape Ltd. Reprinted by permission of the Executors of the Samuel Butler Estate.

TRUMAN CAPOTE: from *Writers at Work, The Paris Review Interviews*, edited by Malcolm Cowley. Copyright © 1957, 1958, by The Paris Review, Inc. Reprinted by permission of The Viking Press, Inc.

STUART CHASE: from "Writing Nonfiction," written for *On Writing, By Writers*, William W. West, Editor; copyright 1966 by Ginn and Company. Reprinted by permission of the publisher.

JOHN CIARDI: from "Work Habits of Writers," written for *On Writing, By Writers*, William W. West, Editor; copyright 1966 by Ginn and Company. Reprinted by permission of the publisher.

SIDNEY COX: from *Indirections for Those Who Want to Write*. Reprinted with permission of the publisher. Published by Alfred A. Knopf, Inc. Copyright © 1947 by Alfred A. Knopf, Inc.

T. S. ELIOT: from *Writers at Work, The Paris Review Interviews*, Second Series, Copyright © 1963 by The Paris Review, Inc. Reprinted by permission of The Viking Press, Inc.

PAUL GOODMAN: from *Growing Up Absurd*. Reprinted by permission of the publisher. Copyright © 1956, 1957, 1958, 1959, 1960 by Paul Goodman. Published by Random House, Inc.

MICHIHIKO HACHIYA: from *Hiroshima Diary*, published by the University of North Carolina Press, reprinted by permission of The University of North Carolina Press.

JAMES D. HART: from *Oxford Companion to American Literature*, Fourth Edition. Reprinted by permission of the publisher. Copyright 1965 by Oxford University Press.

ERNEST HEMINGWAY: from *Writers at Work, The Paris Review Interviews*, Second Series, Copyright © 1963 by The Paris Review, Inc. Reprinted by permission of The Viking Press, Inc.

LOIS PHILLIPS HUDSON: "When the Fields Are Fresh and Green," from *Reapers of the Dust*, published by Atlantic, Little, Brown and Co. Copyright © 1957, 1958, 1959, 1960, 1961, 1962, 1963, 1964 by Lois Phillips Hudson. Permission granted by Atlantic, Little, Brown and Co.

DONALD KEENE: translation of Haiku poem by Kato Shuson from *Modern Japanese Literature*, an anthology com-

Printed in the United States of America

Fourth Printing, 1969

piled and edited by Donald Keene, published by Grove Press. Reprinted by permission of Grove Press, Inc. Copyright © 1956 by Grove Press, Inc.

DOROTHY LAMBERT: "What Is a Journal?" an unpublished MS substantially the same as "Keeping a Journal," published in the *English Journal*, February, 1967, reprinted with the permission of the National Council of Teachers of English and Dorothy Lambert.

ALAN LEVY, BERNARD KRISHER, AND JAMES COX: from *Draftee's Confidential Guide,* published by New American Library, Signet Books. Published by Indiana University Press. Reprinted by permission of Indiana University Press.

WALTER LIPPMANN: from *Public Opinion,* published by The Macmillan Company, copyright 1922 by Walter Lippmann. Reprinted by permission of The Macmillan Company.

ROBERT LIPSYTE: "Mets Beat Giants 8–6 on Swoboda's Homer in 9th," © 1966 by The New York Times Company. Reprinted by permission.

MARIANNE MOORE: from *Writers at Work, The Paris Review Interviews,* Second Series, Copyright © 1963 by The Paris Review, Inc. Reprinted by permission of The Viking Press, Inc.

A. A. MILNE: "The End" from *Now We Are Six,* published by E. P. Dutton & Co., Inc. Copyright 1927 by E. P. Dutton & Co., Inc., © 1955 by A. Milne.

The New Republic: "T.R.B. from Washington" reprinted by permission of *The New Republic,* © 1966, Harrison-Blaine of New Jersey, Inc.

McCANDLISH PHILLIPS: "There's Never a Quiet Moment on W. 15th St." © 1966 by The New York Times Company. Reprinted by permission.

MIKE RECHT: "Mets Shock Giants with Swoboda's Pinch Homer," reprinted with permission of The Associated Press.

G. B. SHAW: from *The Quintessence of Ibsenism,* published by Constable & Co., Ltd., permission of The Public Trustee and The Society of Authors.

JEAN SHEPHERD: "A Midtown Stroll After Midnight," by Jean Shepherd. Reprinted from *The New York Guidebook* edited by John A. Kouwenhoven, Copyright © 1964 by John A. Kouwenhoven and used by permission of the publisher, Dell Publishing Co., Inc.

WILLIAM STAFFORD: from "Writing the Australian Crawl" from *College Composition and Communication,* February, 1964, reprinted with the permission of the National Council of Teachers of English and William Stafford.

WALLACE STEVENS: from *Opus Posthumous,* reprinted with permission of the publisher. Copyright 1957. Published by Alfred A. Knopf, Inc.

ROBERT LOUIS STEVENSON: From "A College Magazine" from *Complete Works of Robert Louis Stevenson,* published by Charles Scribner's Sons.

CHRISTOPHER ST. JOHN: from *Ellen Terry and Bernard Shaw: A Correspondence,* edited by Christopher St. John, published by Constable & Co., Ltd., by permission of The Public Trustee and The Society of Authors.

MAY SWENSON: "The Centaur" (Copyright © 1956 May Swenson) is reprinted with the permission of Charles Scribner's Sons from *To Mix with Time* by May Swenson.

T. R. TEMPLE: " 's' Vonderful," reprinted by permission of *The New Republic,* © 1966, Harrison-Blaine of New Jersey, Inc.

JAMES THURBER: from *Writers at Work, The Paris Review Interviews,* edited by Malcolm Cowley. Copyright © 1957, 1958 by The Paris Review, Inc. Reprinted by permission of The Viking Press, Inc.

WILLIAM CARLOS WILLIAMS: "Poem" from *The Collected Earlier Poems of William Carlos Williams.* Copyright © 1938, 1951 by William Carlos Williams. Reprinted by permission of New Directions Publishing Corporation. "The Dance" from *The Collected Later Poems of William Carlos Williams.* Copyright 1944 by William Carlos Williams.

preface

American taxpayers are paying money to support the teaching of writing which no one wants to read. In English classes most students write dead-end themes. The teachers complain about having to read them and the students never pass them around to their fellows except to solicit aid in grammar, punctuation, or spelling.

Why all this production of writing which carries little meaning or delight? I think for three principal reasons:

1. Teachers have been saying, "Wrong! wrong! wrong!" when they should have been saying, "Right! good! keep going!" even if they said it about only one word or one sentence in a paper.

2. In their study of English, teachers have spent their time reading, not writing. They need to understand and present to their students more fully the processes through which professionals take their writing.

3. English teachers have often allowed themselves to be the only readers students write for. All the students in a class should be readers and critics.

Writing reflects a person's thoughts, feelings, and style of life. It is more an extension of a man's complete self than most other acts. Strong criticism may destroy a beginning writer. He should have achieved some solid successes, however small, in his peers' judgment and his own, before he is subjected to comprehensive negative criticism.

This book shows teachers how to train students to become helpful critics of each other's writing, and how to act as editors rather than correctors, leading a student through draft after draft of his writing until it becomes a work hard for the reader to put down.

A large number of examples in this book were written by students who wrote through the program presented here. Each time this program has been used—whether by teachers in eighth grade or graduate school—it has produced dozens of pieces of good writing. That is the only valid test of a writing course: does it bring forth from every student writing that is alive and valuable?

acknowledgments

Most of the examples of good writing cited in this book are the work of students who have followed part of the program it embodies. Some wrote in my classes; some wrote in classes conducted by participants in the NDEA Institute for High School English Teachers at Western Michigan University in the summer of 1966. Originally I had intended to name all persons whose writing appears in these pages, but when I found that fairness, consistency, comprehensiveness, or discretion had to be disregarded again and again, I decided to name only writers of long pieces, and even then to omit some of those in the interest of protecting them from the perils of truthtelling. I thank all these writers for their contributions.

Among Michigan teachers who sent me writing by their students were Will Brenner, East Grand Rapids High School and Grand Rapids Junior College; Barbara Davis, Charlotte High School; Jean Morell, Portage Central High School; Agnes Haynes, Wayne Memorial High School; Dennis H. Mulder, Grand Rapids Central Christian High School; Bonnie Burd, Northwestern High School, Detroit; Martha Hulings, Ravenna Public Schools; Ruth Hildebrand, Lakeview High School; Katherine Limpus, Portage Northern High School; and Robert Heaton, Reeths-Puffer High School, Muskegon. Sister Mary Lois Glonek of Greater Muskegon Catholic Central High School and Garry Meyers of Westport (Connecticut) Public Schools supplied several of the statements about writing by writers.

My special thanks to John Bennett, for furnishing hundreds of examples of lively writing by his students at Central High School, Kalamazoo, and to Robert Boynton of the Germantown Friends School, Philadelphia, for helping to remove corn shucks from the book.

The notion of free writing, so fundamental to the program presented here, comes from a suggestion to persons who want to become professional writers made by Dorothea Brande in *Becoming a Writer* (Harcourt, Brace, 1934).

K.M.

contents

chapter 1

the language in you

THOUSANDS of persons in the United States believe they don't know how to write well. But look at what children do. A third-grade girl writes:

> **When mother fride my egg this morning it limbered out like corn surp. Then it got buggles. They went up, then went down, like breethen heavy.**

The writer surprised the reader with an original use of the verb *limber,* meaning to become supple or flexible. She compared the movement of the egg to the slow spreading of corn syrup in a pan. She invented her own term, *buggles* (playing on *bubbles*), and showed she knew what she was talking about. She compactly described the movement of a frying egg. This passage is not only fresh and surprising but precise and true. It puts the reader there, watching the egg and feeling its action through his own experience, "like breethen heavy."

1

At times every young child makes memorable statements in writing or speaking. But as he advances in school, his language turns ever duller and emptier. By the time he becomes a senior in high school, he is often submitting papers to his teacher which sound like this:

> **I consider experience to be an important part in the process of learning. For example, in the case of an athlete, experience plays an important role. After each game, he tends to acquire more knowledge and proficiency, thereby making him a better athlete. An athlete could also gain more knowledge by studying up on the sport, but it is doubtful if he could participate for the first time in sport with study alone and without experience and still do an adequate job.**

The writer says nothing new—athletes learn by experience. And he does not put the reader there, watching a player bunt foul or tackle a halfback. A five-year-old boy at breakfast says, "The Rice Krispies are doing the dead man's float." He doesn't tell the reader anything new either, but he speaks originally. With the metaphor he puts the reader in the milk.

A second-grader told to quiet her feet in class said, "They're too Saturday to listen." She expected the listener to make the jump necessary to understand her metaphor. The boy writing about athletes expected nothing of his reader.

A sixth-grader wrote a letter to the custodian of a state park who had showed his class around:

> **Dear Mr. Lemmien,**
> **I liked the trailer ride and the dips got my stomach. Thank you for everything.**
>
> >   **Your Friend,**
> >   **David Booth**

David communicated a significant moment in five short words: "the dips got my stomach." The word *dips* gives the passage authority. The sentence is believable, unforgettable. None of the sentences in the writing about athletes carries as much meaning.

Young children do not always talk and write with such point and liveliness, but they do so often enough that their parents repeat their sayings and writings to other persons with delight. When these children grow up and become high school and college students, they seldom turn in writing that is memorable. Yet outside class, they often use language with power. A student poster for a dance reads:

35¢ Stag. 50¢ Drag.

Metaphor. Rhyme. Economy in words.

Entering the school cafeteria, a girl says that she can't see a clear table. Her friend answers:

> I don't see one either. It's like looking for your best friend at the Rose Bowl on T.V.

At times you have spoken and written skillfully. You can rediscover your tongue—if you've lost it—and bring your writing to life. One way is to take the pressure off for a while. In schoolrooms where students have been asked to write freely, they have written like this:

> I like to go fishing. But I don't like to touch the soft, elongated, repulsive nightcrawlers. They wiggle and contract themselves. Then I can't grab the one I want. Of all the other things in this world I can't stand, baiting the hook is the worst. It's like giving a shot. Sometimes the hook won't go through the worm's wrinkled, slimy body. Then I have to wiggle and force it. That's like stepping on a cockroach and hearing the bones crack, or piercing a stubborn earlobe.
>
> GERTIE BAX

> The wooden bars on the chair look like prison bars as they reflect on the floor from the light. I was in trouble once and getting into trouble makes a person feel bad that it happened and that it never should have happened but it did and there is no way around. I had to sit in a room for three hours waiting, hoping that my brother would be all right and hoping the other boy was too, although from those minutes on, I knew I hated him. Only a chair, a desk, and a man saying, "I'll be back in about a half hour," which really became three. I had to sweat it out walking back and forth in the room with nothing to look at but four lousy walls, I wanted to get out. I wanted them to come and get me out of there. Thoughts passed through my mind as I sat there in the only chair. Chairs can be made to look like different things when their shadow is lying on the floor. The chair over there in the corner looks like part of a ladder. The chair in the police station was uncomfortable and I couldn't sit in it. It was a cheap looking chair in a cheap looking room meant for people who are wrong.
>
> (NAME WITHHELD)

A girl once told her teacher that she couldn't write any kind of paper because she had been raised in a Polish-speaking home and couldn't compose sentences in idiomatic English. Encouraged to write freely of what she cared about, she wrote this of her father:

> **The only difference between him and a lion is that a lion does not laugh. Upon meeting up with him, one most naturally will see the strict lines on his face and his mouth set just so. He may appear tough, but he also has the devil in him. His appearance is stirring. He looks like a foreign foreigner. His voice is low and scary. It really frightens my friends, even male ones. Sometime when I call to say I may be home later, he answers the phone with a deep, husky, and broken "Haaallooo" and I feel I should apologize for calling.**
>
> (NAME WITHHELD)

Outside of class, and in the years of childhood, you and every other person have at times expressed yourself forcefully, with art. It is nonsense to say you cannot do that again when you want to.

> *Man's maturity: to have regained the seriousness that he had as a child at play.*
> FRIEDRICH NIETZSCHE

COLLECTING ONE: Listen for what children say and look for what they write. Use a tape recorder if available. Write down five statements you think are memorable. Include the age of the child if possible and the situation in which he spoke or wrote. Ask your parents if they remember a phrase you spoke when you were young. Perhaps they preserved a bit of your writing. Record children's statements that are remarkable because they reveal freshness, accuracy, and invention in language. Do not record statements that are humorous only because the child speaks out of ignorance of the world or of language.

On a huge hill,
Cragged and steep, Truth stands, and he
that will
Reach her, about must, and about must
go . . .

JOHN DONNE

chapter 2

writing
freely

TELLING THE TRUTH

ALL GOOD writers speak in honest voices and tell the truth. For example, here is Eudora Welty in her novel *Delta Wedding* writing about India, a girl of nine, watching her Uncle George make up with his wife after a quarrel:

> Just now they kissed, with India coming up close on her toes to see if she could tell yet what there was about a kiss.

Asked what makes students write badly, Eudora Welty once said:

> The trouble with bad student writing is the trouble with all bad writing. It is not serious, and it does not tell the truth.

This is the first requirement for good writing: truth; not *the* truth (whoever knows surely what that is?), but some kind of truth—a connection between the things written about, the words used in the writing, and the author's real experience in the world he knows well —whether in fact or dream or imagination.

Part of growing up is learning to tell lies, big and little, sophisticated and crude, conscious and unconscious. The good writer differs from the bad one in that he constantly tries to shake the habit. He holds himself to the highest standard of truth telling. Often he

5

emulates children, who tell the truth so easily, partly because they do not sense how truth will shock their elders.

A seventh-grade boy once wrote:

> **I'd like to be a car. You get to go all over and get to go through mud puddles without getting yelled at . . . that's what I'd like to be.**

The style of this passage is not distinguished. *Get* is here not a key word and yet it is employed three times. The writer switches confusingly from *I* to *you*. The language of the passage is not exciting. No memorable pictures are projected. Yet the statement strikes with force because the boy speaks truly: his shoes and the tires of the car do become muddy. He gets yelled at by his parents and the car does not. The comparison surprises. Its candor draws a smile from the reader.

> *I never think I have hit it hard unless it rebounds.*
>
> SAMUEL JOHNSON

Any person trying to write honestly and accurately soon finds he has already learned a hundred ways of writing falsely. As a child he spoke and wrote honestly most of the time, but when he reaches fifteen, honesty and truth come harder. The pressures on his ego are greater. He reaches for impressive language; often it is pretentious and phony. He imitates the style of adults, who are often bad writers themselves. They ask questions. So he asks questions in his writing: "Did you ever think what might have happened to South Africa if the Boer War had not been fought?" A false question. The writer knows most—if not all—of his readers have not thought of this possibility. However well meant—a false question. In class this person is anxious to impress the teacher, so he begins his paper by saying:

> **The automobile is a mechanism fascinating to everyone in all its diverse manifestations and in every conceivable kind of situation or circumstance.**

His first remark is simply untrue. Cars do not fascinate everyone.

In this paper the writer has placed his vocabulary on exhibit (*mechanism, diverse, manifestations, conceivable, situation, circumstance*) rather than put it to work. An honest writer makes every word pull its weight. In this writer's opening sentence, the words *kind of* are not working at all. They could be dropped with no loss. What does he mean by "all the diverse manifestations" of a car? Cars don't occur in manifestations but in models. If the cars he is referring to are custom-made and not strictly speaking "models," then he should say he is writing about hybrid cars. At the opening of his paper, his reader has no inkling that he is talking about home-made cars. And nothing could be more untrue than the thought conveyed by the last phrase—that everyone finds cars fascinating "in every conceivable kind of situation or circumstance." When the valves need regrinding at 17,000 miles at a cost of $125.00, even the car lover finds his loved one repulsive.

Compare this writer's pretentious and untrue statement about cars with this account:

> Thundering down a Northern Michigan highway at night I am separated from the rest of the world. The windows of the cars are all rolled down and the wind makes a deep rumbling as the car rises and falls with the dips in the pavement. The white center lines come out of the darkness ahead into the beams of the headlights only to disappear again under the front edge of the hood. The lights also pick up trees, fenceposts, and an occasional deer or raccoon standing by the roadside, but like the white lines they come into view only for a few seconds and then are lost in the blackness behind me. The only signs I have that any world exists outside the range of the headlights are the continuous cheerping and buzzing of the crickets and the smells from farms and sulphur pits I pass. But the rushing wind soon clears out these odors, leaving me by myself again to listen to the quickly passing crickets I will never see. The faint green lights and the red bar on the dashboard tell me I'm plunging ahead at 90 m.p.h.; I put more pressure on the pedal under my foot; the bar moves up to 100 . . . 110. The lines flash by faster and the roar of the wind drowns out the noise of the crickets and the night. I am flying through. I can feel the vibrations of the road through the steering wheel. I turn the wheel slightly for the gradual curve ahead and then back again for the long straightaway. I press the pedal to the floor and at the same time reach down to touch the buttons on my left that will roll up the windows for more speed; the bar reads 115 . . . 120, buried. With the windows up, the only sound is the high-pitched moan from the engine as it labors to keep the rest of the machine hurtling blindly ahead like a runaway express

train. Only I have the power to control it. I flick on the brights to advance my scope of vision and the white lines come out of the black further up ahead, yet because of the speed, they're out of sight even faster than before. I am detached from the rest of the world as it blurs past. I am alone.

HENRY HALL JAMES

This boy may have been driving at an immorally high speed—even for a relatively uninhabited region—but he was writing morally, because he was staying true to the feel of his experience. Writing this way requires a quick jump in the car and a zooming away before one remembers all the driving habits he has picked up watching bad older drivers. Try writing for truth.

Never say that you feel a thing unless you feel it distinctly; and if you do not feel it distinctly, say at once that you do not as yet quite know your own mind.

SAMUEL BUTLER

WRITING FREELY WITHOUT FOCUS

WRITING ONE: Write for ten minutes as fast as you can, never stopping to ponder a thought. Put down whatever comes to your mind. If nothing comes, write, "Nothing comes to my mind" until you get started. Or look in front of you or out the window and begin describing whatever you see. Let yourself wander to any subject, feeling, or idea, but keep writing. When ten minutes is up, you should have filled a large notebook-sized page. Remember you are hitting practice shots. If what you write is bad or dull, no one will object.

Save all the writing which you produce while reading this book. Keep it in a manila filing folder so you can go back to it to revise it or look for paragraphs or pages that may be combined or expanded into stronger work. As time passes, you will see your words differently and sometimes learn from them without doing further work.

Here's what one student wrote in ten minutes:

I still haven't gotten used to the dull routine of school. I still feel like I should sleep in the morning until I wake up—naturally. Usually the only things that get me up, even naturally, are an empty stomach and a full bladder. I haven't seen half the new TV shows yet. Those that I have

> seen don't look too horribly bad. It's funny how the week-
> ends always have the worst TV and the weekdays the best.
> My aunt's been in the hospital lately, so all my cousins
> are over. It's funny how all these "little kids" are now all
> grown up and almost ready for high school. I can still
> remember when I, as the "big cousin," always directed the
> tricycle rides up the street, always got to carry the money
> out to the popsicle man, and always got to go to the Santa
> Claus parade and stand on Grandma's shoulders while the
> rest groveled underneath.

That free writing probably kept your attention because it was honest, but it is not memorable. You will probably remember the following free writing longer. In the third sentence the writer says, "this time" and with that phrase begins to tell a story. Most good writing, fiction or nonfiction, depends a great deal on stories—a long story, or maybe a number of little stories used as examples. Professional writers know The Secret of Once. It opens a writer and gets him going, telling of this real object and that uttered word, and soon he has created a world which compels his reader to enter it. For example:

> My Grandma and Grandpa had always lived on a farm in
> Alabama. I used to love to go there when I was young. I
> loved the cows and chickens and the smell of grass. But this
> time things were different; I didn't smell the grass, or see
> the cows, or hear the chickens. Everything was still. The
> funeral was held the day after we arrived. I couldn't un-
> derstand why one bunch of ladies sat around the body
> until I heard them talking. They talked about who cried
> the longest and who cried the least. I hear the same bunch
> gets around to all the funerals.

That statement impresses but does not let the reader touch a cow or hear one chicken's feet scraping the doorsill of a particular chicken coop. And it doesn't tell who died.

A good part of the time he is writing, a writer must sense his reader out there. The poet William Stafford said, "When you write, simply tell me something." Vague advice, but valid. In a sense a writer becomes his own reader while he writes. He talks to his reader and hears that talk himself. When you acquire that knack, other persons will come along with you. Easy as this habit is to learn, many persons never learn it. They are like those who try to turn a piece of pottery on the wheel and never create a cup which holds coffee.

The following free writing forgets the reader out there, talks big, but does not tell the reader enough. It does not employ The Secret of Once.

> I don't want to grow up yet! I'm too young to be burdened with all the responsibilities of adulthood. Someday I'll get married and have a home and children of my own, but for now, I'm going to enjoy every moment of my youth in freedom.
>
> I want to be an unique individual. I spent much of my junior high years trying to act mature, seldom allowing my real self to emerge for fear of non acceptance. I only succeeded in mimicking others. Life is so brief. When I think of all the time I've already wasted conforming, it makes me sad.

Mr. Stafford would say, "Tell me something you did." This writing lacks an authentic voice. No individual person seems to be speaking, but rather a recording of excerpts from textbooks and magazine articles about contemporary youth. In contrast, here is a real girl speaking:

> Everyone around here is having an awful time getting along with me. I'm being positively intolerable. Mom is trying really hard not to say anything in the wrong tone of voice, so that I feel kind of—what's that old-fashioned word, *ashamed* of myself. One day I'm in a great mood, and you could yell at me all you wanted without making me mad or hurt. The next day (or the next hour for that matter) you could say "Good morning," then yawn, and I'd burst into tears. I suppose that is not awfully abnormal (at least that's what Mom says—in her psychological tone, "It's just a phase. You'll grow out of it.") By the way, that makes me mad, too. I don't like to have my life summed up in a series of phases. It seems like she's saying, "You can't help acting like an idiot. It comes natural at this age. But don't worry, you'll outgrow it. It'll pass."

The writer of the next statement used The Secret of Once and puts the reader in the situation.

> He swore at me. It was the first time he ever had. I deserved it but that didn't lessen the shock any. I had gone out on him, then lied to him about it. It was always easy

for me to bring on tears when I was hurt by his actions, but this time I'd hurt him. I couldn't feel sorry for myself. My eyes burned. My fingers picked at my knee. I kept twisting my ring around my finger while he repeatedly and very calmly asked me to please get out. The quiet summer night and full moon seemed to mock my every word. Ironic. I wanted to explain but I couldn't. I wanted him to hold me but he seemed repulsed at my touch. I couldn't leave. Earlier, I could have tossed my head, laughed it off, maybe saved face. But I confessed. Playing on his mercy. He wasn't being merciful. Disgusted, as his elbow brushed my knee, he leaned over and shoved open the door. When I look at the black scar in the street, I can always hear the screaming tires and feel the force of his arm.

Most of these ten-minute free writings keep the reader awake. At times disconnected and perhaps meaningless for a reader, they are full of surprise, as so much writing is not. Some of their surprises came because the writers were not trying hard, but riding with the waves, letting strange and exciting things drift up from the bottom. Most are not finished pieces of writing to be published for an audience, but they come alive.

WRITING TWO: Write three or more of these absolutely free writings. Choose times when no one will disturb you, before breakfast or late at night perhaps. Go beyond ten minutes if the river keeps flowing. But don't expect anything. You're just warming up. Maybe none of your ten-minute writings will produce an interesting sentence. Don't worry. Write. And don't think about punctuation or grammar or style. Put down one word as a sentence if you wish. Maybe your writing will be completely uninteresting to others. As long as you are trying to write honestly and you are writing fast and steadily to fill up a page or two without stopping, you are practicing.

WRITING FREELY WITH FOCUS

Free writing is practice. It involves no pressure on the practicer. It never requires perfection. If the practicer goofs, he has not lost the game or produced a work disgraceful in the public eye. He can forget the bad shots. They do not penalize him. If a writer produces a good passage, he can show it to other persons because he has it down on paper. He is luckier than the golfer, who cannot take a shot off the practice tee home to show his family.

After a game of golf, an amateur spends hours complaining that he missed three short putts. Before a game of golf, a professional spends hours in putting practice. If he hits bad putts, he tries a different stroke, and when he finds one that produces good putts, he grooves it.

WRITING THREE: Now try free writing with more purpose. Stay on one subject as the writer did when she said that everyone thought she was being positively intolerable. But if you find that subject takes your mind off to another related subject, let yourself go to that. The one necessity in such practice is that you keep writing freely and quickly.

> *Thought is an infection. In the case of certain thoughts it becomes an epidemic.*
>
> WALLACE STEVENS

Here is a free focused writing:

> The building was old and dingy. We opened the doors and an even older odor hit us; it smelled of must. I followed the group closely. I was afraid of this quiet solitary place. I walked through the halls peeking around every corner cautiously. I might bump into one of them. Through every open door I saw their faces and bodies. In beds. Sitting looking out windows. Holding dolls, silently humming. I couldn't understand. Would I end up here some day? I'd rather die. Being old was a torture, not the pleasure I'd thought it to be.
>
> After a slight tour of the building, we stopped to eat our sack-lunches. The food didn't taste very good. It was dried-up and molded—I couldn't erase the feeling. Even the bathrooms provided were old like the people using them. Oh God, I prayed, why do they have to live on?
>
> The clocks seemed to never move. Suddenly, walking through a sun-deck, I found her grabbing at me. Her bony little fingers clutched my arm. I was afraid. I imagined her bones cutting into my flesh. I wanted to jerk away. I looked in her face for a long time; she just stared. Her eyes were the first young things I'd seen. They reflected my friends and me. I saw it coming. I understood. That one big tear made everything clear. How much I loved her. She tried to

rise. Her clumsy bars wouldn't let her. It was like she knew she'd die there. She touched my hair. "Angel-hair," she said. All I could hear as I walked away were sobs.

JANE LENARDSON

This passage speaks with authority. The writer passed on to her reader enough of what made her respond so that he could respond also. She found surprising realities and communicated them: old ladies holding dolls, young eyes in an aged head.

Free writing is random rehearsal. Don't let it become dress rehearsal or first night. If you insist that you speak in an honest, not phony, voice, and you write freely and fast, you will write foolishly at times, and at other times with astonishing wisdom.

Here is another focused free writing:

I keep slugging that yellow rubber ball harder and harder. It's tattooed by the skin off my knuckles and comes back for another mark. My hands sting. The kids behind the net can't return those hard balls. Sweating. I gulp down a cold Coke and go over to the trampoline. This web is huge and the air belching from the pressure of bouncing bodies cools me off. It's my turn to show off. As I jump, my sweatshirt parachutes and my jeans come unsnapped. Enough of that. I charge Mike just as he throws a long pass at the rim of the basket. He misses. I run after it and bounce it in. Mike grabs it and I'm right behind him trying to steal it. I sink it from the middle of the floor. Stop it! Girls aren't supposed to do that.

> *If you have had your attention directed to the novelties in thought in your own lifetime, you will have observed that almost all really new ideas have a certain aspect of foolishness when they are first produced, and almost any idea which jogs you out of your current abstractions may be better than nothing.*
>
> ALFRED NORTH WHITEHEAD

As you dash off these writings, don't plan ahead. Write. Spill out whatever comes to mind and eye. Put down honestly what you feel and see. A day after you have finished them, read them over aloud and underline those sentences which you think say something alive for a reader. If you find no such sentences, don't despair. Keep writing. If you find a great many consecutively lively lines, mark a vertical pencil stroke next to them in the margin. Soon you will be writing more and more good lines.

> . . . *what is always provocative in a work of art: roughness of surface. While . . . [these writings] pass under our eyes they are full of dents and grooves and lumps and spikes which draw from us little cries of approval and disapproval.*
>
> E. M. FORSTER

Here is a young hunter's free focused writing. It speaks with terrifying truthfulness.

> I had always wanted a BB gun, but I never had one until now. We were going out to a friend's farm near Paw Paw and my dad bought me one to take along. At first I took it home to practice. I thought it was a big thing to hit an empty Joy bottle from twenty feet.
>
> After I got to the farm, the owner asked me to shoot some blackbirds for him. For a long time no blackbirds came around. At last one landed in a walnut tree in the yard. I walked under it quietly so I wouldn't scare it. The stupid thing just sat there begging to be shot. I fired my first shot. I saw the little gold BB fly past his head. Dumb bird. It still didn't move. I shot again and the bird's face reacted with pain. It fell over, hanging upside down by one foot from its branch. I shot again. It still hung there. I could see blood on its feathers even from where I stood. With the fourth shot it fell, its black feathers red.

Here is one more free focused statement by a beginning writer. In this book "beginning writer" refers to one who has not been frequently published. He may be talented but not yet know his worth because he has not received responses to his work from a number of persons. Most professional writers are often writing freely. When producing by steady daily effort, they frequently break a log jam in the river of their associations and find their thoughts and words flowing rapidly downstream. Making anything well is a combination of conscious and unconscious production.

He doesn't have legs. Not ones that feel or move. It's been that way almost four years now. Wheels. I was scared to talk at first, felt like a kid asking what it is that everyone's talking about. But we did. We used to goof around and tell dirty jokes. I always felt a little fake. Dan and I took him to the bathroom every day. Had to be done in a special way. Were there once. Dan asked a question. I don't remember. I answered, "What do you think I am, a cripple?" That's what I said. I didn't look at anyone, just the wall. For about half an hour, I felt very whole, but my stomach was tin foil. They were quiet, both of them. Quiet as being alone. I wished someone would cut off my arms.

> . . . I sometimes begin a drawing with no preconceived problem to solve, with only the desire to use pencil on paper and make lines, tones and shapes with no conscious aim; but as my mind takes in what is so produced a point arrives where some idea becomes conscious and crystallizes, and then a control and ordering begins to take place.
>
> HENRY MOORE, SCULPTOR

WRITING FOUR: Write freely for twenty or thirty minutes about something or somebody you stumbled upon once. Let yourself record the lumps and grooves, the dents and spikes.

chapter 3
what
is
good
writing?

ONE DAY Philip Booth took one of his three daughters out in the bay for her first swimming lesson. He intended to teach her to float. Later, he wrote this statement about the experience, which he hoped she would read when she was eighteen, or twenty-five, or sixty:

FIRST LESSON

Lie back, daughter, let your head
be tipped back in the cup of my hand.
Gently, and I will hold you. Spread
your arms wide, lie out on the stream
and look high at the gulls. A dead-
man's float is face down. You will dive
and swim soon enough where this tidewater
ebbs to the sea. Daughter, believe
me, when you tire on the long thrash

16

to your island, lie up, and survive.
As you float now, where I held you
and let go, remember when fear
cramps your heart what I told you:
lie gently and wide to the light-year
stars, lie back, and the sea will hold you.

This is good writing. It speaks tenderly without sentimentalizing. It puts the reader in real water—a tidewater bay where lying on her back Mr. Booth's daughter sees gulls. The writer does not kid himself or his daughter: she had better learn to float face up because a person who doesn't learn may float face down dead. A long swim to the island is not easy: she will thrash her way there.

Mr. Booth's statement is true to life. It does not waste words. Its verbs say a lot: *lie, let, tipped, hold, spread, lie out, look, is, dive, swim, ebbs, believe, tire, lie up, survive, float, held, let go, cramps, told, lie, lie, hold.* The verb *lie,* which embodies the father's principal command to his daughter, is repeated strongly.

> *There is no wing like meaning.*
>
> WALLACE STEVENS

Any kind of writing improves as it approaches the skills with which Mr. Booth wrote "First Lesson." For example, economy. The man who writes directions for opening and storing a jar of peanut butter improves as a writer as he learns to say more with fewer words. The writer for the Sears Roebuck catalog improves as he learns to dramatize more fully the product in use—to put the reader there, seeing and feeling what he will buy. Here is a good piece of writing from the *Sears Spring Through Summer Catalog,* 1966:

Dropped in mid-summer from a helicopter when loaded with 25 pounds of sand . . . also dropped when frozen at 20° below zero . . . IT BOUNCED." But Sears new exclusive Trash Can simply wouldn't break! (and because it's all heavy-weight plastic, there was *no noisy metallic clang*).

Sears Best . . . because of these important reasons:

Because Handy Bottom Grips plus side handles and lid handle for easy portability. No hand-cutting bail handle here.

Because friction-fit Top stays on without twisting, fits snugly without getting stuck.

> Because No Seams. Holds water, won't leak. The utility
> area stays cleaner . . . won't be as likely to attract pests.
>   Because Stands Boiling Water, "boiling" hot sun . . .
> "boiling" hot concrete. Made to withstand the weather.
>   Treated with SANI-GARD to retard odor and bacteria
> . . . Won't "pick up" odors . . . resists the growth of fungi,
> mildew and bacteria that cause them.

In some senses, Philip Booth's "First Lesson" cannot be compared
with an advertisement for a trash can; its intention is different, its
achievement greater. But the Sears writer comes closer to creating
good literature than many admen. He does not shoot off a roman
candle of unsupported adjectives—Magnificent! Unheard-of! Stupendous! Instead he tells clearly how the can was tested for durability.
Like Philip Booth he makes the reader believe, because the details he
presents suggest that he knows what he is talking about.

Writing a sports report, "Orioles' 16 Hits Rout Yanks, 9-4," for *The
New York Times*, August 11, 1966, Joseph Durso shows that like a
poet he knows how to make his words speak to each other as well as to
the reader:

> The barrage consisted of these consecutive elements: a
> triple to left by Russ Snyder (leading the Yankees to draw
> their infield in), a single past the infield by Frank Robin-
> son, a single past the infield by Brooks Robinson and a
> home run past everybody by Powell.

"Past the infield . . . past the infield . . . past everybody." Philip
Booth wrote: "Lie back . . . lie out . . . lie up . . . lie gently and wide
. . . lie back . . ."

Steve Smith begins his column "Sport" in *Car and Driver,* September, 1966, with this paragraph:

> After completing our six-car comparison road test (else-
> where in this issue), we started back to the city on the
> Long Island Expressway, known variously as the L.I. Dis-
> tressway, and the world's longest parking lot. It was a quiet
> Tuesday afternoon, so we weren't expecting much traffic.
> Soon, however, the three westbound lanes reached the
> saturation point, slowed to a crawl and then to a stop.
> Temperatures and tempers rose. Some of the traffic bled off
> onto the two-lane parallel service road, allowing about
> half-a-mile of progress before clotting. Somebody had the
> bright idea of trying three abreast, and traffic telescoped

another few hundred yards. In desperation, drivers veered off the roadway onto the center mall and the outside verge, becoming trapped by cars that had pulled off to let radiators cool. Finally, those that were able inched north and south the width of the island, then turned east. Within three hours, every major artery into the city was hopelessly snarled. Nothing moved. The System had broken down once again.

Mr. Smith cites two humorous names for the Long Island Expressway, employs sound beautifully in ending his sentence "slowed to a crawl and then to a stop" and makes the words *bled* and *clot* speak to each other in a metaphor. Like Mr. Booth he seldom uses dull and empty verbs like *have, make, is,* and *come.* Instead he says *telescoped, veered, trapped, pulled off, inched, snarled,* and *broken down.*

In *The Field Book of Ponds and Streams* (G. P. Putnam's Sons, 1930), Anne Haven Morgan writes:

> Mayfly nymphs are of many shapes and sizes; some have flattened heads and bodies and their sprawling legs are held akimbo as in *Heptagenia.* Active runners, like *Calliboetis,* are set high on spindling legs, while the little creeper, *Leptophlebia,* almost drags its low slung body.

Like Mr. Booth, Dr. Morgan employs adjectives that are not vague and inert, but precise and active: *flattened, sprawling, spindling, low slung.*

Guidebooks are usually crammed with fact but written without flavor. *The New York Guidebook* edited by John A. Kouwenhoven (Dell Publishing Company, 1964), includes a chapter by Jean Shepherd, a disc jockey, who writes:

> After midnight you can fuel up for your stroll at Riker's Corner House on the northeast corner of Sixth and 57th. By day it is filled with quick-lunch office types, but after midnight (it's an all-night, seven-day-a-week operation) there's as motley a crew as you can find this side of an average painting by Hieronymus Bosch. Good guys and bad guys, reverends and chicks, all assembled for a plate of scrambled eggs with onions, or a slab of chocolate cream pie. There are no tables, only a horseshoe-shaped counter, which is served from somewhere in the kitchen by an endless belt on a high podium in the center. At Christmastime the podium is covered with elves, brownies, and a tiny

electric train that I once saw derail and crash into seven
banana splits. The applause was deafening. In the spring,
this same treadmill is decorated with plastic daffodils and
rubber tulips, and so each succeeding season is celebrated
amid the hamburgers. It's the only way some of the customers can tell what time of year it is. Many of them have
not seen the sun since they were kids.

Before you start east on 57th, look up Sixth Avenue. Two
blocks north you will see the dark mass of Central Park,
unfortunately an excellent place to stay out of after dark.
There are romantics who will disagree with this. But there
are equally large numbers of experienced patrolmen and
unfortunates who have been mugged, who will tell you the
truth.

Like all good writers Mr. Shepherd chooses from his experience
what surprises him and will surprise his reader, and he delivers it in
sentences that hammer the surprise: ". . . a tiny electric train that I
once saw derail and crash into seven banana splits." He knows the
strategy of using unexpected words together: "each succeeding season
is celebrated amid the hamburgers." And he is not willing to gloss
over truth in order to make Central Park at night seem romantic to
tourists.

Writing is good not because of who writes it or where it appears.
Shakespeare and William Faulkner have written badly at times, and
good publishers have marketed bad work. Writing is good because
of what it says, how it opens up a world of ideas or fact for readers.
And how accurately and memorably it speaks, a voice issuing from
a human being who is fascinating, surprising, illuminating. But still
a man and a writer who does not always strike sparks.

> . . . *failure . . . is the poet's only real*
> *business. The one hope is for a better*
> *and better failure . . .*
>
> JOHN CIARDI

Most good writing is clear, vigorous, honest, alive, sensuous, appropriate, unsentimental, rhythmic, without pretension, fresh, metaphorical, evocative in sound, economical, authoritative, surprising,
memorable and light. If you set out to collect examples of good
writing you will be surprised to find how many writers you admire
are humorous or light. *Hamlet*, a story of decadence and tragedy, is

at the same time one of the lightest plays ever written. Mark Van Doren, a professor at Columbia University who encouraged many young persons in America to keep writing until they became successful authors, used to say in his literature classes that a great work of art possesses a quality of lightness. It is never like a ponderous public building that looks as if it is going to sink into the ground. Lightness can be achieved in many ways—by varying style; by continually lifting the reader with genuine, rather than trick, surprises; by not taking oneself too seriously for the circumstances. For example, directions for cooking need not be boring and deadly: Irma S. Rombauer and Marion Rombauer Becker take space in *The Joy of Cooking* to put some joy into their opening discussion of salads:

> I remember the final scene of a medieval Maeterlinck play. The stage is strewed with those dead or dying. The sweet young heroine whimpers, "I am not happy here." Then the head of the house, or what remains of it, an ancient noble, asks quaveringly, "Will there be a salad for supper?"

This in a cookbook. Here is a college teacher's dittoed instructions for her students:

> Trippers will meet at 7:15 (Kalamazoo time) in front of the Union. The bus will leave promptly at 7:30 a.m. There will be no watering stops between Kalamazoo and Chicago, so I strongly recommend that you all eat something vaguely resembling breakfast before we start—something substantial and comforting like a Hershey bar.
>
> At 11:15 (Chicago time) we will go en masse to the Berghoff for lunch. The Berghoff is a marvelous old German place where the food is good and the prices are low. I think that the $1.50 lunch will make you all feel genial and broad-minded about Chicago, the museum, and modern art.
>
> After lunch everyone is on his own in the museum. Museum fatigue is a very real phenomenon and I caution you to use some restraint in your viewing, taking the 20th century first and whatever else you can manage after that.

The teacher who wrote these directions did not strain to be funny; she simply let her own voice take over instead of the voice of doom we often take on when we feel ourselves in a position of authority.

We can all find an honest voice (yet different voices for different circumstances) in which we can speak with life and vigor. Alan Levy, Bernard Krisher, James Cox, and Richard Flaste, the writers of the

Signet paperback book *Draftee's Confidential Guide* (1966), succeeded in conveying wittily their honest feelings about life in the army. On the first page they said:

> This book is not an exposé; it won't tell you the Army is rotten. The Army isn't rotten. It varies from post to post, but in each place it's the product of our country's needs and of the people who are in the Army—including you. This book will give you quite a few hints, however, that may keep your own Army life from being rotten.

Later in the book they present excerpts from diaries they kept. The passages are dramatic. Persons speak and create tension between each other. Some of these excerpts show army life to be cruel and sadistic, but the last one ends with a note of tolerance that proves the writers were honest when they said earlier they believed the army isn't rotten.

> At formation this morning Sergeant B———— made us hold our rifles above our heads for 10 minutes. Then we had to lift them up with one hand and hold them for another five minutes. It seemed like hours. He looked at us and said: "I know what you're thinking of me. You're calling me all sorts of names. I'm not running a popularity contest, so I don't give a damn what you think. And whatever you're thinking—'gentlemen'—the same to you." . . .
>
> We always have our share of surprises waiting when we return to the barracks after a weary day at the range. Sometimes the inspecting officer turns our beds upside down. Tonight we found all our spit-shined boots muddied.
>
> We began bayonet training yesterday. Whenever we practice with the weapon we have to shout, "Kill . . . Kill . . . Kill." The instructor said anyone who didn't want to say "Kill" could say "Lollypop." No one did.
>
> The cadre and officers are puzzled that we haven't griped as much as we're supposed to—according to Army regulations, I guess. They're not too happy about our strange, passive attitude and consequently we haven't had a night off in a week. One officer said he didn't believe we were capable of showing any emotion. He said it was unhealthy not to let off steam. He directed us to growl for five minutes. We complied, but he wasn't satisfied. It wasn't sincere enough, he said, but he finally gave up.

The worst thing about basic is not the KP, or the lack of sleep, or the harassment, but the fear of the unknown. Everyone was afraid of the gas indoctrination chamber, the infiltration course, and the first day at the rifle range. But hardly anyone would hesitate to go through them now. Much of the griping in basic (and the diarrhea) is the result of anxiety. If we had known beforehand that everything had been planned down to the minutest detail in Washington, that hundreds of thousands of men had gone through the same thing before and were none the worse for it, and that every safety precaution is taken, I think many of our fears would have been considerably calmed.

Part of the power in this writing comes from the lively words the authors have quoted.

If you feel you can never write as well as John Steinbeck, Charles Dickens, or the writers quoted in this chapter, you may be right. But you can write as well as you spoke at your brilliant best when you were five years old, and you can write as well as some of the catalog or guide book writers presented in this chapter—if you find a voice that rings true to you and you learn to record the surprises of the world faithfully. The free writing by beginning writers quoted in the preceding chapters displays many of the characteristics of good writing discussed here; for example:

Surprise: I sink it from the middle of the floor. Stop it! Girls aren't supposed to do that.

The author speaking in an authentic voice: I hear the same bunch gets around to all the funerals.

Economical use of words: The next day (or the next hour for that matter) you could say "Good morning," then yawn, and I'd burst into tears.

Words that put the reader there: My eyes burned. My fingers picked at my knee. I kept twisting my ring around my finger while he repeatedly and very calmly asked me to please get out.

Strong metaphor: I felt very whole, but my stomach was tin foil.

Words that speak to each other: . . . an *empty* stomach and a *full* bladder.

A record of the authentic voice of another person: "It's just a phase. You'll grow out of it."

Strong adjective: Her eyes were the first *young* things I'd seen.

Strong, full verb: The stupid thing just sat there *begging* to be shot.

Strong repetition: It fell over, *hanging* upside down by one foot from its branch. I shot again. It still *hung* there.

Powerful rhythms: I knew I hated him. Only a chair, a desk, and a
  man saying, "I'll be back in about a half hour," which really
  became three.

The persons who produced these free writings are on their way. They
may need to master additional skills, but they have already produced
many sentences that ring true and stay in the reader's ear.

> *The best writing, both prose and poetry,*
> *as Shakespeare pre-eminently shows,*
> *makes use, with condensation and selec-*
> *tion, of playful, impassioned, imagina-*
> *tive talk.*
>
> SIDNEY COX

chapter 4

tightening

GOOD WRITERS meet their readers only at
their best. If you should read the sentences in their wastebaskets, you
would find them full of bad starts and complete misses. When you
write, you can discard your bad tries and forget them.

Benjamin Franklin, who helped Thomas Jefferson write the
Declaration of Independence—a skillfully revised document—once told
this anecdote to Mr. Jefferson:

> When I was a journeyman printer, one of my companions,
> an apprentice Hatter, having served out his time, was about
> to open a shop for himself. His first concern was to have a
> handsome signboard, with a proper inscription. He com-
> posed it in these words: "John Thompson, Hatter, makes
> and sells hats for ready money." with a figure of a hat
> subjoined. But he thought he would submit it to his friends
> for their amendments. The first he shewed it to thought the
> word "hatter" tautologous, because followed by the words
> "makes hats" which shew he was a hatter. It was struck out.
> The next observed that the word "makes" might as well be
> omitted, because his customers would not care who made
> the hats. If good and to their mind, they would buy, by
> whomsoever made. He struck it out. A third said he thought
> the words "for ready money" were useless as it was not the
> custom of the place to sell on credit. Every one who pur-
> chased expected to pay. They were parted with, and the
> inscription now stood "John Thompson sells hats." "*Sells*

hats" says his next friend? Why nobody will expect you to give them away. What then is the use of that word? It was stricken out and "hats" followed it, the rather, as there was one painted on the board. So his inscription was reduced ultimately to "John Thompson" with the figure of a hat subjoined.

You can cut out the unnecessary words in your writing in this way. The principle is simple: don't repeat words or ideas unless they strengthen what you want to say. "Hatter . . . makes hats" repeats *hat* to no avail. Don't tell your writer that "Mr. Smith is a man who—." The words *Mr. Smith* reveal that Smith is a man. Don't say "Lincoln School is a *school* that I really like." Look at what happens when a writer cuts out weak repetitions:

Original. He looked at Mike. Mike was his brother.

Tightened. He looked at his brother Mike.

Original. The beginning of the play shows Richard as a confident and strong man while the end shows him as a desolate and weak man.

Tightened. The beginning of the play shows Richard confident and strong; the end shows him desolate and weak.

Before you get carried away with cutting out weak repetition, remember that strong repetition is the heart of all good writing, in fact the heart of all good music making, hurdle racing, hammering, walking, or courting. Repetitions set up pattern. Only with pattern can you achieve emphasis and variety. Da-da-da, da-da-da, da-da-dum. That *dum* is smart because it comes after all those *da's*. It picks up its power as you wait through all those *da's* for something to happen. Repeat and vary. That is the secret of achieving significant form in all art and communication.

This book will demonstrate how the repeat-and-vary pattern strengthens writing in many ways, but for the present, consider only how to omit those repetitions in your writing which are not working powerfully, which get in the reader's way rather than drive them down your road. If you can learn to say in a few words all you want to say, with precision and fullness, you will delight yourself and your reader. We all love a man who says a great deal in a few words. Most of us feel that life will be too short; so we praise the man who can hammer the nail with only three blows. We don't want to hear:

> In order that the ruling organization of a country that is
> committed to a democratic organization organized to give

the people a voice in its procedures, and thinks of their well-being, shall not become disorganized and come to an end in these times . . .

And we don't want to hear:

That government of the people and government by the people and government for the people shall not perish from the earth.

That's so much government that we can't hear the people. We want to hear

. . . that government of the people, by the people, for the people, shall not perish from the earth.

That statement repeats *people,* not *government.* The man who wrote those words respected people and knew his *repeat-and-vary* principle. Further examples of how to repeat words powerfully will be presented in Chapter 8.

REVISING ONE: In your WRITING ONE and WRITING TWO papers, lightly circle all repeated words. Then consider each one. Do you want to retain it? If you want to omit it, draw brackets in pencil around it so that after you show the revision to others and give it time to cool off, you can restore an omitted word easily if you choose. Thomas Jefferson used brackets to recommend omissions to others, and most editors today follow him.

> *Life is the elimination of what is dead.*
> WALLACE STEVENS

The words *which, who,* and *that* often clutter up sentences. Good writers remove excessive Whooery, Whichery, or Thatery.

1. Mr. Rendew, Alice's father, [was a man who] actually liked to have his lawnmower go wrong so he could tinker with its motor.
2. George [is the type of man who] always shines his shoes before going downtown.
3. [The people that] I would like to tell you about [are] Father and Mother.

Other words, for example *all* and *what,* often fail to add meaning to a sentence and need cutting.

1. [All] I wish [is that] he would admit that passion has a respectable place in our lives.

2. [What I mean to say is that] no child should eat his grandmother.

The careless use of the word *thing* is more serious and damaging.

Original. The thing that enrages me is mosquitoes inside my open shirt collar.

Revision. Mosquitoes inside my open shirt collar enrage me.

3. [The] first [thing] I'd like to say [is] . . .

Original. Of all the things in the world I can't stand, boiled hot dogs are the worst.

Revision. I can't stand boiled hot dogs.

Why do schools turn out students so masterly in word wastery? Simple. Knowledge consists to some extent in naming and ordering things. So schools teach categorizing—how to place things in classes, species, etc. (Note that the word *things* is used twice in the two preceding sentences, but meaningfully, not emptily. These two uses of *things* are necessary and justifiable.)

Thus educated persons become addicted to such categorizing words as:

type	situation	phase	factor
kind	area	aspect	one

Often the words are not pulling their weight in a sentence.

Original. The first level of the poem gives the situation of a dull sergeant speaking to a group of new recruits.

Revision. The first level of the poem presents a dull sergeant speaking to a group of recruits.

1. The Queen realized that her life was not [a] carefree and spotless [one].
2. He was a typical [type of] fraternity man.

When a writer must categorize and generalize, these words are valuable, but often they are abominations.

Namery, another sickness, is the habit of naming things which do not need naming. Consider this passage:

> **Juliet and Rosalind are women who fall in love. This is one of the few similarities between these two characters. They are different in age, with Juliet being an impetuous adolescent and Rosalind being a mature adult. This difference is illustrated by the manner in which each character falls**

in love. Juliet rushes into romance and gets married as quickly as possible while Rosalind makes sure of her love for Orlando—a much more rational and logical choice than Juliet's.

This paragraph is devastated by Namery. The author says that Juliet and Rosalind fall in love and then unnecessarily says these acts are similar. He says the two are different in age and then later says one is an adolescent and the other an adult. He wastes completely the sentence:

> This difference is illustrated by the manner in which each character falls in love.

because the next sentence shows the difference specifically. The paragraph could be cut in half without losing essential meaning:

> One of the few similarities between Juliet and Rosalind is that they both fall in love; but Juliet rushes into romance while Rosalind makes sure of her love for Orlando. Juliet is an impetuous adolescent, Rosalind a mature adult.

Essentially Namery is a failure to recognize that one's audience may possess brains. The writer says:

> George came in with a new idea. It was a thought that had never struck his boss.

The reader doesn't need to be told that an idea is a thought. All he needs is

> George came in with an idea that had never struck his boss.

In schools, Namery usually involves a special vocabulary.

> The causes of the basic difficulties in the area of mathematics are manifold. Fractions present the student with an entirely new set of assumptions.

The introductory sentence stupefies the reader with its dull buzzing. The writer should have said:

> Fractions are hard to learn because they present students with new assumptions.

Too often writers introduce everything to their audience: "Now we are going to look at large cities and then we are going to compare them with small towns," they say, when all they mean to do is compare Chicago, Illinois, with Bad Axe, Michigan.

REVISING TWO: Take one of your free writings you like best and tighten it by removing all Whooery, Whichery, Thatery, and Namery.

When you examine your own writing for weak repetition, you may not be able to see it. You need a way of looking for it. Ask yourself where you have said something twice without meaning to. The following passage from a student paper shows weak repetition of both words and ideas. Try cutting it in about half.

> **Hands, did you ever notice how many different kinds of men's hands there are? I first began to notice hands when I found that all men's hands were not as large as my Dad's hands. They were large, strong, and forceful, yet always gentle like the man. His hand encompasses mine even now when he takes it gently yet firmly, as though providing it with a cover of protection against the outside world. But he has always been like that, strong and protective, yet gentle. When those hands hold a baby, the baby stops crying and is quiet as though calmed by their strength and gentleness. When those hands take a pencil and draw an idea, the lines are firm and confident. Other men seem to respond when they shake his hand to the friendliness and strength behind the handshake.**

The assertions in that passage are simple and unsurprising. They do not need a lot of repetition to be clear to the reader.

REVISING THREE: Look over two of your past writings for meanings unnecessarily repeated. For example:

> Valerie scrutinized my face [carefully].

The word *scrutinize* means to examine carefully.

Original. Richard has a consistently bad habit of not listening to what people are saying to him unless he is sure it will please him.

Revision. Richard consistently fails to listen to people unless he is sure they will please him.

The word *habit* means a consistent or frequent action. Because *consistently* is used, *habit* can be eliminated.

> The ground felt [peculiar. It was] soft as clouds.

If the ground was soft as clouds, it must have felt peculiar, and the writer need not make the opening comment. In the revision he hits the reader with his surprise. He does not waste a word telling him a surprise is coming. Note how the following verbose statement is brought alive by simple tightening:

Original. I see a man whose face is hidden by shadow except where the sun reveals it.

Revision. I see the sun-lit half of a man's face.

You may properly think of wasting words as a form of dishonesty. No one means to do it; but when he does, he risks losing both the reader's attention and trust.

> *A young author is tempted to leave anything he has written through fear of not having enough to say if he goes cutting out too freely. But it is easier to be long than short.*
>
> SAMUEL BUTLER

*Start out with the conviction that abso-
lute truth is hard to reach in matters
relating to our fellow creatures, healthy
or diseased, that slips in observation are
inevitable even with the best trained
faculties, that errors in judgment must
occur in the practice of an art which
consists largely in balancing probabili-
ties—start, I say, with this attitude of
mind, and mistakes will be acknowl-
edged and regretted; but instead of a
slow process of self-deception, with ever-
increasing inability to recognize the
truth, you will draw from your errors
the very lessons which may enable you
to avoid their repetition.*

SIR WILLIAM OSLER

chapter 5
deceiving
oneself

SOMETIMES writers set out to deceive
their readers, as Roget's *Thesaurus* puts the words, to hornswoggle
or bamboozle them, to throw dust into their eyes; to engage in window dressing, hanky-panky, chicanery, pettifogging, flam, bam, flim-
flam, or cajolery; to speak mealy-mouthed buncombe, to beat about
the bush, to quibble, counterfeit, fake; to write two-faced, bare-faced,
or smooth-faced; to tell taradiddles and whoppers, to gild the pill.

But more often they set out to tell the truth and speak seriously,
as Eudora Welty advises them, and still they gild the pill and throw
dust into their own eyes as well as the reader's. No writer knows how
often he deceives himself and his reader until he becomes a professional and listens to the complaints of editors and readers. Then he
often sees that he has unconsciously

32

(1) not written about what really motivated him to put pen to paper, or

(2) not spoken truly when he thought he was being faithful to the world he experienced, or

(3) told only a small part of the truth, or

(4) forgotten to tell the reader the facts that make convincing what he insists the reader must be overwhelmed by, or

(5) grandly asked questions that everyone knows the answer to, or

(6) apologized for not being an expert on what he writes pages and pages about, or

(7) used awkward and phony language that does not belong to him, or

(8) used six words where his reader only needed two.

The best writers commit these sins. You cannot rid your writing of them, but you can reduce them if you learn the identifying marks of the snakes and where they are likely to slither into your paragraphs.

Any writer, beginner or professional, feels pressed to imitate successful writers. Often the beginner echoes an idea he has heard before without remembering how the thought was imbedded in a fact of his life. He generalizes on his knowledge instead of putting his reader through the experience that led to the generalization. He presents a conclusion but does not tell the story that led him to it. Here, for example, is a poem published in a high school newspaper:

PLAY TODAY

Yes, my child, use this time for play,
Tomorrow will be too late.

Play with your soldiers, cannons and guns,
Use them while they are a toy.

Be happy that the world is not yours.
Tomorrow it will be, but today it is mine.

Let him live today as a time of freedom and play!
Tomorrow he will work and he will have no time to play.

This is a time for pleasure and a time so short,
So be a child of joy and of troubles forgotten.

Tomorrow is too late my child.
Tomorrow, you are a man.

The writer may have seen her small brother playing with soldiers and then her father came home from work too tired to do more than eat, read the paper, and go to bed. The thought she wishes to convey, that a child should enjoy his life of play while he can, is old and moldy. No reader wants to encounter it unless it is brought alive with power and originality. If the writer had revealed her brother and father in the uniqueness of their experience, she might have produced a good poem. In the following writing, note how a mother showed her child at play and opened the lid on a mystery. She did not deceive herself about what story she wanted to tell.

MY SORCERESS

> My daughter is a spare-toothed, seven-year old sorceress. Her brown hair is too short for a ponytail, too long for anything else. Yet if her hair were cut, some of her magic power would disappear. Her sparkle and infectious laugh assure control of her victim. When her thirteen-year old brother says, "I hate your guts," she dances around him and chants, "I love you, I love you." Then she breaks a vial of laughter in the room and he is in her power. Although his words do not change, he has taken up her chant.

> CAROLINE BOWMAN

Often an author generalizes on his experience but does not relate it: double mistake. One experience usually makes an unconvincing base for a generalization. Without the personal story, the writer may not be able to keep his reader awake. A writer must learn that his authority resides in his knowledge, not in an attempt to sound like someone else. What led a writer to begin writing often can tell him where his subject hides. The young man who began a paper with this paragraph (part of which was quoted in Chapter 1) probably didn't realize that he was faking his way through every sentence:

> I consider experience to be an important part in the process of learning. For example, in the case of an athlete, experience plays an important role. After each game, he tends to acquire more knowledge and proficiency, thereby making him a better athlete. An athlete could also gain more knowledge by studying up on the sport, but it is doubtful if he could participate for the first time in a sport with study alone and without experience and still do an adequate job. I think that this is the very important point which Thoreau is trying to show. He is not opposed to education, but thinks that we can be educated many times better with ex-

perience. I have the impression that he feels that it is better for most people to gain experiences and not waste so much time on unrelated things that will be of little value to them in gaining their goals more quickly in life.

What spurred this boy to spend so many words telling the obvious fact that an athlete gains from experience? Who doesn't? Probably he was thinking of a football game in which he made three mistakes: missed a tackle because he hit too high, threw an interception because he couldn't see over the red-dogger's hands, and failed to make a clear signal for a fair catch. If he had put the reader dramatically through these experiences, he might have written a memorable paper. But he didn't. He wrote as if he were a philosopher instead of a football player, and his philosophy was old and dully stated.

> *. . . creativity is continual surprise, and only because it is surprise can it be truth. When we grow self-conscious we hide, we cloak, we disguise, we lie. So the true writer artist always hopes, through working swiftly with his emotions to spring forth the delights and terrors, to trap them before they escape.*
>
> RAY BRADBURY

Another way writers deceive themselves is to speak only to themselves and yet expect the public to be fascinated. This act might be called private writing. For example, a girl publishes a poem in a high school paper:

SORROW
MY TRUE STORY

Now, I want to tell you people
My true story and it's sad
I will shout it from the hill tops
How I really had it bad

How I cried each night just for him.
How I missed him when he left.
I believed the lies he told me.

Then his heart grew tired and restless
And he soon stopped loving me.
He would flirt behind my back
And he thought I didn't see.

Now, I know he was unfaithful
But my hurt just wouldn't show
For I loved him, too much even
To ever let him go.

I wonder as I look back if
I did right, or was I wrong?
To let him think he deceived me
When I knew it all along.

He finally asked for his freedom
So, I had to let him go
Now my friends say to forget him

But they don't even know
That when I hear his name or see him
All the memories creep inside
Then my heart is filled with
Sadness and the tears are hard to hide.

I'm sure you recognize my story
For it happened to you too.
That's why I'm shouting from this hill top
How did it end with You???

The person who speaks in this poem cried, she missed her boy friend; he told her lies, he stopped loving her, he flirted behind her back. A pattern of experience that almost every girl has known, yet the writer tells not one convincing detail—what was the boy like? how did he treat her? Blatant or devious lies? Finally, she says, she let him go. Was she in a position to let him go? He had already gone in the sense of being unfaithful. She asks what might be a penetrating question:

I wonder as I look back if
I did right, or was I wrong?
To let him think he deceived me
When I knew it all along.

Does she really wonder? She accuses him of deceiving her and then admits deceiving him. If she had faced this question squarely and probed the reasons both deceived each other, she might have found truth valuable to herself and her readers. She says she felt such sorrow that she is now shouting from this hill top "How did it end with You???" What does this question mean? It may be false, covering up some other question or attitude. Is she really interested in knowing how other students' loves worked out? Or does she mean only to suggest her superior knowledge—that love turned sour for her and will for others? In the next to the last stanza she says:

> But they don't even know
> That when I hear his name or see him
> All the memories creep inside.
> Then my heart is filled with
> Sadness and the tears are hard to hide.

Unless her friends are inhuman, they would expect that when she heard his name or saw him she would remember moments with him—whether she had despised him or loved him. But what memories? She never tells anything about this boy that convinces the reader she loved him or even knew him as a person.

> *"If the artist does manage to be ruthless with himself," said the voice, "must we not think of him as the luckiest of men? How many men can afford the luxury of being ruthless with themselves in their dreams of doing a perfect thing?"*
>
> JOHN CIARDI

Consider another love poem, also written by a high school girl:

MISSING

> You belong here with me
> on a night like this.
> You are part of it.
> Your leaky old car
> parked outside the house,
> the dry smell of your hair
> the man-sweet smell
> of your freshly washed shirt.
>
> But tonight
> all that are left
> are oil stains
> in a drip-drop pattern
> by the curb.
> And they get dimmer
> with every rain.
>
> DOLORES WISE

This writer doesn't say she has gone up on a hill top to shout her sadness or even that she loved the boy she writes to, but the evidence is there to show she knew him and cared for him. Her love comes through so sensuously that many readers will call to mind their past loves as well as this girl's. No pose here, no self-deception. The writer of "Sorrow" sounds as if she is happy that a boy left her so she can parade her anguish in public, and yet she writes what is essentially a private statement that does not communicate. The writer of "Missing" speaks memories that belong to her but in such a way the public can share them.

Poets, novelists, newspapermen, scientists—all writers—constantly face the same questions: How can I tell my story? What, really, is the story? It may be that a rat injected with hormones changed from a tired old fellow who slept in the corner all day to a classic high jumper leaping over six matchboxes in a row twenty times every day before dinner. A great advance in hormone research. But how to convince the readers of its greatness? Relate the theories of the scientist first? All the failures of past scientists? Concentrate on the rat? Show how he looked sleeping in the corner or simply say how many hours he spent there every day? Describe the height, color, and durability of the matchboxes? Put the scientist into the story and say what he did to carry out the experiments? What will convince? A good piece of writing does more than assert. It convinces, by relating a body of experience or possible experience. It embodies ideas or opinions in fact. But to find the right body is not always easy. You may deceive yourself in the hunt.

> *Communication involves at least two things: securing the wanted response from the person addressed, and the feeling of meaning on the part of the utterer.*
>
> P. W. BRIDGMAN

Often a writer deceives the reader and himself by attempting a trick ending or beginning, holding back the identity of someone or something when such holding back does not heighten meaning. The materials of a story or experiment should determine whether the writer is justified in reversing the natural order of events or holding back information that normally would be communicated at once. The reader is always out there. The best writers forget him at times but finally remember that writing is to be read. Life is full of ambiguity. A writer is justified in building mystery into his work. But to pump false suspense into writing is to cheat the reader. The beginning writer often destroys the excitement in an experience by insisting to the reader that he is about to be amazed. For example:

> **I began wading across the river on the sandbar. Deeper and deeper I went into the water. Up to my waist, then chest, then shoulders. The sandbar was narrow here—only about a foot wide. One misstep and off I would go. I was just about midway when IT HAPPENED.**

The IT forgets the reader. He wasn't there. What actually happened may have been exciting, but the writer must give the reader a chance to determine how exciting the happening was. Note how the story goes without the false suspense signal.

> . . . I was just about midway when I tripped. I fell, went under the water, and the sandbar disappeared beneath me. I was carried downstream.

Holding back is justified when the significance of a series of events or progression of ideas is enhanced by the mystery. For example, the following passage opens with a sentence that puzzles the reader:

> Grandma, Dad's stepmother, welcomed us warmly, but gave us whole wheat biscuits with our meals.

What is the point of whole wheat biscuits? A mystery. The next sentence reveals the answer:

> Many times we watched from another room as she served her own grandchildren the preferred biscuits made from white flour.

This is the way the experience came to the writer, as a mystery revealed later when she saw the white biscuits. She makes the reader wait for understanding, but the wait is rewarding. A writer should expect intelligent reading from his audience, but the line between writing privately and publicly is difficult to draw. Suspense is a common ingredient of life, but in writing it should not be artificially introduced. It should exist in the materials the writer has discovered.

And so with questions. They should belong to the writer and his body of materials or he should not ask them. "Did you ever fall down a basement stairway while eavesdropping and land in your sister's boy friend's lap?" The answer is easy. "No, I never did." Not only does this question give away what might be a smash ending to a humorous story, but it is not really meant. Ask questions when you mean them, when you have really wondered about what they ask. Avoid them when you know your readers know the answers. "Are children wiser than grown-ups?" The reader knows the writer is going to say next: "Yes, sometimes." But the writer deceives himself about his job. He should not be running a question and answer show. He probably wanted to tell his reader about a time when he saw a child act wisely. He should forget the hanky-panky and get on with the story. A writer who frequently asks lame questions ultimately becomes as irritating as a six-year-old child who prefaces every assertion with the words, "Mom, you know what?"

Closely related to false questions are apologies and irrelevant introductions. Any editor will tell you that most manuscripts he sees wind up three times before they deliver the ball. Begin the paper. Wind up once and throw the pitch. The difficulty with beginnings comes from that sticky old relationship with the reader. Will he believe me? Will he like me? How can I impress him with my wisdom or honesty? One sure way to depress the reader is to apologize before starting a long article.

> I may not know much about politics, but I'm sure of one
> thing.

A reader may be tempted to say, "If you don't know much about politics, why are you writing this long article about it?" Modesty is one thing and false modesty another. To pretend he knows almost nothing of a large subject he is writing about is inexcusable in a writer, but to admit that he does not know this or that bit of information, or that he is not sure of his understanding on one point, is proper and even persuasive to the reader. For example, Stephen Spender, poet and critic, writing about another man's poem, says:

> The idea—if I understand it—is that the poet, through
> allowing his isolated self to die, enters into that life . . .

Mr. Spender admits that the poem is hard to understand; he does not deceive himself or his reader.

Naturally beginnings are difficult for a writer because they establish or fail to establish a strong relationship with the reader. Often the writer doesn't know all the persons who will read his work. And even when he does, he cannot be sure how each reader will comprehend his sentences. When a person is uneasy about how others will understand him, he often acts pompous, speaking words that he has not really made his own. And so he does not find his own voice. Everything becomes strained and artificial rather than easy and sure and winning. The urge to impress readers at the outset is so powerful that in their first drafts of a piece of writing writers feel obliged to make sweeping statements about mankind when they actually have a much smaller story to tell. For example, here is a professional writer beginning an article in a magazine about high-performance boating:

> Time has a way of perpetuating events, situations and people. As one event dies another is born. As one situation dissolves, another is conceived. As one person disappears, another appears. The cycles of life's activity renew themselves constantly.
>
> In the unlimited circle a few years ago sports reporters bemoaned privately the loss of colorful figures. Lee Schoenith had mellowed from blustering "bad guy" of the pits to Chairman of the Unlimited Commission: Bill Muncey, Peppery Willard Rhodes and their *Thriftway* retired, and with them went the possibility of fiery hassles and pungent statements. Col. Russ Schleeh of plumber's helper fame left the sport (and Air Force) for staid duties behind a desk of industry. And so it went. "Story material," said one tired writer, "is lacking—and that's an understatement."
>
> Into this void strode big, bouncing, boisterous Bernie Little and his beautiful buoyant, bewitching four-seater, *Tempo.*

The opening paragraph of this article is highly pretentious. Everyone knows persons die and are born, and men rise to fame and retire. The writer speaks these obvious truths in a voice that should belong to a prophet. All she is trying to do is introduce the story of Bernie Little, an attractive racing boat driver who appealed to her for his humor and manliness.

Nothing helps a writer more than immediately finding a voice in which to speak—one natural and right for him and fitting for his material and audience. This writer didn't find it here. After beginning in prophetic voice, she shifts in the third paragraph to corny repetition of "b" sounds that would sound right only in the mouth of a carnival barker on the Midway who knows he is kidding himself and his audience as he says, "A bevy of buxom beautiful Bunnies."

But she wrote well in other parts of her article. In the opening she experienced a common difficulty of all writers—finding words that speak honestly and validly.

A writer must test every word for its pitch: does it hit the note he was aiming for? Does it say what he meant it to say? The simplest word can be falsely used. *And* looks innocent, but often gets writers into trouble.

> She came by our house swinging her ever-present black
> parasol *and* Dad was trying to fix the fertilizer distributor
> so he could get the potatoes planted faster.

And is the wrong word there. Ordinarily it joins like or equal things. The woman swinging the parasol and Dad fixing the fertilizer distributor are not equal or related until the writer brings them together. He should drop the *and*, make two sentences, or replace *and* with a word like *while*.

Frequently writers employ the loose, imprecise language of casual conversation which will not stand scrutiny as it must if it is to be writing that tells the truth and speaks seriously. A writer says:

> I saw the victim lying beside the car, his left leg separated
> from his body and blood all over the highway. I was rather
> shaken . . .

Rather is here a false word and should be omitted. In this use it belongs in the family of expressions like *not exactly* and *not too nice,* permissible in informal conversation but often sloppy and inexcusable in writing.

> Again and again he had lied to his daughter about what her
> fiancé had said about her. As a father I guess he wasn't
> exactly nice.

No, not exactly.

Phony language like this creeps into the best writers' work. They must be ever on guard against it. They like the sound of their sentences and don't listen closely enough to hear that they have said:

> Johnny was hanging suspended from the highest branch.

or

> The talk has a tranquilizing effect on him.

when they could have made the same point in fewer words:

> Johnny was hanging from the highest branch.

and

> The talk tranquilizes him.

The ways of deceiving oneself about what he is saying are too numerous to illustrate completely here. One more conversational habit that may lead writers into trouble:

I *did* have to disarm one student last year.

Something interesting *did* happen when the sisters came to that camp.

Sometimes, but rarely, this use of *did* to emphasize a verb signals the reader that what is being told now is unexpected. Something said earlier implied otherwise. But usually the writer will save words and lose no meaning by saying:

I had to disarm one student last year.

Something interesting happened when the sisters came to that camp.

"Something interesting did happen" sounds dull. Make it happen. If it was so interesting, tell it so the reader will be fascinated. Hit him with the surprises you have collected. Don't weaken them with excessive *did's*.

I hope you did like this chapter on Deceiving Oneself and that it did teach you many valuable and important things that you did find interesting.

Shams and delusions are esteemed for soundest truth, while reality is fabulous. If men would steadily observe realities only, and not allow themselves to be deluded, life, to compare it with such things as we know, would be like a fairy tale and the Arabian Nights' Entertainments.

HENRY THOREAU

chapter 6
finding reality

MOST OF US go through each day looking for what we saw yesterday and we find it, to our half-realized disappointment. All our todays become dull yesterdays. But the man who daily expects to encounter fabulous realities runs smack into them again and again. He keeps his mind open for his eyes.

Asked to expect surprise, a number of students explored their nearby worlds for fabulous realities. Here are some they found:

1. A Band-Aid on a small tree.
2. A roll of toilet paper on the lawn of the university Maintenance Building.
3. A pregnant woman carrying a globe of the world in front of her up a steep sidewalk in the city.
4. On Sunday morning a boy walking down the main street wrapped in a pink blanket with a New Era potato chip can over his head.
5. Sign in a downtown arcade: "Four Barbers. No Waiting." And then below: "Television While You Wait."
6. Under a parked car, a lollipop lying in oil.
7. On the envelope, the postage meter message: "Fly the fastest route to the Orient via Northwest Orient Airlines." Next to

44

it, the Detroit Post Office's cancelling message: "Discover a new world, see the U.S.A."

8. "Help the poor kitty, Honey!" screamed the girl at the curb. Her boy friend stopped and looked down at the grey and white mangled, lifeless animal with the label on it reading "Made at Sears Toyland."

9. At a busy intersection I saw a white-haired woman scooping up spilled dry oatmeal from the street after the bottom of her grocery bag had burst. She was explaining to a honking motorist that she didn't want to waste the oatmeal—she was going to take it home to her ducks.

10. Last fall a blind man with a white-striped cane passed a kindergarten class searching for leaves. A boy walked all the way back to school with his eyes closed.

Each of these statements surprises. It is not fairly surprising, but absolutely surprising, because it is unique. A robin sitting in the April snow in Illinois or Massachusetts would not qualify as a fabulous reality. Often these states experience a late short snow after robins have arrived. Tension is necessary—two things which do not belong together touch in some way. And their touching creates waves of further suggestion that are not stated. The boy is not walking down *a street* wrapped in a pink blanket *on Monday*, but down the *main street* on *Sunday*, when others are dressed in Sunday-go-to-church clothes. Going to the Orient and discovering a new world in the United States are notions that create more than a simple contradiction together. They make the reader think of how little he knows of China or how persons quick to give him advice like "Go west, young man" are telling only half the possibilities of life. Written in concise form, these fabulous realities are complete in themselves and at the same time pregnant, like the woman walking up the hill, with worlds of thought yet to be explored—doors, beginnings, for further writing. They may be suggestive on several levels. The person who reported the woman explaining about her ducks to the honking motorists might note that ducks honk, too.

COLLECTING TWO: Keep a piece of paper or a notebook in your pocket this weekend and jot down five fabulous realities you see. When you come home, write them in sentences and keep revising them until you have built up to the surprise rather than given it away weakly early in your statement. Tighten your sentences. Note how this little story fails to bring out its point excitingly:

Original. Mr. Berger got up from his brown easy chair and walked across the room to the color television set. He expertly began adjusting the knobs of the set to sharpen the picture and bring out stronger colors. When he finished, the performers had stunning green faces against a bright orange background. Mr. Berger smiled, walked back across the room to his easy chair; then everyone in the room began to roar with laughter. Mr. Berger was color-blind.

This story is explained rather than presented. It could be written so the reader shares the experience as it happened. If the onlookers *roared* with laughter, most of them must have known that Mr. Berger was color-blind. Then the surprise lay in the garish picture he created, and the tension came from the contrast between his expert manner and the resulting picture. Instead of respecting the fact of the incident, the writer tried to play a trick on his reader by not revealing that Mr. Berger was color-blind until the end. This version misses the point of presenting fabulous realities.

Here is a shorter, more dramatic version:

Revision. Color-blind Mr. Berger got up from his easy chair and walked across the room in front of everyone to the television set. He expertly adjusted the knobs until the performers' faces came through sharply, green against the bright orange background.

A writer must remain sensitive to his own anticipations or expectations as well as the reader's, if he is to perceive the tension between a fact and its context which creates surprise. That is a matter of seeing truth and writing it honestly.

The writer who tries for truth will not pretend he sees fabulous realities constantly; for if everything is surprising nothing is surprising. In a writing class, a student submitted this statement to his classmates:

> **I went out to my car Friday afternoon, stuck my finger in the radiator and found ice particles floating round. Just a few days before, it was 70 degrees.**

The passage did not strike his classmates as surprising. They lived in Michigan, where the temperature in November frequently changes rapidly. In Hawaii the ice particles would have been unusual. A writer cannot force surprise artificially. Henry Thoreau warned of the dangers of trying to manufacture such wonder:

> We are eager to tunnel under the Atlantic and bring the Old World some weeks nearer to the New, but perchance the first news that will leak through into the broad flapping American ear will be that Princess Adelaide has the whooping cough.

COLLECTING THREE: Collect five or more additional fabulous realities. Do not be easily satisfied. Tension. Punch at the end. Uniqueness. Implications or suggestions which spread beyond the statement.

WRITING FIVE: Look over all the fabulous realities you have recorded. Inspect them to see whether one may be expandable into a longer piece of writing. Here is an example:

> Friday night we were "phone-sitting" at the ambulance funeral home when the doorbell dinged incessantly as if someone were leaning on it. We found a chartreuse-faced woman collapsed on the stoop choking that her husband was having a heart attack. There he was in the back seat, his chartreuse face and his gray body jumping and jerking in unconscious convulsions. Nobody mentioned the chartreuse boy slumped in a twitching heap on the front seat. We couldn't get the oxygen tanks there too quickly. All three of them were dying. Carbon monoxide. There wasn't any time to panic or to be repelled by the trio of now grayish dying faces; one face on the fourth step of the porch, one face in a gray trance on the back seat, the third face hidden in the torn beach towel that tried to camouflage the worn front seat. Oh, Lord! No time to get help. Funny how easy it was to carry those soft bodies to the openness of the front lawn. Their rasping vomiting brought a garish red tinge to their ear lobes and nostrils. Get the ambulance from the garage. Oh, no, don't let it rain. Please!
>
> Honey, they don't know. They can't hear that thin siren. They don't mind that half of the red flasher has burned out. Who knows what life is for as it screams down the shiny pavement?

Such looking, such discovery, is not a trick and not an exercise. It is the way good writers see. Because their eyes are not tired, their readers turn their pages with surprise. In *People of the Abyss,* a book about the city of London, Jack London wrote:

> From the slimy spittle-drenched sidewalk, they were picking up bits of orange peel, apple skin, and grape stems, and they were eating them. The pits of green gage plums they cracked between their teeth for the kernels inside. They picked up stray crumbs of bread the size of peas, apple cores so black and dirty one would not take them to be apple cores, and these things these two men took into

their mouths, and chewed them, and swallowed them; and this, between six and seven o'clock in the evening of August 20, year of our Lord 1902, in the heart of the greatest, weathiest, and most powerful empire the world has ever seen.

Note that Jack London is here not just telling an unusual incident but is writing toward an idea—that the great English capital city did not save its citizens from degrading poverty. Surprising realities suffuse good essays and articles as they do good stories. One of the reasons students in schools seldom write powerful themes or essays is that they mistakenly think good nonfiction writing is abstract and dull. Actually, the best writers of nonfiction (articles, essays, autobiography, history, etc.) continually surprise their readers with fabulous realities.

When you put a fabulous reality on paper, it may lead to a general idea or even an essay. Note how the following close look at four daffodils starts the writer into a paragraph that might easily flower into an essay:

Our four daffodils look like they are ready for burial. Two of them look like puckered-mouthed old women who just got poked in the ribs. The petals are reaching toward the cup in search of water, but all the water is beneath. What stupid plants. If they could look down, they would see the water through the transparent side marked "No Deposit; No Return; One Quart." One of the other daffodils looks like a banana skin with the banana sucked out of it. Its onion skin petals are gnarled and coiled like an old farmer's hands with rheumatism. The color has gone from a sunrise yellow to an autumn brown and evening amber. The odd part is that the leaves are still healthy and vibrant green in color. It seems backward that the beauty dies first. What am I supposed to do—throw the flower out and keep the leaves?

ROBERT THOMPSON

Eventually an imaginary world is entirely without interest.

WALLACE STEVENS

When you read accounts others have written of surprising realities, you may feel they were lucky but you were never blessed. But reality is often fabulous for the man who remains awake.

> *He [Thoreau] knew how to sit immov-*
> *able, a part of the rock he rested on,*
> *until the bird, the reptile, the fish,*
> *which had retired from him, should*
> *come back and resume its habits, nay,*
> *moved by curiosity, should come to him*
> *and watch him.*
>
> RALPH WALDO EMERSON

The unfamiliar frequently appears amazing, as does the familiar when it is scrutinized more closely than usual.

COLLECTING FOUR: Look up the names of wildflowers, or car parts, or any terms that belong together, and do them the honor of listening to their sounds as you read them aloud. Rearrange them on a page so their sounds and meanings harmonize or conflict. Or some day while you're waiting for a long freight train to pass, write down the names on the cars. Here, for example, is a selection of adjectives used to describe the parts of mushrooms:

violaceous	sinuate
flocculently tomentose	pruinose
decurrent with a tooth	emarginate
glabrous	bulbously incrassate
gibberulous	fibrillosely squamulose
irregularly flexuous	

Your list may be a description of a world others don't know. What you know best you know by name and the names are apt to be exotic to others. You do not have to travel abroad to amaze others, or yourself. Such ordinary fabulous materials may enrich a piece of your writing if you remember they are available. Walt Whitman became a famous poet compiling lists of the realities of his America, and James Thurber made up his own names for the animals and birds in his head, to the delight of many readers. He was thinking of the names of real animals and birds and insects when he captioned his pictures "A Grope approaching, unaware, a Clinch in hiding," and when he called a bird on a limb "The Huff" and a fat bird under a flower "The Peeve (or Pet Peeve)."

Hoping for publication, many beginning writers construct tales designed to shock the reader out of his shoes, but they forget that the fantastic world of their creation must at some point capture the reader's belief or he will never be surprised by its fantasy. A reality must underlie the fantasy. Often a true recital of actual events is the surest way to wonder. The following story written by a college freshman shows how the fact of her life, looked at honestly through the space of intervening years, flowered into a reality as fabulous as any in the Arabian Nights:

> Have you ever heard of anyone who has grown up with a tree? Well I did. When I was born my father planted a new tree in front of our house. Each year my parents would watch me and the tree grow. Each birthday they would measure my height; then they would measure the tree so I could see how much it had grown in the last year. That tree grew so much that I often thought it would never stop. I can remember that my parents were worried about me when I was in the fifth grade because I began to have back trouble. I was leaning to one side and was growing off balance. My parents took me to a doctor and I received help. That same year the tree in front of the house began leaning to one side. It was growing out of its natural way. Dad put sticks all around it and tied it in such a way that it would straighten up. Now we have both gone through that younger growing period, and I should really just be beginning to live my life. But our tree has lost so many of its limbs that its life is almost over. I feel that a part of my life is rapidly dying with it.

Except for an opening false question, that is a strong piece of writing. The girl who wrote it was not speaking from imagination but from life. She wore a brace on her back.

Life is routine more than it is fabulous; without the steadiness of the expected, newness would be impossible or chaotic. But most of us would gain from confronting a great deal more newness than we do.

If you stand right fronting and face to face to a fact, you will see the sun glimmer on both its surfaces, as if it were a cimeter [scimitar], and feel its sweet edge dividing you through the heart and marrow . . .

HENRY THOREAU

Sit down before fact as a little child . . .

THOMAS HENRY HUXLEY

chapter 7
writing
case-
histories

FOG IS BEAUTIFUL from above or outside —rolling, wispy. But once your car enters it, your journey becomes nightmare. Where you are, how fast you are going, what direction, or what other vehicle will loom up, you do not know. You cannot drive at a reasonable speed and you may very well slide into a ditch or river before you know it. There is simply too much unknown.

This is what happens often to students in school. The beginning writer should take his journeys on the back of his hand or in his own yard. And simply tell us what he knows. A case-history of how he carried his papers on the route one morning, of how he prepares for school in a family of seven in a house with one bathroom, of how he got ready to play his first game of varsity basketball. A day, a week, an hour—some interval of his life through which he takes us as he carries out one connected action or watches someone else or something else go through a process. No fog should be involved.

A person does not have to be a professional writer to tell a case-history with authority and power. He has only to know his

journey intimately and carry some attitude toward it which enables
him to select details that keep the history alive and significant—
something more than a bad list of names and dates. Michihiko
Hachiya, a medical doctor in Japan, was wounded on August 6, 1945,
by the first nuclear explosion directed against human beings. The
next morning he awoke to groans of patients and a new Hiroshima.
He told the story of his experiences, a simple case-history of what
happened to him then.

> Dr. Katsube looked me over and after feeling my pulse,
> said: "You received many wounds, but they all missed vital
> spots."
> He then described them and told me how they had been
> treated. I was surprised to learn that my shoulder had been
> severely cut but relieved at his optimism for my recovery.
> "How many patients are in the hospital?" I asked Dr.
> Koyama.
> "About a hundred and fifty," he replied. "Quite a few
> have died, but there are still so many that there is no place
> to put one's foot down. They are packed in everywhere,
> even the toilets."
>
> •   •   •
>
> Downstairs, I ran into Mr. Hirohata sitting on a bench and
> sat down beside him. Mr. Hirohata had been employed in
> the Telephone Bureau and was at work in the building
> when the explosion occurred. Despite the fact that he was
> less than four hundred meters from the hypocenter, Mr.
> Hirohata escaped injury.
> "How did you avoid injury when nearly everyone around
> you was killed or hurt?" I asked.
> "The thick concrete wall of the building protected me,"
> answered Mr. Hirohata, "but people standing near the
> windows were killed instantly or died later from burns or
> cuts. The night shift was just leaving and the day shift coming
> on when the explosion occurred. Forty or more were killed
> near the entrance. About fifteen employees in the construc-
> tion department, stripped to the waist, were outside taking
> gymnastics. They died instantly."
> "Doctor, a human being who has been roasted becomes
> quite small, doesn't he? Those people all looked like little
> boys after the explosion. Is there any reason why my hair
> should be falling out and I feel so weak? I'm worried,
> doctor, because I have been told that I would die and this

has already happened to some people I know who didn't seem to be hurt at all by the *pika*."

"Mr. Hirohata, I don't believe you need worry about yourself," I answered, trying to be reassuring, "Like so many others, you've been through a dreadful experience, and on top of that have tried to work night and day here at the Bureau. What else could one expect? You must go home, stay absolutely quiet in bed, and get all the good nourishing food you can."

This excerpt from a 233-page book shows that Dr. Hachiya wrote down his experience in incidents and conversations as they came to him. He called the book *Hiroshima Diary: The Journal of a Japanese Physician, August 6–September 30, 1945.* He told what he did, what others did, whom he saw, what they said to each other. The writer of a case-history tries to put the reader there, right in the process, the place, the action. If he sees a man riding a bicycle with a broken red reflector on its rear bumper, he does not write: "I saw a man riding a damaged bicycle," but "I saw a man riding a bicycle with a broken red reflector on its rear bumper."

If you record the details of a process or experience and then write them into a case-history, in one sense you are an authority. You may not know more about that process or experience than some others, but your written record commands respect by its truth to particular fact. Here is a case-history written by a student:

THE BIRTH OF A LAMB

As my father and I fed our ewes at night, I could easily pick out which ones had serious thoughts for the long night ahead. Their ears would be streamlined like the wings of a jet. Their sides would be concave from their backbones like the sides of the pup tent. After we finished chores, I would climb into the straw mow where I would be the king looking down on a command performance. Tonight I would watch a miracle people never have the opportunity to see —watching the coming of a new life.

I couldn't tell how long the birth would take. If it were hard, it might take three or four hours—only an hour if it were easy. First came the water bag. I was surprised to see it because in my excitement I was looking for the lamb. My anticipation bounces me over many surprises because I remember only the end.

The bag was pliable like a transparent sack made of rubber bands. It held nearly a pint of antifreeze colored liquid. As the birth progressed, the water bag bounced lower and lower like a spider coming down his web. When the bag touched the dirty straw in the pen, it acted like an anchor as it pulled the rest of its container from the ewe. This accomplished, it opened, spilling its deep purple antifreeze onto the straw like a fallen handkerchief full of BB's that has been held by the corners. The new element sponging through the dirt-freckled straw united the freckles into a solid dirty brown.

A gummy material followed the water bag, threatening the worn straw again. It was thick and sticky; it looked and felt like petroleum jelly with gum added. The work was coming heavier to the ewe as a pair of tar black hoofs covered by a slimy plastic bag emerged. The ewe pushes from her front shoulders down. I can follow the strain down to her rear shoulders, then up again as she relaxes. She holds her breath and pushes so hard that her lips curl outward, sometimes emitting a little "ma-at"—not a "blat" like most people think.

The nose and eyes are out, but the hardest part remains. The straining eases now. The anxious ewe thinks her labor is over. She gets up expecting to find the lamb behind her, but finds nothing. She licks the spot where his head has touched and lies down to try again. Once the lamb is out past his shoulders, the rest is easy. Now I sigh and realize that I've pushed and strained with the ewe for the last hour.

The lamb doesn't need me, but I rush down from my throne, stumbling because my eyes see only him. He lies coughing to clear the phlegm from his throat. I reach into his plastic puddle and force my finger into his throat, clearing it.

The mother communicates with me. A recognizable smile unites me with her feelings. I could have had the birth and she could have been the king.

She doesn't have a doctor to hand her the baby, so she forces herself up to lick off his sticky coating. Our union of feeling ends; she's a sheep and I'm a curious little boy. I can't understand how the slimy plastic sack tastes. Too many people can't understand.

MAX SLISHER

Writing a case-history will point you in the opposite direction from which this high school student went when he wrote the following comment for his school newspaper:

DAYS GONE BY DON'T RETURN

> Everyone has heard the expression from their parents, "Well when I was young . . ." What parents need to realize is that life is different now; the problems of teenagers are still present, but the problems are new and different.
>
> Today's teenagers are pressured more than any other generation has been before. A constant threat to this age is one of worrying about college and being "in" a crowd at school.
>
> These problems existed when parents of today were younger, but not to the extreme that they do now. A job today requires a college education; before, this was not necessary.
>
> Teenagers are more socially conscious now than in past generations. Fads must be met, the new places must be visited, the group must be followed in order to be considered "in."
>
> Times change; with them come joys and problems. Life for the teenager seems easy to most parents but it is difficult. New problems arise before old ones are solved. It is a never-ending battle of pressures and difficulties.

Maybe a good point, but never made convincing. Had this writer presented a short case-history of a student learning to observe a fad, or visiting one of the "new places that must be visited," or going through the actions necessary to become "in" with a group, he probably would have produced a valuable piece of writing.

> *The momentum of the mind is all toward abstraction.*
> WALLACE STEVENS

WRITING SIX: Write a case-history of some job, process, action— what happened through a period of time. An hour working at the telephone switchboard, a day in the body shop, one swimming lesson you gave a five-year-old, one vacation day when you did "nothing" for eight hours. If possible, take notes as you go through the experience, or right after the act, and record details you can remember.

Choose an action that is fun or misery for you, exciting or boring. Speak factually most of the time, as did Mr. Hachiya and the author of "The Birth of a Lamb." Make your reader respect you as an authority on this action by the way you reveal its intimate workings, but remember not to lose him in meaningless technical terms.

Pack in the detail but make it add up to reveal the essence of the job, or your feeling toward it. A case-history should be useful and fascinating. You can make it alive by remembering to keep asking "So what?" as you assemble materials and write. When the reader finishes your history, he should go away with one or two major impressions in mind, and possibly feelings, as well as a memory of close details.

Note how the following case-history of a few minutes at a music festival reveals the feelings of a performer and a judge. Like all good writing, it does not oversimplify. It centers on the embarrassment of one person and goes deeply into its complex causes. And so humorously.

REED

Maybe I could faint again. I did at the Solo-Ensemble Festival. Almost, anyway. That's where instrumentalists memorize a solo and go play it for a rating from some judge who knows all about whatever instrument it is and spends all his Saturdays listening to the same solos over and over. But I was playing along on mine and hoping I'd remember the next note because I'd only memorized the piece the night before and I kept getting short of breath and gulping. Pretty soon I felt faint but I thought I better keep going instead of being one of those whimpering fainting females. I began wondering what would happen if I did faint right there.

It would wreck the reed for sure. The reed is what makes the noise. No reed, no sound, and the hellmost torture for a clarinetist is wrecking a reed because the good ones cost forty-five cents apiece and only come in boxes of ten and only two or three of these will work with luck, and two or three won't work at all and the rest will just kind of thud a lot.

So when I thought of falling over on my good reed, I decided I better stop, so I asked the judge if I could stop for a while, except I said, "Sir, I feel faint." The judge was a heavy man who looked like he should have been bald, but he wasn't. Anyway, my accompanist hadn't heard me and

it was at the end of a rest and I was supposed to come in again, so she kept playing my cue over and over. I walked over to the judge's desk and said I felt faint and wanted to sit down. He wore black glasses and looked at me over them like what was I doing stopping in the middle of a piece like that? I was supposed to just play and not interrupt his judging routine with sudden stops. He took my elbow and my clarinet, which he put on his desk after checking the make of instrument and mouthpiece I had because he was a devoted clarinetist and probably hated fainting whimpering females. I hoped then that I was using a fifteen dollar Kaspar mouthpiece some character sits around making by hand in Ann Arbor, except he's retired now. This is like my mother telling me to always wear pretty underwear in case I get hit by a car and have to go to the hospital. Maybe she said that because once she fell down the stairs and broke her leg and was embarrassed to tears at having to ride all the way to the hospital in an ambulance with ugly underwear.

The judge kept my elbow and showed me to a chair. He told me to "take a whole bunch of deep breaths." While I was doing that, a group of people came into the room because they thought I was through playing. It was supposed to be a science classroom regularly except that Saturday when clarinetists performed in it and people were only allowed to come in between performances. When I got up and started in the middle of the solo it puzzled them a little, but when I was through they clapped anyway and the judge told them they hadn't heard very much, but the rest was just as good. That's one of those devious, double-sided comments people say and leave a person wondering exactly what they meant for some time afterward. I volunteered to play the whole thing again but the judge kind of shoved me out to the hall and collapsed in a chair.

LOUISE FREYBURGER

If you prefer, you may write a history of someone else's actions. Choose what you can observe first-hand, clearly and completely—an incident or event you can sit and watch like a cat. Take notes. Ask questions if necessary. Get the facts right.

You might sit in the library and write down what you see for an hour. Sit opposite the circulation desk, close by, where you can hear and record what the clerk does and says in a half hour.

Think of what your finished writing will look like. Choose a process or event small enough in time and limited enough in scope that you can cover it with satisfactory thoroughness. Don't write a case-history of your high school career or a year's performance by the basketball captain. Each would require volumes. Aim at a paper of two to six pages, double-spaced if typewritten, a little more if in longhand.

REVISING FOUR: When you have finished your first draft of the case-history, put it aside for a day. Then read it aloud to see whether any leading idea or feeling emerges. If you find one stirring a little, consider cutting out those parts that do not touch this idea or feeling, and adding more details that strengthen it.

If you care about what you write, and know or observe it closely, you will reveal to your reader things he doesn't know. Stay awake when you observe. If you or other human beings are in action, the chances are high that you will be recording some fabulous realities.

One professional caution: Change any real names in your case-history to fictional names. What if your work becomes published, or passed around locally? What you consider an unbiased report of how Mrs. Smithweather, the science teacher, swore at John Saunders in lab may not strike Mrs. Smithweather in that way. If you had money, she might properly sue you for libel. Some real names you must keep in your writing or its point may be lost, but inspect all names and weigh the need to change them. Samuel Butler wrote a long book which became the classical English story of a sensitive son and a tyrannical, self-righteous father. Butler's real father was a sadist to him, but he refused to publish this book until after his father had died. And then it came out as a novel, with Butler's father carrying a fictional name. Butler himself died before *The Way of All Flesh* was published and he never knew that he had written one of the finest novels in the English language. The least you can do is protect Mrs. Smithweather and yourself by changing names.

> *It is much easier to sit at a desk and read plans for a billion gallons of water a day, and look at maps and photographs; but you will write a better article if you heave yourself out of a comfortable chair and go down in tunnel 3 and get soaked.*
>
> **STUART CHASE**

Repeat: *to double, re-double, renew, parallel, echo, match, mirror, reproduce, regenerate, reincarnate, multiply, revive, reaffirm, reassert, accentuate, emphasize, build, hammer, slap, thump, beat, bang, punch, jab, convince, charm, lull, caress.*

chapter 8
repeating

WEAK AND
STRONG REPETITION

IF SOMEONE you love keeps saying he loves you, the repetition is beautiful. But if someone you dislike keeps saying he loves you, the repetition is unbearable. And there are places and moments where you don't want to be told you are loved. Even the heartbeat, with its repetitious but slightly irregular liveliness, can become monotonous—for example, if recorded day after day in a laboratory.

Repetition can comfort or bore, clarify or confuse, astound or outrage. Consider these repetitions:

> **I think Ethel was rebelling when she refused to follow my suggestion. She was rebelling against her ability to recover, her ability to heal, her ability to retain her youth. She had lost her youth, yet she was still fighting. Fighting for a lost cause.**

They clog the passage rather than emphasize what needs to be emphasized.

The professional writer reads his work aloud to himself and to others. He hears repetitions his eyes did not see. The beginner and the professional need to find ways of getting inside their writing and hearing it objectively. One way is to listen for repetitions, which are easily detected. Those that the writer is surprised to find are usually weak: he didn't intend them. They may become valuable to him as flags indicating other failures or surrenders. If he didn't notice them before, he probably missed other weaknesses. Read the following passage aloud and you will find weak repetition. It will help you spot other weaknesses.

> One of the specific aspects of the speech was the question and answer period. I feel that the panel during the question and answering period was very biased in their questions to Governor Barnett of the state of Mississippi. In so much as the questions directed toward Governor Barnett were mostly concerned with segregation in general.

The passage needs massive cutting. Here is a possible revision:

> In the question and answer period, the panel was biased toward Governor Barnett of Mississippi. Most of the questions concerned segregation.

In another part of his column, this writer ran into a snag with the word *fact*.

> Governor Barnett has said that the North is just as segregated as the South. This is of course an overstatement of fact, but it still does contain a certain amount of fact. There are no signs forbidding Negroes from using a drinking fountain or from buying a bottle of Coke from a vending machine, but I have experienced prejudice in the North and even helped the cause of segregation in Lansing, Michigan.

The second sentence might be revised in this way:

> This is an overstatement but still contains a certain amount of fact.

Note that in both excerpts from this column, the writer employed weak repetition when he was generalizing, not when he was giving particular evidence. His last sentence in the second excerpt ("There are no signs . . .") is well written. In it he has found his voice and speaks with his natural powers.

Often weak repetition blooms when a writer tries to impress his reader, as in this passage:

> When one sits before an open hearth and can see the flames shooting from the burning wood, hear the crackling of the fire as it engulfs its source of fuel, and feel the

> warmth given off, one enters another "world," a "world"
> which is quiet and peaceful . . . You may ask why we
> spend so much time by the fire, and that should be a diffi-
> cult question to answer. But I believe it is the "mystery" of
> the fire that intrigues us. This "mystery" of the fire has a
> way of captivating your thoughts and putting you in a
> trance-like atmosphere.

Here again words appear close to each other in ineffectual repetition.
To show how unprofessional he is, the writer also puts quotation
marks around *world* and *mystery*—which he uses in the commonest
way—and insults his reader. Instead of saying the crackling fire
"engulfs its *wood*," he says "engulfs its *source of fuel*." He so feared
repetition that he went to ridiculous lengths to find a synonym. Wood
is fuel, but here the general subject of fuel is not being discussed.
If the writer cannot stand to hear the word *wood* repeated, he should
remove its first use, not its second. Then the passage would read:

> When one sits before an open hearth and watches the
> shooting flames, hears the crackling as the fire engulfs the
> wood, and feels the warmth given off . . .

Avoidance of repetition sometimes leads writers to silly substitutions
for a key word in a passage. If the principal subject of your writing
is *cats,* use the word *cats* frequently. Don't say *cats,* then *felines,
furry friends,* and *four-legged bundles of fur.* Sports writers often sin
with this "elegant variation." For example, a good sportswriter in a
student newspaper began his article with *The Rich track team.* Then
he calls them by their name *The Olympians.* Next he says, "Then
the squad began to show." Up to that point his variation in naming
is inoffensive, but next he says:

> Still improving, the Central cindermen then overran T. F.
> South and Lockport West, finishing the season in grand
> style. The Olympians captured nine firsts . . .

By that point the paper's regular readers are probably fatigued by
the writer's attempt to avoid repetition, and an outsider is probably
lost, wondering whether *the Central cindermen* still refers to *the Rich
track team* or to one of their opponents.

The writer who has found a voice that belongs to him repeats
words with power, not with weakness. If he wants to hit a word
hard, he repeats it. Dr. Seuss does:

Then Horton the elephant smiled. "Now that's that . . ."
And he sat
 and he sat
  and he sat
   and he sat . . .
And he sat all that day
And he kept the egg warm . . .
And he sat all that night
Through a *terrible* storm.

Thomas Paine, the pamphleteer who helped persuade colonists to join George Washington's army, wrote:

> I call not upon a few, but upon all: not on this state or that
> state, but on every state: up and help us; lay your shoulders
> to the wheel; better have too much force than too little
> when so great an object is at stake.

These repetitions helped create the United States.

In Shakespeare's *Macbeth,* Macduff speaks to Malcolm, reminding him of the sad state to which Scotland has fallen under the rule of the murdering King Macbeth:

Each new morn

New widows howl, new orphans cry, new sorrows
Strike heaven on the face, that it resounds
As if it felt with Scotland and yelled out
Like syllable of dolor.

Here the word *new* murders husbands, fathers, happiness, and creates widows, orphans, sorrows. It is not at all like the *new* which appears on so many packages of detergent, toothpaste, and shampoo in the supermarket. The manufacturer thinks the word will sell his product and he changes the product ever so slightly once a year, or changes it not at all, and stamps *new* on the package. Too many *new's* on packages have killed the force of them all.

Professional writers usually avoid starting a sentence with the same word that ends the preceding sentence:

> I found out his name was John. John was an engineer.
>
> The last topic on the program was rehabilitation. Reha-
> bilitation is an urgent matter in Michigan because prisons
> are overcrowded.

In his second or third draft, the professional writer looks for repetitions of this sort—he knows they will be there—and expunges them. But frequently he achieves his best repetition unconsciously. An idea, or a fact, often epitomized in a key word, dominates his mind. He repeats it when he writes.

A good way to utilize repetition without being dull is to shift the form of the repeated word, or play with it in some way. Here a writer makes the word *uncivilized* speak to the word *civilized*:

> I don't like picnics. That's against the great American tradition, I guess. I don't like to combine the civilized way of eating with uncivilized surroundings.

When you write out a first draft hurriedly, you may find one key word appearing again and again. Before you eliminate the repetitions of it, think twice. Some of the repetitions may give strength to your writing and let the reader know what objects or ideas dominate your thought. Here is a memory of childhood that needs cutting. It contains too much good writing to be allowed to remain in this state marred by weak repetitions. But some of its repetitions are essential; for example, of the word *outside,* which is central to the writer's point. (Some of the major repetitions are indicated here in italics.)

> Summer seems more fun during childhood. I remember those *screen-door days.* The back *door* to my house was covered with two sections of *screen* that bulged from being pushed by an endless chain of small hands. I doubt that the *door* was ever shut without a *bang*; in fact it seemed to be there for the sole purpose of shutting with a *bang.* To butt out that *door* without hearing the familiar b-r-r-zing *BANG!* would have been as unnatural to me as giving my sister some of my candy—well almost. I was always in a great hurry to get *outside.* Summer is an *outside* time. I had an outside mind. I could only think in *outside.* Sometimes in my haste to join my mind *outside,* I would fly at the *door* only to discover, too late, that a security-conscious grandmother or some such menace of childhood had locked it. I would come to a tire-tearing halt, like a cartoon car stopping on a dime. I had to peel my face off the *screen* like a waffle, and looking very much like one only with much smaller squares. I would *cuss* at whoever locked the *door.* If I did not know who the culprit was I would *cuss* at

everyone just to be on the safe side. However my anger was silent, or mutterings at best. My mother's children left much to be desired where brains are concerned, but she did not rear any of us to be *stupid*, at least not so *stupid* as to be caught *swearing*. My father was a great strong *swearer*. He could invoke deities and conjure up demons that made my bottom sore before the *belt* was even off his waist. I was always puzzled by the fact that I could say *"god-darn"* this and *"god-darn"* that depending on whatever I wanted *God* to mend, and yet *"goddamn"* always removed the belt from my father's waist. The sin was in the "damn" not in the "God." I always wondered what God thought about it and how big a belt he had.

MICHAEL MANUEL

In this reflection on childhood, the notion of *outside* is crucial to the story because it is the urge to get outside quickly that led the boy to swear and to confront his father and think upon the effects and causes of profanity. But too much emphasis on *outside* and the screen door makes the ending discussion of profanity seem like an afterthought rather than the major subject the writing builds toward.

Here is a revision of the story with a number of the repetitions cut out:

The back *door* to my house was covered with two sections of *screen* that bulged from being pushed by an endless chain of small hands. That *door* seemed to be there for the sole purpose of being slammed. To butt out it without hearing the familiar b-r-r-zing BANG! would have been as unnatural to me as giving my sister some of my candy.

I could only think in *outside*. Sometimes in my haste to join my mind *outside*, I would fly at the *door* only to discover too late that a security-conscious grandmother had locked it. I would come to a halt like a cartoon car stopping on a dime and would peel my face off the *screen* like a waffle. Then I would cuss—at everyone, just to be on the safe side—but silently, mutteringly. Mother did not rear us to be so stupid as to be caught *swearing*.

Father was a great strong *swearer*. He could invoke deities and conjure up demons that made my bottom sore before the *belt* was off his waist. I was always puzzled because I could say *"god-darn"* this and *"god-darn"* that, depending on whatever I wanted *God* to mend, and yet *"god-damn"* always removed the belt from Father's waist. The sin was in the *"damn"* not in the *"God."* I always wondered what *God* thought about it and how big a *belt* he wore.

Repetitions remain but they are necessary, therefore not tedious but powerful. To gain their full effect, some words should not be repeated at all. The writer should save them strategically for one best moment. In the above story if the word *bang* is to sound loud, it should be heard only once.

Rhyme is a form of repetition, of sound, not word. It can be used in prose if the writer remembers that its effect there is customarily humorous. Lilian Moore wrote a book she called *A Pickle for a Nickel* in which she had Mr. Bumble say truly, "Boys like noise."

REVISING FIVE: Examine your story about childhood. Omit the weak repetitions and consider adding strong repetitions. Use penciled brackets so that you may restore words or phrases should you later change your mind.

WRITING SEVEN: Dash off two 10- to 15-minute free writings in which you play frequently with repetition. Repeat words in as many different patterns as you can. Repeat a word three times in a row, then repeat it as the key word in three phrases: "He was a bumbling carpenter, a bumbling father, a bumbling fisherman." Then separate the repeated words even more from each other. Try repeating all kinds of words—verbs, adverbs, prepositions, adjectives, nouns, etc. Use a word once with one meaning and then with another meaning. If you feel stalled, study advertisements in magazines and commercials on television to find still other ways to repeat. Study poems; almost all good ones repeat words skillfully. In all your practice in repeating, do not make up nonsense phrases or sentences that are lists of words unrepresentative of thoughts or feelings in you. Try always to say something you mean but play while you do that. Play around—seriously.

PARALLEL CONSTRUCTION

One of the fundamental beats in all good writing is parallel construction, which is based on repetition. No competent writer's ear is deaf to it. Take this statement:

George liked Jean and often walked beside her on the way to school. Jean was also sometimes accompanied to school by

Ronald, who also liked her, but who often could be seen walking behind her.

Here is a shorter version:

George liked Jean and often walked beside her on the way to school. Jean was also accompanied by Ronald, who walked behind her.

But it is still awkward. Seeing that the sentences compare George's and Ronald's walking with Jean, the professional writer would cast each part of the comparison in parallel form:

George liked Jean and walked beside her to school. Ronald liked Jean and walked behind her to school.

Tightened and paralleled in this fashion, the sentences now emphasize that Ronald was bashful. They could be paralleled in another way:

The boys liked Jean. George walked beside her to school and Ronald behind her.

At the same time that most parallel patterning throws into simple and dramatic comparison two or more ideas or persons or things, it shortens a statement so severely that it requires work from the reader. This is an ideal combination of qualities: challenge and delight.

The writer who wonders how his words will strike his reader need only ask how they strike him as he patterns them. If he finds himself unchallenged or bored, he should know he is not writing well. His words should speak to him as well as to his audience—and to each other. Parallel patterning helps give them voice. Here is a beginning writer making words speak to each other:

I like to bounce when I get into bed, and pick up my pillow and throw it down, then pick up my head and drop it into the pillow, like someone picking up a little kitten and dropping it in some out of the way place so that it won't get _under_ foot. Good thing I've got the upper bunk . . . I couldn't be any more _out_ from _under_ foot.

Train your ear so you hear a word when you write it, and then ask whether it needs an answer from another word soon. Here is a beginning writer who was listening as he wrote:

Why not be natural, free, untimed, unlimited?

Here is a professional advertising writer listening as he wrote:

> You ought to watch Longchamps meat experts buying beef for your dinner. They stride through the refrigerators, sniffing and poking each rib on the rack. They know what's what. So butchers give them their best. Well marbled steaks, tender as butter. Naturally aged meat, with a rich, beefy taste. Longchamps experts are tough. That's why Long-champs steaks are tender . . .

All writers who want to hammer an idea employ repetition and parallel construction. A high school girl gets out her hammer in the following article from the Lakeview High School *Crystal* of Battle Creek, Michigan (May 6, 1966):

NASTY NAZI SYMBOL OR HARMLESS FAD?

> **Most teenage fads are inoffensive and short-lived. A current fad in Battle Creek is far from inoffensive and should be stopped at once.**
>
> **Teenagers are adorning themselves with symbols of German militarism such as German army helmets. Some are wearing an Iron Cross on a chain around their neck. Elsewhere, the Nazi swastika is in style.**
>
> **These symbols recall the death of 291,000 Americans and the slaughter of six million Jews.**
>
> **They recall an upheaval during and after the war, started by a man who used the swastika as the symbol of an evil philosophy.**
>
> **Human memories are short, but not so short that they blot out this devastating period of history.**
>
> **These military symbols are probably just an expression of rebellion. Some kinds of rebellion are healthy. This kind is sick.**
>
> JANICE NEMRAVA

IMITATING ONE: Practice parallel patterning so you can see how easy and hard it is. Read the following examples and imitate their structure while you are writing thoughts of your own:

1. Every day, the sun; and, after sunset, Night and her stars. Ever the winds blow; ever the grass grows. Every day, men and women, conversing—beholding and beholden.

   RALPH WALDO EMERSON

2. We have rates by the hour, day, week, month, or by the job.

DICK'S KALAMAZOO JANITOR SERVICE,
YELLOW-PAGES ADVERTISEMENT.

3. Other people cannot see what I see whenever I look into your father's face, for behind your father's face as it is today are all those other faces which were his. Let him laugh and I see a cellar your father does not remember and a house he does not remember and I hear in his present laughter his laughter as a child.

JAMES BALDWIN

4. Cut flowers at proper stage of development. Dahlias when fully open; gladioli when first floret is open; peonies when petals are unfolding; roses before buds open. In general, cut while in bud.

The Pocket Household Encyclopedia

5. Remember that young uncooked spinach makes a good salad; that cooked buttered spinach and grapefruit salad are an ideal reducer's luncheon; and that cooked spinach greens are superb with Hollandaise Sauce . . .

IRMA S. ROMBAUER AND MARION ROMBAUER BECKER

WRITING EIGHT: Write two 10-minute free writings comparing two objects, acts, or persons. Let yourself drift frequently into parallel patterns. Do not try to make every sentence parallel, but seize upon whatever opportunities present themselves.

Before you start writing, read this passage by Emerson aloud twice, listening for parallelisms:

> A foolish consistency is the hobgoblin of little minds, adored by little statesmen and philosophers and divines. With consistency a great soul has simply nothing to do. He may as well concern himself with his shadow on the wall. Speak what you think now in hard words and to-morrow speak what to-morrow thinks in hard words again, though it contradict every thing you said to-day.—"Ah, so you shall be sure to be misunderstood."—Is it so bad then to be misunderstood? Pythagoras was misunderstood, and Socrates, and Jesus, and Luther, and Copernicus, and Galileo, and Newton, and every pure and wise spirit that ever took flesh. To be great is to be misunderstood.

There was a Boy . . .
many a time
At evening, when the earliest stars began
To move along the edges of the hills,
Rising or setting, would he stand alone
Beneath the trees or by the glimmering
lake,
And there, with fingers interwoven, both
hands
Pressed closely palm to palm, and to his
mouth
Uplifted, he, as through an instrument,
Blew mimic hootings to the silent
owls . . .

WILLIAM WORDSWORTH

chapter 9

remember-ing childhood

ACHIEVING DISTANCE

REMEMBERING CHILDHOOD is not childish, but wise and sweet and necessary. We go back because we loved those years of play. We go back because remembering moves us closer to the children around us today. We go back because in writing through these years we gain a second life.

The best writers take this journey. Mark Twain wrote *Huckleberry Finn,* a novel about a boy with a gifted tongue, who once said:

It would get so dark that it looked all blue-black outside, and lovely; and the rain would thrash along by so thick

that the trees off a little ways looked dim and spider-webby;
and here would come a blast of wind that would bend the
trees down and turn up the pale underside of the leaves;
and then a perfect ripper of a gust would follow along and
set the branches to tossing their arms as if they was just
wild; and next, when it was just about the bluest and
blackest—*fst!* it was as bright as glory and you'd have a
little glimpse of tree-tops a-plunging about, away off yonder
in the storm, hundreds of yards further than you could see
before; dark as sin again in a second, and now you'd hear
the thunder let go with an awful crash and then go
rumbling, grumbling, tumbling down the sky towards the
under side of the world, like rolling empty barrels downstairs, where it's long stairs and they bounce a good deal,
you know.

J. D. Salinger wrote about another boy with gifted tongue, who
cherished his little sister Phoebe:

She was laying there asleep, with her face sort of on the
side of the pillow. She had her mouth way open. It's funny.
You take adults, they look lousy when they're asleep and
they have their mouths way open, but kids don't. Kids look
all right. They can even have spit all over the pillow and
they still look all right.

And the best poets go back to childhood. May Swenson went back
like this:

THE CENTAUR

The summer that I was ten—
Can it be there was only one
summer that I was ten? It must

have been a long one then—
each day I'd go out to choose
a fresh horse from my stable

which was a willow grove
down by the old canal.
I'd go on my two bare feet.

But when, with my brother's jack-knife,
I had cut me a long limber horse
with a good thick knob for a head,

and peeled him slick and clean
except a few leaves for the tail,
and cinched my brother's belt

around his head for a rein,
I'd straddle and canter him fast
up the grass bank to the path,

trot along in the lovely dust
that talcumed over his hoofs,
hiding my toes, and turning

his feet to swift half-moons.
The willow knob with the strap
jouncing between my thighs

was the pommel and yet the poll
of my nickering pony's head.
My head and my neck were mine,

yet they were shaped like a horse.
My hair flopped to the side
like the mane of a horse in the wind.

My forelock swung in my eyes,
my neck arched and I snorted.
I shied and skittered and reared,

stopped and raised my knees,
pawed at the ground and quivered.
My teeth bared as we wheeled

and swished through the dust again.
I was the horse and the rider,
and the leather I slapped to his rump

spanked my own behind.
Doubled, my two hoofs beat
a gallop along the bank,

the wind twanged in my mane,
my mouth squared to the bit.
And yet I sat on my steed

quiet, negligent riding,
my toes standing the stirrups,
my thighs hugging his ribs.

At a walk we drew up to the porch.
I tethered him to a paling.
Dismounting, I smoothed my skirt

and entered the dusky hall.
My feet on the clean linoleum
left ghostly toes in the hall.

Where have you been? said my mother.
Been riding, I said from the sink,
and filled me a glass of water.

What's that in your pocket? she said.
Just my knife. It weighted my pocket
and stretched my dress awry.

Go tie back your hair, said my mother,
and *Why is your mouth all green?*
*Rob Roy, he pulled some clover
as we crossed the field,* I told her.

These persons wrote of childhood at the height of their mature powers. If you are under twenty, you need even more than they to write of childhood. A writer requires about seven years of distance between him and the events he recalls. Then he is unfamiliar enough with them to feel the need to relate them fully for his readers and for himself. If he writes of yesterday's or last year's events, he usually remembers them so well he leaves them shrouded in his nearby intimate memory, which the reader does not share. James Boatwright, editor of *Shenandoah* magazine, says that few writers in their teens can write strongly of anything but their childhood. You may hope he is not right but you should start where you are most likely to achieve success. Do not search for tasks in which you will probably fail. Proceed, as this book suggests, from success to success.

> *But don't expect to write well about the love affair that you are in the midst of, or have just mailed a letter to break off. One principal figure in that situation you can't see. At least one. Probably two. You are "involved." You don't surround it. You suffer or you triumph; you do not comprehend.*
>
> *Later, all those feelings will become your knowledge. They will be of your knowledge and your wisdom when they no longer possess you. Your subject must be something you possess and can move all the way around. The former feelings that come together in your sub-*

ject may include the most glorious or
devastating that you ever had. And you
will re-experience them. But you must
emotionally enclose and dominate them.
                                    SIDNEY COX

Consider the skill with which this high school student wrote of her childhood. Her name is withheld because she is writing candidly of her family.

BIRD

I sneaked back into my room, waited. I heard the light thud on the stairs. The floor creaked. The dress hangers swung squeakily on the door as it opened, then closed. I counted to ten, held my breath, listened. A soft shuffling sound came from the darkened room next to mine. Then with the squeak of springs came the shrill cry. A click. A spurt of choked sobbing began when the light went on. Rapid thuds sounded across the floor, door slammed, footsteps pounded down the stairs.

When the sound was gone, I crept from my bedroom to the stairway. Holding myself with my feet, I stuck my head through the bars and leaned down over the ledge. The room at the bottom of the stairs was dark, but I saw a light shining from the kitchen. Still, I could only hear a disturbed mumble and irregular sobs. My head was feeling heavy and since my position didn't let me hear the talk below, I inched back to bed without anyone else hearing them.

I didn't think Suzie would act like that. She was a smart big sister, not the sissy type to get upset by a dead bird on her pillow. After all, the soft, smelly part had rotted off long before I found the bird. Now all it was was a delicate spine and skull with a few feathers sticking out at the neck. I liked it because of its pink and purple colors. No one else liked it. But my mother let me keep it when I told her I would keep it in my bedroom with my piece of driftwood. She didn't like my driftwood, either. Suzie had even handled my bird before. Now she had probably smashed its spine when she lay on it and maybe pulled some of the feathers off. She had been downstairs now long enough to stop her crying bit and to tell on me.

I heard someone; maybe she was coming. I started to go tell her that I didn't think she was going to take it so hard. But, no, it was a heavy, steady beat on the stairs. The sound came near my closed door. Silence. The beat, steady again, moved into Suzie's room. I fell asleep as the sound closed in on my room, but I woke up the next minute to see my father staring down. He had turned my bright light on, so I squinted up, looking sleepy and innocently asked what was going on. I knew that was a bad question when I saw my bird in his hand. He replied by asking where my driftwood was. I told him and he got it. And I told him I didn't see why everyone was making such a big fuss about the bird. He gave me the usual line about "never do that again." Then he told me how Suzie was really upset and that she was going to spend the night on our play room davenport. He left without really scolding me. He probably didn't see how my bird could scare anyone, either.

I didn't really believe that Suzie would stay on the davenport all night. And I thought she would want to come get mad at me herself. So I fluffed my pillow, lay down, and waited. All I heard was the garbage can lid slam down.

The humor of this story comes from the writer telling matter-of-factly of her childhood outrage at her sister's refusal to enjoy going to bed with a skeleton of a bird, yet at the same time letting the reader know that now she knows her sister had reason to be upset. The writer tells the reader enough, but not too much. She puts the reader there, listening for the sister's reaction down below. She makes the bird really dead, remembering "the smelly part had rotted off," and liking it "because of its pink and purple colors." She chose surprising attitudes to write about; so she keeps the reader off balance while telling him consistent and believable truth. She knows that bird and her family. When her father comes up the stairway, the reader probably expects a bawling out. Instead, father disapproves without scolding, and thus comes over as a real man, not a stereotyped parent.

This story is almost professional in its skill, but it could be polished further. It communicates sounds precisely: "a spurt of choked sobbing," "The beat, steady again, moved into Suzie's room." Almost every sentence makes the reader want to know what is going to happen next. And yet the repetition of *thud-thuds* and *squeakily-squeak,* all in the first paragraph, is weak.

Here is another young person's story about childhood:

ORANGE

A pitcher of orange drink fell over in the refrigerator and trickled out onto the floor, creeping along, where the tile meets the green of the living room carpet. I hate orange pop. It makes me think of our church picnics, which always had an over abundance of that too sweet nectar—the junk that kids consume by the gallon and end up vomiting up by the end of the day under some dwarfed tree in the corner of a baseball field. I was a champ at it—only I intermingled bottles of orange drink with cups of soft, white ice cream that slid down my throat (after the tenth or so) like chunks of plaster of Paris. Still I shoveled it in and then ran in the races. I won, of course, to the delight of my ego and the sorrow of my stomach.

Splash! We were in the creek. About a half dozen of Mrs. Sallay's Sunday School sweethearts couldn't make it through the day without plunging into the muddy creek while walking the narrow branches stretched from bank to bank. I never missed the fun, year after year. Was I sick by the end of the day! I remember clinging to the trunk of a very small friend, watching fat, bald shirtless men loudly oppose the young boys in softball. While the women squealed at flabby forms puffing around third base, I threw up my ten bottles of orange pop, now the gravy over my once-downed lumpy ice cream. The day was complete. I could go home.

GEORGIA TODHUNTER

A reader probably would not say that the writer of "Orange" was making up this story. It contains the authority of closely recorded fact: a "dwarfed tree in the corner of a baseball field," orange drink and white ice cream that "slid down my throat (after the tenth or so) like chunks of plaster of Paris." Parts of the story may have been made up but they are true to life, deeply. "Orange" is a fine piece of writing but probably would not be published in a magazine because it does not develop any incident through time, as does the following memory of childhood:

THE PIRATE SHIP

I can still remember the time two of my buddies, Jim and Tom, and I decided to leave home. We were all avid Captain Kid fans, and we decided to build a pirate ship and make our fortunes by looting and plundering other vessels.

After three agonizing days of searching for a ship, we discovered an old discarded casket crate drydocked in the cemetery. It was ideal. Just large enough to hold all three of us and yet small enough to make the fancy maneuvers demanded of a pirate ship. Finding our ship solved one problem, but getting it back to our hideaway created another, because it was well guarded by Mr. Snod, the groundskeeper. We waited until he went into his office for lunch to avoid capture and then charged the ship and overpowered the sole crew member, Snod's angora cat.

We hoisted the ship upon our wagon, lashed it down securely, and set out of the cemetery full sail, knocking over two small tombstones due to the faulty navigation of Tom who was steering the wagon. This part of the operation went along without a catch until we started down a long hill a block away from my house. One minute we were towing the ship and the next minute it was towing us. About halfway down the hill, the ship got second wind and lurched ahead, breaking our grips on the rope.

Twenty crushed tulips and one trampled hedge later it came to rest in my mother's flower garden. Now more than ever, if we had a reason for leaving home, this was it.

We tried to fix the mangled tulips by breaking uncooked spaghetti sticks into pieces and inserting them into the stems, hoping to make them straight again. After twenty-five minutes of failure we gave up and dragged the ship into the back yard and tried to get it seaworthy before one of my parents discovered the disaster area in the front yard.

I went into the basement and rummaged around until I found some tar and old rags. Dipping the rags into the tar, we managed to seal up the slits in the ship. By now we looked more like the Bre'er Rabbit tarbaby than pirates.

Our mast and sail were made up of my mother's clothesline pole and a white sheet she had hung out to dry. We needed a Jolly Roger to identify our ship so we borrowed Jimmy's grandfather's V.F.W. flag. We nailed spikes into the bottom of the ship to prevent the sharks from eating us up.

All good pirate ships had a ram to destroy other ships at close range, so we had to have one, too. After a lot of fast talking I persuaded Tom to lend us his father's moose head which would serve as the battering ram. We needed a cannon for long range warfare and we found it in my father's pump-type fire extinguisher, which we first emptied and then refilled with soap water. This would blind the crews of other ships long enough for us to make use of our twelve-point battering ram.

At last we were ready. Tugging and straining, we lifted our coffin onto the wagon and embarked toward the river to launch it, taking the short-cut through Mr. Freeland's backyard and Mrs. Murphy's flower garden. The ship was now top heavy from the sail, and the moose head fell off the wagon every fifty feet or so. Every time our ship fell, the nails in it would gouge the ground.

By the time we had crossed Mr. Freeland's lawn and Mrs. Murphy's flower garden, they looked like battlefields ripped apart by bombs. We used everything in sight to cover these areas. Tables, chairs, incinerators, toys, wet laundry, lawnmowers, bikes, play pens, empty milk bottles, and a sleeping dog. But to no avail. Within minutes, Mr. Freeland and Mrs. Murphy attacked like dive bombers, forcing us to abandon ship and flee for our lives.

Where could we run, what could we do? Head toward my house and the ruined front yard, or surrender and face the wrath of Mr. Freeland and Mrs. Murphy? We never got to make a decision because we were intercepted by our parents, who had discovered the disaster in their front yard and were following our poorly disguised trail. Trapped, we surrendered and tried to explain our actions. It was useless. Our tar-covered pants were yanked off and we were flogged all the way home. Our ship was destroyed and we were confined to our room indefinitely, let out only to eat.

Whenever I see Jim or Tom today, we stop and look at each other with that knowing smile and say, "It woulda' floated!"

MICHAEL MAY

The writer chose his details skillfully: they never become tedious; they take the reader on the dry voyage. The ship metaphor is continued in the telling of the story: the crate is *drydocked*, the wagon faultily *navigated*, the crate made *seaworthy*, the flag is a *Jolly Roger*, they *embarked* toward the river. The story is more than just a tale of a day's play: it shows how kids become engrossed in playacting and run smack into their parents' world without realizing they come from another.

WRITING NINE: Choose from your childhood a moment you can't forget and write it down. Put the reader there as these three stories do. You may tell of the experience in simple narrative—this happened, then that happened—as did the writers of "Bird" and "The Pirate Ship." Or consider a persistent joy or annoyance in your childhood and find examples which illustrate the feeling as do the events in "Orange."

BEGINNINGS AND ENDINGS

Most good published pieces of writings have been created in several drafts—each version tighter and sharper than the last. What you see in print is almost never the first effort. No professional writer expects to dash off a piece of writing that is beyond improvement. Each version he thinks of as preliminary to another better version until finally he has had enough of drafting and says, "Done."

About eighty percent of the time, professional writers and editors find that the beginning of their first draft is no beginning at all. It is a mess, a series of false beginnings in which the starter's pistol goes off once, then twice, and the runners burst from their blocks only to stop and come back again. A writer must expect these bad starts because when he first meets his reader he has been thinking through *all* that he wants to tell him, not just the beginning of it. So he tells him too much—what concerns the end of the story or the chain of ideas, as well as the beginning—or too little, on the false assumption that the reader has just gone with him on this journey of reflection. In fact it cannot for the reader be a journey of memory. It must be a trip into an unknown woods in the partial dark where the stumps and branches leap at his feet and the hanging spider webs clutch his face.

Look at the first draft of your story. Is there some place on the first page where the reader could begin satisfactorily? Look for a spot where the story itself starts up, not simply where you began to write.

I write my first version in longhand (pencil). Then I do a complete revision, also in longhand . . . Then I type a third draft on yellow paper, a very special certain kind of yellow paper. No, I don't get out of bed to do this. I balance the machine on my knees. Sure, it works fine;

I can manage a hundred words a minute.
Well, when the yellow draft is finished,
I put the manuscript away for a while, a
week, a month, sometimes longer. When
I take it out again, I read it as coldly as
possible, then read it aloud to a friend
or two, and decide what changes I want
to make and whether or not I want to
publish it. I've thrown away rather a few
short stories, an entire novel, and half
of another. But if all goes well, I type
the final version on white paper and
that's that.

TRUMAN CAPOTE

In its first draft, "The Pirate Ship" began like this:

I can still remember the time two of my childhood buddies and I decided to run away from home.

Even today I'm still not sure what happened to bring
about this idea of ours.

Anyway, since we were all avid Captain Kid fans, we
decided upon building a pirate ship . . .

The second sentence is all wrong because it confusingly returns the
reader from childhood to today. The third shifts again to childhood
with an apologetic "anyway," a word persons use in conversation
when they have become mixed up in telling a story. The writer has
the advantage over the speaker: he can unconfuse himself by rewrit-
ing his story until he gets it right for the reader. If he presents in
the final draft confusion, he had better have intended to represent
confusion or he is a lazy writer.

As "The Pirate Ship" appears in its complete and revised form, it
begins competently and moves in a clear line. The writer introduces
himself and his buddies, says they decided to build a ship, and then
tells in ordinary narrative sequence how they searched, found, built,
and launched their vessel—on land. What happened first, second, and
so on. The revised opening is adequate. It might be more powerful
written this way:

My buddies Jim and Tom, and I searched for three days
for a ship. We looked in Mrs. Grigg's junk pile beside her
garage. The old steel swing wouldn't do, too heavy [and
then more examples] . . . We were Captain Kid fans and

had decided to build a pirate ship and make our fortunes
by looting and plundering other vessels.

On the third day, we discovered an old discarded casket
crate . . .

This opening sounds more like a story and less like an explanation
or lecture. An opening should start something going. If possible,
arrest the reader with your beginning. Make him feel as if you've
pulled him over to the curb and are getting out of the patrol car.
Create tension, suspense, or surprise, or begin an action that carries
along the reader, making him continually ask: "What next?"

One of the simplest ways to create a good beginning is to look
down the first page until you find an arresting line and cut out all
that goes before it. Or move it into first position. Few writers, beginners or veterans, can throw a high hard one on the first pitch. They
have to warm up first, and they should not present their readers with
the beginning practice tosses they made in the bullpen. Anton
Chekhov is considered by many critics the best of all modern short
story writers. Notice how in his published draft—we don't know how
many earlier drafts he threw in the wastebasket—he began two stories:

MY LIFE

The director said to me: "I only keep you out of respect
for your esteemed father; otherwise you would have been
sent flying long ago." I replied: "You flatter me, Your
Excellency, in assuming that I am capable of flying." And
then I heard him say: "Take that gentleman away, he gets
on my nerves."

IN THE RAVINE (1900)

The village of Ukleyevo lay in a ravine, so that only the
belfry and the chimneys of the cotton mills could be seen
from the highway and the railroad station. When passers-by
would ask what village it was, they were told:

"That's the one where the sexton ate up all the caviar
at the funeral."

And here is Reynolds Price, author of the novel *A Long and Happy
Life,* beginning a story:

THE WARRIOR PRINCESS OZIMBA (1961)

She was the oldest thing any of us knew anything about,
and she had never been near a tennis court, but somewhere

around the Fourth of July every year, one of us (it was
my father for a long time but for the past two years, just
me) rode out to her place and took her a pair of blue tennis
shoes.

These three beginnings to stories do not go off like cannons, but
neither do they go *poof* like a puffball kicked in the woods. They say
something. They do not beg, or back up, or curtsey. Whether you
are writing stories, articles, editorials, or answers to an examination,
start solidly.

In writing an opening beware of the windy generalization:

Everybody likes hot rods and I am no exception.

Not true. Many persons detest hot rods and consider them the most
likely transportation to Hell. Don't turn off the reader by pretentious
or coy behavior. In the beginning you establish your voice. If you
begin squeaking like a monkey or thundering like an elephant, you
have ruined your chances with the reader, who will be astounded
later to find you writing in natural human voice. Beware of phony
introductions, voice changes, and unnecessary apologies.

An opening often gains by being new, surprising; but if your
writing is crammed with surprises all the way through, you may do
well to begin quietly and conventionally. You do not have to amaze
or stun or mystify your reader at the beginning. But you have to
avoid alienating him with emptiness, phoniness, or unsuccessful
attempts at humor. You may simply begin factually:

East High School is located two miles from the center
of the business district in Clarksville.

but don't use that fact unless it makes a point relevant to your story.
Later in this story, the distance from the school to the business district
should come up.

Think hard how your reader will take your first words. Consider
this opening:

**What's going on? This question might have gone through
the minds of the grocery store owners when the students of
Mr. McMahon's psychology class went to the different stores
for an assignment that was done over vacation.**

"What's going on?" is a question that might be asked by anyone in
any situation. Here the reader is required to wait too long before the
question gains any significance.

Revision: "What's going on?" said the grocery store owner when
he saw twenty-five students from Mr. McMahon's psychology class

walking up and down the aisles writing in their notebooks. They were carrying out an assignment during Thanksgiving vacation.

When you have found or created a good beginning to your story, consider its ending. At both ends of a piece of writing, a writer is driven to explaining, almost as if he wanted to give advice to the reader on how to read what he has written, and nothing is worse than advice. If the Explainery comes at the beginning, it is lost on the reader who does not know the story yet. If it comes at the end, it tastes like soggy bread. The reader has read the story and is insulted by being told what he has read.

The first draft of "The Pirate Ship" ended like this:

> And since we had taken the "short-cut" across our neighbor's lawns, I'd say that it was approximately four phone calls and one crushed fence later that our parents finally caught up with us.
>
> Our ship was contrabanded and we "pirates" were sentenced to three long weeks of reforesting various islands, along with a looooong lesson from the "Board of Education"!

When the writer read his first draft to other students, they told him they wanted to know more about what happened on the journey through the neighbors' lawns. They didn't like the tired joke about a Board of Education being used to spank the boys. It was a pun that didn't spring from the experience itself, a canned joke. Discussing his story with critics, the writer said, "We really were upset to be stopped by our parents. Why, even today, when I see Jim or Tom, we look at each other and say, "It woulda' floated!" The critics and the writer knew instantly that he had stumbled on to a fine ending.

Study the ending of "Bird." It asks the reader to guess the significance of the garbage can lid slamming down. The story ends: a lid is put on it.

Look over your story for a spot near the end which is exciting or surprising. Or consider stopping a little before you believe the reader expects you to. Near the end find a good detail, an example of one of the main feelings or ideas in the story and chop everything else off that follows it. Or move the good passage to the end position. Don't drool an ending. Wipe your mouth, say the last word. Leave the reader.

Think of and look at your work as though it were done by your enemy. If you look at it to admire it you are lost . . . If we look at it to see where it is wrong, we shall see this and make it righter. If we look at it to see where it is right, we shall see this and shall not make it righter. We cannot see it both wrong and right at the same time.

SAMUEL BUTLER

chapter 10
criticizing

CRITICIZING WRITING is painful and valuable. One cannot say "good" or "bad" unless he has developed standards. One of the best ways to build standards is to sit with five to ten persons who discuss each other's writing, which they read aloud. Then the novice critic can judge his responses against those of his companions. In their faces he can see which writing holds or loses them, makes them laugh or smile. In weeks and months of such sessions, he develops bases for judgment, and all the while his own writing stands in his mind, receiving a silent, secret criticism.

When his turn comes to read his writing aloud, he hears his words as if detached from him. He instantly notes slips he failed to see when he read over his work in his room. While he is reading before critics, he finds himself saying "oops" and reaching for a pencil with which to change a word or line. At first the experience of reading to the group may be so frightening that he does not learn from the responses (or lack of responses) because he does not fully perceive them. But after a few readings, he comes to this awareness, and the silence of the group at a moment when he thought his writing funny or stirring shows him that he needs to take the writing home and put it on the workbench, or perhaps throw it in the wastebasket.

> *I learnt to speak as men learn to skate*
> *or to cycle—by doggedly making a fool*
> *of myself until I got used to it. Then I*
> *practised it in the open air—at the street*
> *corner, in the market square, in the park*
> *—the best school.*
>
> GEORGE BERNARD SHAW

If the group responds positively in the right places, the writer will go home anxious to write more. Encouragement is the battery that motivates the car. Once the motor is running, the car can go for hundreds of miles on a small charge of praise.

Every writer needs encouragement, whether beginner or prize-winning novelist. Loren Eiseley, the naturalist and anthropologist who wrote *The Immense Journey* and other books which are the envy of professional writers for their style, said of his learning experience:

> My greatest fortune was in having understanding teachers
> . . . I shall always be grateful for the interest they took in
> my work, for their encouragement expressed or silently
> affirmed.

Here, briefly, is the history of a beginning writer learning to revise, to criticize, to take criticism, and thus to write more professionally:

Having finished his first draft, he reads it aloud to himself. He writes a second draft, cutting, adding, rearranging. He puts the writing away for several hours—or if he has time, a month, three months. He then reads it aloud and sharpens it. The next morning he polishes it.

> *. . . the mere act of reading aloud put*
> *his work before him in a new light and,*
> *by constraining his attention to every*
> *line, made him judge it more rigorously.*
> *I always intend to read, and generally*
> *do read, what I write aloud to some one;*
> *any one almost will do, but he should*
> *not be so clever that I am afraid of him.*
> *I feel weak places at once when I read*
> *aloud where I thought, as long as I read*
> *to myself only, that the passage was all*
> *right.*
>
> SAMUEL BUTLER

Then he takes it to a group of other beginning writers and reads it aloud to them. He listens to what they say. He tries to hold their responses in mind without accepting or rejecting them instantly. At home a day later, he reviews the criticism, follows the suggestions he thinks helpful and ignores those he finds invalid. He writes his fifth draft and submits it for publication or files it with his finished work.

A program for improving writing such as the one presented in this book will not succeed unless the beginning writer becomes experienced through engaging in critical sessions with his peers. The person directing the program needs to encourage the writers to criticize upon their own two feet, and to evolve their own standards; but he also needs to state his own opinions of what is good and bad about writing—both the writing of those who sit with him and that published by established professionals.

He may help beginners become better critics by reading a paper or two before the group, preferably one that has been reproduced for each member, pointing out its strengths, and inviting further comments from the group. Then he can break the group into smaller sections of seven, eight, or nine, and ask them to read aloud their papers to each other for criticism. Nine is an ideal number because it makes a sufficient audience to put pressure on the writer. He hears his words differently when they are read to an audience of that size than he does when he reads to two or three listeners. If most of his nine listeners say his writing is good or bad, he cannot dismiss their opinion lightly. But if he reads to only two or three, he may say, "Well, Jim was just trying to be nice to me" or "Abigail never did like me anyway."

Preferably, small groups should meet in separate rooms, or only two to a room, so that they will not disturb each other; but that is not always possible. When the leader finds time does not permit a reading of all papers in groups as large as nine, he may cut groups to four or five, or even three when the writers have become more trustworthy and honest as critics.

The remarks of critics who take writing seriously are the most valuable response a writer can receive. Marginal comments pointing out slips or mistakes in grammar, spelling, or mechanics are not ordinarily useful to a writer until he is polishing his work in final draft. The experience of thousands of teachers in American high schools and colleges has showed that such reading for correction rather than helpful editing has had little positive effect. Once beginners sense they are improving rapidly and can write papers that move their peers, they take pride and care in their work, which improves every aspect of their writing. A man is not going to learn the fine points of catching a football on the run, over the heads of defenders, or near the sidelines, until he can first hang on to it when it is thrown straight at him softly.

Giving criticism in a small group session asks a great deal of the critic. If he is impressed, he must sense his reaction and make it verbal. Some persons say that criticism must never be vague—"Good," or "I liked that." Those persons were never writers; they don't know what encouragement means. Perhaps they fear such general remarks are mere flattery. If so, the criticism is immoral and damaging. If honest, it is valuable. It will be more valuable if the critic learns to state it specifically: "I liked your descriptions. They were fresh. I wrote down this one: 'The hands looked stiff, as if they had just weeded a garden, and her fingers were yellow and brittle.' "

The wise critic knows that the beginning writer is vulnerable to almost any blow. He has little confidence, is easily knocked out. He feels his writing is all him; he has developed no objectivity. Any criticism of his sentences is an attack upon his self. Therefore the critic who would help a beginning writer, rather than destroy him, starts with positive criticism. He looks for what he can praise. A sentence. A paragraph. An incident. One word. If he can find nothing he can honestly admire, he says nothing but "Keep writing." Everyone has a command of words if he can find the troops that belong to him, and the wise critic finds ways of assuring the beginning writer of this fact.

As the beginner continues writing, he more often speaks with force and tells experiences or ideas that strike with surprise and truth. The critic keeps before the beginner his successes. He tries to move him from success to success.

The critic remembers he is part of a group. He volunteers only two or three criticisms during a half-hour period, knowing that if he talks more than that he will usurp others' time and lessen his chances of being heard with attention and respect. So he takes notes as the writer reads and he selects from all his responses to the writing those he thinks will most aid the writer.

Only when the writer has achieved enough successes to recognize his abilities and potentialities does the intelligent critic engage in thorough and negative criticism. Once the writer senses that a number of honest and keen-minded persons have admired some of his words, he is strong enough to take negative criticism and use it to create a success.

A professional editor demonstrates model behavior. He considers himself not so much a judge as a helper—one who assists the writer in improving a piece of writing that both persons have a stake in. He is not a public critic sounding off to impress others with his wisdom or wisecracks. He is not trying to get one up on the writer he works with.

> *He [Ezra Pound] was a marvelous critic because he didn't try to turn you into an imitation of himself. He tried to see what you were trying to do.*
>
> T. S. ELIOT

In his manner he must convince the writer he is not out to needle him but to help. Only then will the writer think objectively about what the critic is saying. Striking back at the critic is pointless. At the moment of criticism, no one enjoys being told his writing contains weaknesses. Learning to write communicatively is painful, but if the writer builds confidence slowly and solidly, he will rise to the level where he exclaims in joy with the critic at their mutual discovery of a weakness and how it may be strengthened.

To learn to do something well rather than simply to learn *about* something requires failure. Not final failure, but a number of small failures alternated with successes. The learner who never anticipates failure is doomed to continue without improvement or to collapse into perpetual inactivity. He is fortunate if he has an expert coach who makes sure many of his first small tries are successes.

The wise writer expects his fellows to say they don't like something in his work. He tries to find out what and why. When his writing is praised, he says "Thank you" or nothing. He does not apologize and say, "This is really not very good. I needed to take more time on it," or "You've all probably heard this kind of thing before." If he really possesses such feelings toward his work, he does not bring it to the group for criticism. He presents only what at the moment looks good to him, in the best form he can put it in. He tries to be honest. When he receives criticism he never says, "Well, I wasn't trying very hard when I wrote that." He does not agree with a critic just to be friendly, but he does not engage in long hostile defenses of his work which imply the critic is committing a crime to speak against what he has written.

> *A writer is unfair to himself when he is unable to be hard on himself.*
>
> MARIANNE MOORE

Disciplining himself in group critique sessions, a writer trains himself to be a better critic of his own work when alone with it. He knows he must stand by his words or change them upon criticism. The critics may praise and censure, rave and rant, but he must make the final decisions. He is ultimately responsible for his sentences.

[George Bernard Shaw often sent his early drafts of his plays to his friend Ellen Terry, the actress, for criticism. Once she said she feared to suggest changes on his manuscript. He wrote back:]

"Oh, bother the MSS., mark them as much as you like: what else are they for? Mark everything that strikes you. I may consider a thing fortynine times; but if you consider it, it will be considered 50 times; and a line 50 times considered is 2 per cent better than a line 49 times considered. And it is the final 2 per cent that makes the difference between excellence and mediocrity."

chapter 11
sharpening

REHEATING a piece of writing after it has cooled, tempering it, and sharpening it is enjoyable—if you know how. Otherwise it may turn out worse, brittle or misshapen. Look for the common sicknesses or dullnesses professional writers try to eliminate: Is-ness, It-ache, There-ache, excessive use of adjectives, adverbs, and passive verbs.

Consider this column of opinion printed in a high school newspaper. Its first paragraph makes its point dramatically; its verbs are vigorous and its adjectives full of meaning.

[THE FEMININE ERA]

Waltzing down the corridor in a velvet-collared, ruffled shirt, clutching a pink hairbrush, a teenager hurriedly skipped into the school lavatory between classes and began labor over a hair-do with side-swept bangs for four and a half minutes of agony and disgust; the door was marked "BOYS."

5

Is this the beginning of a new feminine era today among the boys of our country?

As they walk down the hall fussing and swishing with 10 their hair with an occasional pat on the bangs, it becomes more apparent that this is a generation of feminine men coming up.

Once it was the style for boys to carry small combs in their hip pockets; now it's brushes, brushes with pink and 15 baby blue handles.

By a recent poll it was revealed that until a few years ago, a boy got up in the morning, ran a quick one-stroke combing through his hair, jumped into the same old pair of Levis he'd taken off the night before and headed for school 20 in less than ten minutes.

Today, an act like this would be considered a tragedy in a boy's life if he wasn't allowed at least a couple of hours to himself for the care and parting of his hair.

It seems that of the both groups, the boys are more con- 25 scious than girls about subtleties of dress.

Although occasionally they are apt to go a little more overboard, when they begin wearing ruffled embroidered shirts and more cologne than girls do perfume.

Boys have adopted hair styles popular with the girls . . . 30 The boys have joined the co-eds in going to the "mod" or "natural" look with moderately short hair and side-swept bangs that shade their eyes.

Today, it is not unusual for a receptionist at a beauty salon to pick up the phone and find out that it is a male 35 customer who wants to make an early appointment to have his hair thinned, washed, set, and then sprayed for a big school event coming up. In some parts of the state, there are even special beauty salons for only the male customer.

Why this drastic change? Is it because the boys see the 40 feminine world as a privileged one, and they want to join it too?

Is it the feeling that the demands of the traditional masculine role are more than they can tolerate and they are abandoning it? Whatever the reason may be, "BOYS," stand 45 up and hold your role as a "MAN."

Through the first 38 lines, this writing makes a strong case. Then it asks several good questions which it fails to probe or answer. It ends in a thicket: asking boys to fulfill their traditional role without understanding why it may be changing or whether it should change or whether males were at other times just as feminine in personal habits.

The author, a girl, is quick to condemn boys for following feminine hair and clothes styles. She neglects to admit that many girls of the time follow masculine hair and clothes styles.

The column needs rethinking. But for the moment, consider only how its expression might be sharpened in lines 7 through 45. It suffers from Is-ness, a dullness marked by weak uses of forms of the verb *to be*. If *am, is, are, was, were, shall, will,* or *been* connects trite or empty adjectives or vague nouns, it probably needs replacing with a verb that carries more meaning. Often a form of the verb *to be* can be eliminated from a sentence without losing any meaning. Write down all uses of this verb in lines 8 through 46 and study whether or not eliminating them would strengthen the writing. Here is the way a professional editor might make such an inspection:

Lines 5 and 7: adequate *was* and *is*. Don't change.

Line 11: Is-ness. Revise sentence:

Original. As they walk down the hall fussing and swishing with their hair with an occasional pat on the bangs, it becomes apparent that this *is* a generation of feminine men coming up.

Revision. As they walk down the hall swishing and fussing with their hair, occasionally patting it on the bangs, they embody a new generation of feminine men.

Line 13: Is-ness (*was*). Revise sentence:

Original. Once it *was* the style for boys to carry small combs in their hip pockets; now it's brushes, brushes with pink and baby blue handles.

Revision. Once boys carried small combs in their hip pockets; now they carry brushes with pink and baby blue handles.

Line 16: Is-ness (*was*). Revise sentence:

Original. By a recent poll *it* was revealed . . .

Revision. A recent poll revealed . . .

Lines 21 and 22: Is-ness (*would be, wasn't*). Revise sentence:

Original. Today an act like this *would be* considered a tragedy in a boy's life if he *wasn't* allowed at least a couple of hours to himself for the care and parting of his hair. (34 words)

A difficulty in this sentence is that the expression "an act like this" doesn't refer to any words preceding.

Revision. Today a boy denied a couple of hours to himself for the care and parting of his hair would consider himself tragically mistreated. (23 words)

REVISING SIX: Circle other uses of the verb *to be* in "The Feminine Era." In considering possible revisions, try to eliminate empty nouns and verbs, and replace them with persons or things which act through vigorous verbs. The revisions exhibited above do away with these weak expressions:

> it becomes more apparent that this
> it was the style
> by . . . it was
> an act like this would be considered a . . . in a boy's life

Note that these expressions contain no power or color. They consist of abstract and lifeless words, necessary and useful at times, but here pale and empty.

One way to transfuse red blood into a sentence anemic with Is-ness is to substitute a metaphorical verb for *is*. For example:

Original. The poor dog *is* an inferior because he *is* not a symbol maker, says Western Man.

Revision. The poor dog *wags* his tail as an inferior because he *is* not a symbol maker.

Here the second part of the statement retains an *is*. If it were eliminated by saying "because he doesn't make symbols" the sentence would lose part of its balance and parallel construction: "an inferior . . . a symbol maker." So you can see that you should not eliminate *is's* wherever they appear without considering how they are functioning.

Shakespeare was a master of the metaphorical verb. In *Macbeth* he made Malcolm say:

> This tyrant whose sole name *blisters* our tongues,
> *Was* once thought honest.

Suppose Shakespeare had written with Is-ness:

> This tyrant whose sole name *is* a blister on our tongues,
> *Was* once thought honest.

Again, one use of the verb *to be* is enough in the statement.

REVISING SEVEN: In one of your past longer pieces of writing circle every use of the forms of the verb *to be*. Consider which need to be eliminated and revise the sentences in which they appear. Remember that Is-ness stands for a *weak* use of a form of *to be*. No writer can write many sentences in a row without usefully employing *is*.

It-ache and There-ache are dullnesses marked by unnecessary uses of *it* and *there*. They are often associated with Is-ness. Diagnosis of It-ache and There-ache in "The Feminine Era":

It-aches in lines 10, 13, 16 were eliminated along with the Is-ness. It-ache in line 24:

Original. *It* seems that of the both groups, the boys are more conscious than girls about subtleties of dress.

Revision. The boys are more conscious than girls about subtleties of dress.

There-ache in lines 37-38:

Original. In some parts of the state, there are even special beauty salons for only the male customer. (17 words)

Revision: In some parts of the state, special beauty salons serve only male customers. (13 words)

REVISING EIGHT: See if you can find other examples of It-ache and There-ache in "The Feminine Era." Often you will discover you have already eliminated them in dealing with Is-ness.

You are hunting for uses of *it* and *there* which do not carry solid meaning, but act merely as convenient handles for introducing other expressions. Sometimes they operate well as handles. They are hard to replace in these two sentences:

> It is cold out tonight.
> There are only four houses on the other side of the street
> on our block.

Too often, vague uses of *it* and *there* lead a writer to wasting other words as well:

Original. It is the task of the school to train all the students.

Such an It-ache as that may be cured by making a noun the subject of the sentence. At the same time, an editor would probably change the possessive construction "of the school" to "school's," a more informal but vigorous expression:

Revision. The school's task is to train all the students.

A sentence does not ache from a healthy use of *it* or *there*. For example:

> The ball rolled and rolled until it hit the fence.
>
> "He's sitting over there," said the witness, pointing.

In these sentences *it* represents the ball and *there* tells a place. These are different uses from those involved in *It is* and *There are*.

Now look for It-ache and There-ache in the longer paper you examined in REVISING SEVEN and make the needed changes.

Dullness also results from the excessive use of passive verbs.

Passive. It was brought to our attention by the manager that we had not sent out the invoice.

Active. The manager told us we had not sent out the invoice.

Passive. The play was a performance that was observed by George with amazing indifference.

Active. George observed the play with amazing indifference.

Passive verbs suggest that nobody is doing anything. Just sitting around being acted upon.

Passive. The object that was stepped on by me was a ladybug with lavender spots.

Active. I stepped on a ladybug with lavender spots.

Passive. The scheme was conceived by John at four in the morning.

Active. John conceived the scheme at four in the morning.

Dullness may also be imparted to sentences by excessive use of the verbs

make	go	get
have	move	come

They are not full of specific meaning. Circle each use of them in your writing and question it: can the verb be replaced with a more particular and meaningful one? For example, *making* might be supplanted by

constructing	gluing	joining	stringing
building	piling	digging	sticking

and many other verbs. Even these are fairly general; for example, a writer might say "I *cemented* two stones together" rather than "I stuck two stones together." Choosing more precise and vigorous verbs puts life into writing because life is particular, not general.

Like Is-ness, the shoddy use of *make, have, go, move, get,* and *come* leads to a frightening waste of words:

Original. This land *has* the appearance of being arid.

Revision. This land looks arid.

These verbs frequently seed sentences with unnecessary nouns.

Original. He finally *came to* his decision. He would run.

Revision. He finally decided he would run.

You should remember that these suggested revisions are made out of context. The last revision above saves three words from the original sentences, but if the author's purpose was to slow down the reader and delay the divulging of the decision, he might better use the original version, which carries a different rhythm.

Beginning writers often insist on establishing the ownership of an object with the verb *have* before they let the owner use the object. Good way to clog the story.

Original. He *had* a bicycle. He rode it to work every morning.

Revision. He rode his bicycle to work every morning.

The principle involved in sharpening is to fill words with precise meaning or get rid of them. Beginning writers splatter adjectives and adverbs like buckshot. Consider this passage:

> I summoned up courage and *boldly* set forth through the pathway. Suddenly loomed in sight five male patients sitting outside only a few feet from me. Too late to turn back, I consoled myself with the idea that an attendant was probably *unobtrusively* hidden from view but there, nevertheless, for protection.
>
> Then the thought dawned on me that I was in the wrong and didn't deserve protection because I was trespassing— there were blockades which I had ignored, set up in front of the pathway. The patients, perhaps sensing my *nervous* anticipation, *possibly* evident in my *faltering* steps and *nervous* eye movements, said "hello" to me.
>
> My *natural* reaction to this situation bothers me. In Psych class we consider mental patients just "sick people." I don't want to be guilty of sharing the *common* feelings of the *general* public.

Here in line 1, *boldly* is unnecessary with "summoned up courage" and "set forth," both expressions which imply boldness. In line 5, *unobtrusively* is unnecessary. Seldom does anyone hide obtrusively. In lines 10 and 11, *perhaps* is an honest word but the other italicized words overdo the notion of sensing nervousness. A sharp cutting is needed.

Original. The patients, perhaps sensing my nervous anticipation, possibly evident in my faltering steps and nervous eye movements, said "hello" to me.

Revision. Perhaps sensing my anticipation in my faltering steps and nervous eye movements, the patients said "hello" to me.

In line 13, *natural* is not an accurate word for what the writer wants to say. *Instant* or *stereotyped* would make more sense. In line 15, *common* is unnecessary. *Sharing* and *general* say enough by themselves.

Remembering the *repeat-and-vary* principle, the good writer avoids ruts. He does not allow himself to supply for every verb an adverb and for every noun an adjective until the pattern becomes monotonous and the words flabby. He avoids or changes dead patterns like these:

> He slowly walked up the stairs, nonchalantly pushed on
> the door, and casually entered the room.

> At the picnic were sticky-fingered children, rosy-cheeked
> mommas, and large-stomached fathers.

When he finishes his first or second draft, a good writer tests the adjectives and adverbs: are they pulling their weight? Do the other words around them render them unnecessary? See how freshly and powerfully Shakespeare uses an adverb in giving Regan, King Lear's daughter, these words about her father:

> 'Tis the infirmity of his age: yet he hath ever but *slenderly*
> known himself.

Powerful adverbs and adjectives are not beyond you. On the whole, the writer of "The Feminine Era" made her adverbs and adjectives count. *Velvet-collared* and *ruffled* and *side-swept* are doing their jobs. But in lines 26-27, the writer fell off the ship with the expression "a little more overboard." One can go overboard, but not more or less overboard.

A fundamental in using adverbs and adjectives is not to let one of them smother the effect of another strong word. Don't let your straight man steal the attention from the comic. If you write

She was *unusually* hideous.

you have lessened the force of *hideous* by making the reader attend to the weak word *unusually*. If you write

It was a *tremendously* tall skyscraper.

you have lessened the force of *tall*. In fact, both *tremendously* and *tall* are tired and should be replaced with words that fix the height of the skyscraper in actual or metaphorical scale.

I stood a hundred feet away and yet my neck ached from looking up to the top of the building.

This chapter has talked about weak uses of certain words. All of them may be used adequately or strongly by a skillful writer. Note in this beautifully phrased passage from "Self-Reliance" that Emerson uses many strong verbs but also forms of *to be*. He plants four adjectives within the space of seven words. He finishes with a sentence that carries the normally vague and weak verb *go*.

Travelling is a fool's paradise. Our first journeys discover to us the indifference of places. At home I dream that at Naples, at Rome, I can be intoxicated with beauty and lose my sadness. I pack my trunk, embrace my friends, embark on the sea and at last wake up in Naples, and there beside me is the stern fact, the sad self, unrelenting, identical, that I fled from. I seek the Vatican and the palaces. I affect to be intoxicated with sights and suggestions, but I am not intoxicated. My giant goes with me wherever I go.

The power of this passage comes from its ideas as well as from its expression. Emerson is true to his thoughts and feelings, and therefore his words carry surprise. The words that precede or follow ordinarily weak verbs like *to be* or *goes* are full of meaning—*intoxicated, giant, fool's paradise*.

Sharpening writing is not as black and white a matter as this chapter suggests. Many of the changes dictated here are debatable, and only a person considering the total context of a word or phrase can see whether or not it should be retained. Find ways of probing your sentences so that you see alternative ways of stating them. *Is, there*, and *it* frequently are wasted and breed other unnecessary words. But they are good words in their place. You will find writers as brilliant as Bernard Shaw using *it is* when the words are not absolutely necessary, as in the quotation at the head of this chapter:

> And it is the final 2 per cent that makes the difference
> between excellence and mediocrity.

This *it* doesn't ache much. It could be eliminated and the sentence written

> And the final 2 per cent makes the difference between
> excellence and mediocrity.

but the words *it is* in this passage act as emphasizers. They slow down the reader and make sure he gives attention to *2 per cent*.

The moral of this chapter is not to do away with all uses of the cited words, but to learn where to look for possible weak spots in your sentences. The writer of this book originally wrote the first sentence of the paragraph above in this way:

> Sharpening writing is not as black and white a matter as
> this chapter makes it appear.

Spotting the *it* in the sentence, and thinking about removing it, he saw that he could drop three words, *makes, it,* and *appear,* and substitute only the word *suggests.*

REVISING NINE: Look over two of your past free writings and attempt to eliminate from them weak passive verbs, empty verbs like *make* and *have*, the overuse of adjectives, and the unnecessary use of intensifying words like *tremendously* and *great big*.

Life is a jungle of events whose mean-ings are at once too casual (and to that extent insignificant) and too full of pos-sible implication (without offering us any guidance as to which implication or set of implications we should choose). The skilled storyteller makes those mean-ings at once more significant and less confused.

DAVID DAICHES

chapter 12
finding
an
angle

TEACHER: Write about something that interests you.
STUDENT: But I don't know of anything that interests me.

The student didn't mean this idiotic statement to be taken literally. He meant to say that under the pressure of an assignment he could not think of a subject he thought properly impressive. The American poet William Stafford has said:

> A person writes by means of that meager but persistent little self he has with him all the time. He does not out-flank his ignorance by intensive reading in composition class; he does not become brilliant about constructions by learning the history of the language. He is a certain weight of person, relying on the total feeling he has for experience . . . You know how often students bring something to you, saying, "I don't know whether this is really good, or whether I should throw it in the wastebasket." The assump-tion is that one or the other choice is the right move. No. Almost everything we say or think or do—or write—comes

in that spacious human area bounded by something this
side of the sublime and something above the unforgivable.
We must accustom ourselves to talking without orating,
and to writing without achieving "Paradise Lost." We
must forgive ourselves and each other much, in our writing
and in our talking . . . When you write, simply tell me
something.

Mr. Stafford's six-year-old daughter Kit once said to him:

We'd have a old car, the kind that gets flat tires, but inside
would be wolfskin on the seats and warm fur on the steering wheel, and wolf fur on all the buttons. And we'd live in
a ranch house made out of logs with a loft where you sleep,
and you'd walk a little ways and there'd be the farm with
the horses. We'd drive to town, and we'd have flat tires,
and be sort of old.

Kit told her father what she cared about. She did not reach for
some grandiose subject, but stayed with her own experience and the
wolfskin she had read about in children's books. In this simple
way she told her father she loved him and wanted to live with
warmth, the texture of logs, the excitement of horses. What she was
interested in intersected with what her father was interested in, and
communication took place.

Good writing requires a constant shuttling between a writer's
self and his subject—where do they intersect? If the subject is assigned
and the writer feels no interest in it, he must turn it over and over,
come at it from many angles, until he finds a place where some
aspect of the subject intersects with his past experience or present
interest. Good writing also requires a shuttling between the writer
and his audience. Are he and his readers similar in some ways? How
should *he* talk to *them*? And good writing requires a shuttling of the
writer between his subject and his readers. What parts of it will be
new and significant to them?

That is why good writers often talk of finding an *angle*. They do
not mean some gimmick or trick by which to dupe their readers into
trying what cannot be interesting or useful to them. They mean a
line of direction which will intersect writer, subject, and audience
on the way to a point, an intersection of valuable meaning.

Kit was *talking* to her father in the car, but what she did can be
applied to writing as well. She spoke her true feelings. Only that
which first excites the writer stands much chance of exciting the
reader. But the intersection of meaning could not have taken place if

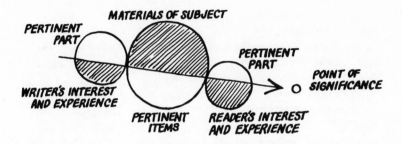

Kit had simply stated her feelings. She had to present some of the experiences she had enjoyed with her father, not catalog them in infinite detail, but select some that produced the feelings or could stand for them—for warmth and coziness, wolf fur and a log house; for sharing an intimate experience, flat tires.

> *But wise men pierce this rotten diction*
> *and fasten words again to visible things.*
> RALPH WALDO EMERSON

WRITING TEN: Write an article about a person, place, or incident that surprises and fascinates you. Choose a particular audience—your classmates or the readers of the school or local newspaper. Ask yourself how long it should be—what will the paper print? How much of the subject as you handle it will your readers take? Think of your angle—how much of the subject does it demand that you discuss? How does it limit what you can cover? Before you write, consider this case-history of how an article was written by a professional reporter, Lane Wick, for the *Kalamazoo Gazette*, August 7, 1966:

A PRETTY MIXTURE OF SKY-DIVING AND SAFETY

Stan Peck, the personable executive-director of the Kalamazoo County Safety Council, says he nearly fell out of his chair when he learned of his new secretary's avocation.

"I'm a sky-diver," pretty 18-year-old Sue Goris told Peck while on her second day on the job.

"A what?" Peck gulped weakly.

Sue, who began her aerial antics March 13, told her boss that she enjoyed sky-diving because "it's so neat, really!"

"I'll admit I was somewhat surprised," Peck told a reporter while managing a grin. "But I told Sue that there is

some danger in most sports and that I guess sky-diving with
the proper precautions and training could be as safe as
many of them."

Sue began work in the safety council office several weeks
ago among posters saying "Darkness Hides Danger, Facts
About Seat Belts, Watch Out for Kids."

She works among the safety slogans during the week, and
then leaps out of airplanes 3,000 feet above the ground on
Sundays. A few square yards of silk, and the ability to pack
the material properly, stand between her and death.

"I think about that sometimes," Sue confides. "When I'm
going up in the plane, usually. You think that it could all
be so very final."

But the thrill of her 10 parachute jumps to date has in-
creased with each venture and she wishes that each trip to
earth could last much longer.

Until last winter, Sue had never been in an airplane.
At Christmastime, she took a round-trip jet plane ride to
the State of Washington.

Her parachuting attempts have been undertaken from
the Austin Lake Airport, in Portage, and at an airport near
Muskegon. The first five jumps were "static-line" leaps,
during which the chute is opened automatically by a line
attached to the plane.

The last five jumps were free-fall ventures with Sue
pulling the rip-cord.

What started her desire to be a sky-diver?

"I used to watch sky-diving programs on television," she
said. "It looked so neat, so I tried it—and it was!"

"The first one was perfect. I jumped off the plane and
when I felt the chute snap open I thought, 'I've done it,
I've done it!'"

But she came in for a landing slightly wrong on the second attempt, and was dragged briefly by the chute. On the
third jump, her feet tangled in auxiliary chute lines.

"I wasn't really worried," she said. "I just didn't know
what to do. I came down OK, but I was shaking after I
landed."

On a recent jump, she got caught in a "thermal"—an
updraft of hot air—and drifted nearly a mile off target.

Sue is a 1966 graduate of Loy Norrix High School. She
plans on enrolling in night courses at Western Michigan
University this fall.

A self-proclaimed tom-boy when younger, Sue now enjoys water skiing, sailing, riding horses and motorcycles, and watching football and basketball.

She lives with her parents, Mr. and Mrs. Frank Goris, at 725 Lakeway.

Sue has a teen-age brother who she says is interested in taking up sky-diving.

"I'm sort of against that," Sue said. "I don't want anything to happen to him."

Part of Mr. Wick's regular beat was to cover the doings of the Kalamazoo County Safety Council. One day Stan Peck, the director said, "You ought to do a story on Sue Goris, my secretary, instead of me. I nearly fell out of my chair when she told me she was a sky-diver." Mr. Peck and Mr. Wick saw a story with an angle: girl working in Safety Council office regularly risks her life jumping out of planes.

A day or two later, after getting Mr. Peck's permission to interview Sue at her job, Mr. Wick interviewed her. For about twenty minutes he questioned her and got her talking freely about sky-diving. During this time he did not take notes because he finds that persons not used to being interviewed sometimes freeze when a reporter is taking down what they say. As she talked, he kept in mind his angle for the story and asked questions that might provide what he calls "critical elements" for the account. Later he asked her again about these matters and took down her answers.

He asked Miss Goris how she had started sky-diving. She said with a club at Austin Lake Airport. She told about some of the men in the club; about her girl friend Sonny, who jumped with her; about learning to pack parachutes, to tumble, and to jump off a ladder without injuring herself. Mr. Wick listened to these comments closely but doubted that he would use them in his story. He felt that the general public had read so many articles about sky-diving in magazines and newspapers in the past ten years and had looked at so many television shows about sky-divers that they would be bored by a recital of how a person learns to sky dive and carries out a jump. "If Sue had hurt herself jumping off that training ladder," he said, "I would have put that in the story because it would have been relevant to my story." Because she worked in the Safety Council office, he was looking for anything she might say that would build the tension between safety and accident. She told him about jumps which came near to being accidents—when she was dragged by the chute, and when her feet became tangled in the auxiliary chute.

He used these facts. She told him about how a diver climbs out of the plane, hangs on to the strut, and in a free fall counts to ten before pulling the cord. She told him how static-line jumps are made. He didn't use these facts. A week later she told him about the time she had been caught in an updraft of hot air and carried nearly a mile off her target. He used that.

Miss Goris impressed Mr. Wick with her beauty. He thought that readers are always interested in pretty girls, that she would look good in news photographs, and that her femininity was in contrast to the rugged act of sky-diving. When she was younger, she said, she liked to ride horses and play ball with the boys. "You'd say you were sort of a tom-boy?" asked Mr. Wick. "Yes," she said, "a tom-boy." When he asked her if she had ever been on an airplane before she jumped for the first time, she said her first trip in a plane had occurred last Christmas. He used that fact.

"When I went to see her," said Mr. Wick, "I knew I could get a good story because it was there. If only I could get the right comments from her. She was free and honest, easy to interview. She didn't try to be cute or jazz up her part in sky-diving. After the first twenty minutes, I began taking notes and trying to put down what she said. I believe these sentences are exactly the words she spoke:

> It looked so neat, so I tried it—and it was!
>
> I jumped off the plane and when I felt the chute snap open I thought, 'I've done it, I've done it!'

When a person I'm interviewing says something the way I want it said for my story, I usually stop everything, even listening, and try to get down the words verbatim."

When he returned to the office after talking to Miss Goris, Mr. Wick checked the newspaper's file of past clippings and found an article saying she had been elected Future Homemakers Queen of Mattawan, a nearby rural town, when she was in high school. He did not use this fact. Often, he said, stories about pretty girls tell whether the girl is engaged to be married or dating one boy or none. He did not use any information on this point. He did not use the names of the two sky-diving clubs she had belonged to. "Another reporter would handle this story differently," he said. "But this is the way it appeared to me—a girl working in a safety office and indulging in a dangerous avocation."

Mr. Wick said that when he began reporting five years ago he used to write feature articles that were full of irrelevant material. "There was a time," he said, "when editors chopped my articles a lot. But I came to realize that a lot of background kills a story and that I should put in only what was critical. I learned to throw out everything that was not interesting to me. I finally learned what I had heard so many times from journalism teachers and editors—that a story should be like a bathing suit, long enough to cover the subject, but short enough to keep it interesting. In school and college, I wrote term papers fifty pages sometimes—put in everything. In this story I used almost nothing about Sue's personal life, just a few short paragraphs near the end to identify her for the readers, but held to a minimum because such facts were not critical to my story."

Asked whether he thought about the possibility of the story making Mr. Peck, the director of the Safety Council, appear to be acting contradictory to his own advice, Mr. Wick said, "I've known Stan for a long time. He has a good sense of humor. I felt I could do it in such a way as to not offend him. In a story like this, you shouldn't ordinarily offend people. Sometimes in reporting you have to offend them when they're charged with crime or some other damaging act. And the fact was, as Stan pointed out, that many avocations and jobs are dangerous. The Safety Council exists to help people learn to take safety precautions in carrying them out."

Asked about the beginning of the story, Mr. Wick said that he didn't think it grabbed the reader as strongly as it might. He picked up Mr. Peck's comment "I nearly fell out of my chair" because it referred to a possible accident, but he wasn't sure that many of his readers got this connection. The ending seemed right to him. "From everything I heard her say," Mr. Wick said, "this comment seemed the natural kicker for the story. It brought together danger and safety. I like to end with my best statement."

Sue Goris said her brother didn't like that last line when he saw it in the paper but she had felt that way and so she made the comment. She thought Mr. Wick did a perfect job of quoting her and saying how she felt about jumping. She was glad he had not used anything about her being queen in Mattawan. "It didn't amount to much," she said.

Reality is often fabulous, as this newspaper story demonstrates. But writing reality into a tightly constructed story like this takes discipline and craft. And experience—for Mr. Wick, five years. Consider now three stories by inexperienced writers, published in school newspapers. The first one contains a number of strong possibilities that are never realized.

SENIOR GIRL MAKES HORSES HER HOBBY

"I have always loved horses, since I got my first rocking horse at two years of age," June Randall, senior, says.

For several years, June has taken lessons in horseback riding at Snider Creek Hunt Club.

Now she is lucky enough to have two horses of her own. Seven-year-old Raffy and ten-year-old Blue's Yankee Pride, called Blue, are both boarded at her grandparents' farm north of Melo.

"To have a good understanding between the horse and the owner, to understand why the horse acts as he does and never to blame anything on the horse, is very important," June says.

As soon as there is an opportunity, June takes part in horse shows.

"My biggest thrill was getting my first blue ribbon with my horse Blue," she said.

She trained Blue herself for the English style of riding. Next fall June is going to Middle State University where she is planning to go into Veterinary Medicine, a six year program.

Right now, she is looking for a place near the university where she can board Blue during her college years.

To race Arabian horses is a future dream for June. She is also planning to have her own veterinary practice. [All names in this story have been changed.]

One might say that this story is so much shorter than Lane Wick's that the writer could not do justice to the many aspects of June Randall's interest in horses. That is all the more reason for the writer finding an angle which helps him select critical elements from the mass of material he confronts.

Suppose the writer had approached his task as Mr. Wick did. A girl likes horses. Nothing unusual there. A girl owns two horses herself—somewhat unusual. She loves to ride horses in shows. Expected. She is planning to be a veterinarian. Surprising. Few women are doctors. A call to the Middle State University veterinary school might reveal what percent of women vets work in the United States. Miss Randall plans to take her horse to college with her. Surprising.

As soon as the writer found out that Miss Randall was planning to study veterinary medicine and take her horse to college, he had a possible angle. Many of the high school readers of this article were thinking of college and of a vocation. When the writer heard her say:

> "To have a good understanding between the horse and owner, to understand why the horse acts as he does and never blame anything on the horse, is very important."

he could have questioned her about what she meant and what experiences had led her to these conclusions. She would have revealed some of the understanding she has for horses which led her to want to become a doctor and would probably make her a good student of veterinary medicine. As it is, the quotation is vague and falls apart at the ending—"is very important." The writer easily could have induced Miss Randall to give examples of understanding a horse and thus shown why the understanding is important.

With this angle in mind, a writer could have omitted a number of elements not critical and saved room for new and significant material. What happened in training and winning a blue ribbon happens to many girls who participate in horse shows. Not critical to this story.

The opening quotation is good; it could be improved by reversal:

> "Ever since I got my first rocking horse at two years of age, I have loved horses."

Then the surprising words *rocking horse* hit the reader at the outset of the story.

The following article, from the same newspaper, has an angle:

JUNIOR GIRL'S LIFE HECTIC

Helping to care for a herd of cows, many chickens, three cats, one rabbit, three dogs, and four kittens is part of the job for Meg Niles, junior.

Meg lives on a 100 acre farm at Tee Lake in Sherview with her parents and six brothers and sisters. Her brothers, George, a senior, and Ren, a freshman, also attended Crestview High. Meg's father, Mr. Robert Niles, is a teacher of physics here at the school. Mrs. Niles is the school nurse for Crestview's neighbors across town, Tee Lake Central.

When Meg was asked how she liked living on a farm she replied, "I like it, especially the fresh air, except when the wind blows your way during manure spreading time."

> **Besides doing her chores on the farm, Meg has a part time job at Community Hospital as a "Miss Messenger."**
>
> **"This job," said Meg, "will give me valuable experience, as I plan to become a nurse."**
>
> **This year Meg has been maintaining an A average and has been chosen as one of the two girls to represent Crestview High at the Wolverine Girls State this summer.**

Meg's hectic life is the angle in this story, but more hectic than what or whose? Many of the materials for exploiting the angle are present in the story, but they need pointing up.

The second paragraph identifies and places Meg Niles but doesn't point up the hectic character of her life, as it should. She lives on a 100 acre farm. How does that make her life hectic? Does she have to do a job that is affected by the size of the farm? "Besides doing her chores," the writer says, but he doesn't tell what they are. She has six brothers and sisters (meaning three brothers and three sisters, or twelve in all?). How does her large family take up her time and make her life hectic?

Which facts must be omitted as not critical to this story? The last statement, for one, because it says how she will be busy this summer away from the farm and school. Not touching the angle. And the quotation from Meg: "This job will give me valuable experience, as I plan to become a nurse." Again off the angle, and a flat statement with no individual flavor.

A little more questioning by the writer and a sharper use of materials and this story would be first-rate. To *point up* material is to write it so the reader sees its pertinence. The opening sentence of this story makes one-half of a good lead. The enumeration of cats, rabbit, dogs, and kittens helps build a hectic life—four kittens make a difference. But the writer should have found how many cows were in the herd and what "many" chickens signifies. If Meg has to feed fifty chickens every day, her life will not be as hectic as if she had to feed a thousand. Helping to care for these animals, says the writer, is "part of the job for Meg Niles . . ." The statement cries for another part of the job to be put right with it. Suppose the facts went like this:

> Helping to care for a herd of forty cows, fifty chickens, three cats, one rabbit, three dogs, and four kittens, and working two hours daily at Community Hospital as a messenger reduces Meg Niles's study time. But she maintains an A average.

Starting this way and cutting the elements not critical to the story would leave space for the writer to tell more about Meg's family obligations—maybe she helps her little brother tie his shoes and get dressed each morning—and establish even more convincingly the commitments she has as a farmer's daughter.

To persuade the reader how hectic a person's life is, many professional writers would take the subject through a day, hour by hour. That would be a good way to present this story. Then the writer could end like this:

> Does Meg like living on a farm? "I like it," she says, "especially the fresh air, except when the wind blows my way during manure spreading time."

This is a lively statement. It reveals an authentic farmer's daughter.

The following story, about a place, is written tightly and with few words that fail to pull their weight. But it forgets its author, subject, and audience.

COLONIAL WILLIAMSBURG OFFERS EXCITEMENT

Being thrown in jail isn't a part of most vacations, but visitors to Colonial Williamsburg delight in being imprisoned in the pillory and stocks. But then, many things are different and exciting about this most enchanting re-creation of America, two hundred years ago.

This is truly painless history. Instead of standing in a museum, gazing at the artifacts of a bygone life, one actually steps into the eighteenth century and moves in the gay atmosphere of this capital whose territory encompassed eight of our present states.

The wigmaker fashions his perukes, the smithy works his bellows, and the militia fires its cannon to the setting sun as the carriages creak across cobblestone lanes.

So much has been written and photographed about Colonial Williamsburg that we will not attempt to duplicate the many books and travel folders now available. However, we do feel that everyone should know how inexpensive, and yet fun-filled, a stay in this Virginian restoration can be.

The Motor House is moderately priced, especially for family groups, and its setting in a forest of tall pines makes it seem like the most fabulous resort. Four swimming pools provide cooling relief from sightseeing.

Free buses tour the area constantly and golf is available at two championship courses. For guests of any of the Williamsburg lodgings, tennis courts, shuffleboard, lawn bowling and badminton are provided.

Williamsburg abounds in fabulous eating places where foods such as "Sally Lunn" and "Tipsy Cake" are everyday items.

John D. Rockefeller, Jr. started this wonderful restoration so "that the future may learn from the past." It is also a place where a family can steep itself in this testimony to liberty, have a fine vacation, and still have money left over for the return trip.

The headline gives away the writer's failure to find an angle. Most of this newspaper's readers have heard and read about Williamsburg and a number probably have seen it. Foods such as "Sally Lunn" and "Tipsy Cake" are not exciting unless described. And even then, perhaps *exciting* is too strong a word. The quotation from Mr. Rockefeller "that the future may learn from the past" is tired, what anyone would expect to hear about a restored city. At one point the writer says:

So much has been written and photographed about Colonial Williamsburg that we will not attempt to duplicate the many books and travel folders now available.

She reveals her awareness that writing on subjects like this often bores readers. Hanging over this whole piece is a cloud of advertising malarkey. It is not serious, as Eudora Welty said, and it does not tell the truth. In the second paragraph the writer says "This is truly painless history." What does that mean? Perhaps that she learned more about history touring Williamsburg than reading a difficult book? If so, she must show some of the history she learned and what it means to her now. If she were writing the truth instead of weak advertising, she would probably admit that her feet hurt from all the walking on cobblestones—painful. And if she really found the food fabulous, she might have shown it to the reader. Did the Southern pecan pie elate her taste buds or did it lie deflated and runny on the plate?

Here are some reminders about how to write a story with an angle:

1. Look for what surprises and interests you.
2. Consider what your readers already know about the subject.
3. Interview persons so they talk freely. Don't ask questions that encourage yes and no answers: "Did you like Mr. Smith the

first time you met him in Detroit?" Ask open-ended questions that keep a person talking. Then he will probably say unexpected things you can use. "Tell me your first impressions of Mr. Smith."

4. If you don't have an angle when you begin interviewing, keep awake for one. The sooner you get it, the easier you will find deciding how much material to gather. But take more notes than you think you will need. A late change in angle or a discovery of new relationships may make some materials suddenly critical.

5. When you hear a statement that sounds valuable or memorable, take it down word for word. If necessary, say, "You said, 'Smith acted like an embarrassed ring-tail monkey'?"

6. Remember that when you write about living persons (and peopled places) you may hurt them by divulging derogatory or private information. Consider showing your final draft to them to check accuracy and approve what information is made public. You do not necessarily have to respect their wishes. In some cases you may decide not to respect their wishes about what should be divulged. If your article reveals damaging information, think about changing all names to hide identities.

7. Once you have chosen an angle, make sure it determines which materials you select and omit. How does the angle touch your interests, the available materials, the audience's knowledge and likely interest?

8. Pull out from your materials what you think will make an opening which grabs and an ending which kicks.

9. Cut your article to the bone of surprise, almost. Leave a little lean meat so the bone will stand out in contrast.

chapter 13

creating
form

PATTERNS

A RECENT TEXTBOOK on writing says:

> Since learning to outline is one of the most important
> steps—perhaps the most important—in writing well, we
> want you to make at least four outlines.

The man who wrote that must never have talked to a real writer.
Eight out of ten writers say they never use outlines and the other two
say they use them only in late stages of writing, in the second or
third draft when they have all the materials captured and need only
to rearrange them strategically.

In the first place, outlines freeze most writers. Professionals are
looking for ways of breaking up the ice and poking around in new
waters. They want writing and ideas to flow.

> *I have often at the beginning of a book*
> *found myself very uncertain what I*
> *would do, and appalled at the difficulty*
> *of knowing what to put where, and how*
> *to develop my incidents. I never have*
> *that feeling now because I have always*
> *found that there is some one point or*
> *other in which I can see my way. I im-*
> *mediately set to work at that point and*

> *before I have done and settled it, I in-*
> *variably find that there is another point*
> *which I can also see and settle, etc.,*
> *etc. . . .*
>
> SAMUEL BUTLER

In the second place—Wait a minute. The second place. By their form, outlines always imply there will be a second place. Maybe there won't be. Or shouldn't be. I.a., I.b., II.a., II.b. "Express all your points in the outline in the same style, all complete sentences or all phrases." The Outliners are full of stuff like that. They get a writer so interested in the form of the outline that he quits thinking of the writing he is outlining.

Yet a reader needs some form or he becomes confused, gets lost, gives up. Making anything—a table, a fishing fly, a piece of writing—involves a struggle between form and content. Only the dull assembly-line maker can avoid that struggle by drawing up a perfect plan, or outline, before he begins creating. Punched out, every one the same, no surprises anywhere. A good planner allows for departures from plan, sidetrips down alleys full of discovery. The best trip you ever took in your life—could you have written an outline for it beforehand?

Yet the reader and writer need form, some direction, some over-riding mood, or they will sense only chaos. When the folks at home send George on a trip, they expect more than a bagful of chaos spilled on the kitchen table when he returns.

Many professionals say that the more experienced they become, the more certain they are of where they're going before they start. But they still keep their eyes and ears open as they go, hoping for fortunate accidents.

Beginning, you may find a direction, even a conclusion, flowering in your mind. Then all you do is find experiences to embody it and bring it alive. But if there is not an example or experience clinging to the idea or direction when you first get it, the chances are you will never bring it alive. Better start with something already alive and kicking. A butterfly caught and squirming in the net, wings flapping wildly. Not a lot of preserved specimens lined up in the glass case neatly and systematically labeled.

But the glass case is good. Something to enclose the things flapping around in your mind and experience. Place something else with the butterfly. Does it go with him? Or does it contrast in some significant way? Is it a leaf in shape—half of the butterfly? And then a bird. Look at him. How do his wings differ from the butterfly's and the leaf's? Let these pieces of experience knock around against each other in the case and in your mind.

> *It doesn't matter which leg of your table you make first, so long as the table has four legs and will stand up solidly when you have finished it.*
>
> EZRA POUND

If what you are thinking about doesn't fit into a case, you may simply jot down the elements in a list, informal, like the one you take to the supermarket.

Any piece of writing needs a point. What that means is hard to say but easier to sense. Everyone knows the meaning of the word when he listens to a person talk on endlessly through boredom into sleep, and someone says, "He talked on and on but to no point." What *point* is and why it is needed can be seen by reading most term papers written in high school and freshman college classes. They have subjects but no points. For example, Harry Smithers writes "about Switzerland." His paper is dead already. The facts he has read about Switzerland or the things he has seen in Switzerland do not make a paper simply because they concern one country. What about Switzerland? Do any of the facts he has collected do anything to each other? Contradict? Surprise Harry in some way when compared with facts he knows about other countries? If he thinks he will write about Switzerland because the library has a number of books on it, or because no one else has written about it recently in school, or because he once heard that watches are made in Switzerland, his paper is doomed. When he starts in on a good piece of writing he will have an itch or he will never scratch hard, with purpose and enjoyment.

Switzerland might be Harry's subject, but never his point. To cover Switzerland would be to write an endless number of volumes, describing its government, postal system, watchmaking industry, role in European and world wars, people's dress, food, social customs— all with that dreadful emptiness of a travel brochure or a bad children's encyclopedia. Take this statement by a writer in a political magazine:

> The Swiss make watches, speak many languages, act as
> peace arbitrators, never commit themselves to the cause
> of right in any war, and act as holding companies for all
> sorts of high-level financial wheeling and dealing, aiding

persons all over the world in avoiding taxes and financial
responsibility.

Maybe this statement is not true. But it is full of assertions, of points
that could be pursued with genuine curiosity. It was not made by
the Chamber of Commerce trying to attract tourists, but by a man
puzzled and inquiring who said what he truly believed. If you
came upon this statement as the opening paragraph of an article,
you would probably suspect that the writer was going to take you on
a journey.

An editor of a university press once said that most Master's and
Doctor's theses submitted to him for possible publication were unpub-
lishable. No one would want to read them, he said. Some contained
ideas and material that could be brought together with point if the
author could bring himself to see why anyone might want to know
what he had found in his research. When he came upon such a thesis,
the editor said he returned it to the writer with the query: "So what?"
If the writer could rewrite his thesis so that it answered that question,
he had made what could be justly called a book.

To construct a good piece of writing you need to go somewhere
in it. If you haven't taken a journey, no amount of outlining or
structuring can make the writing live. Whatever the type of writing—
article, essay, story, case-history, poem—it must contain surprises and
questions. Else it will remain dead for you and the reader. They must
be genuine surprises and questions. Many beginning writers are
affected by the worst, most gimmicky writing. They spin a long
description of a man they have known, disguising who he is and
where they have known him, and then in the last sentence they say:
"There he was, smoking his pipe in the big rocking chair in the living
room—my father." Surprise is valuable, but it must make a point
or give truth to experience. This trick ending about Father does
neither. If the writer told of a man exhibiting behavior shockingly
unlike his father's, then as indication of the shock the writer himself
felt, he might properly hold back the identity of his father until
the end. The first-rate writer produces surprise after surprise for his
reader, in his expression, in the events he records, in the thoughts he
comes to through comparisons. But he does not play practical jokes
on his readers.

What shape will you give a piece of writing? Or better yet, what
movement? It needs a pattern. Formlessness is too hard on human
perception. You will lose your reader if he has no hint of what
journey you are taking him on. He needs surprise and wondering,

but he cannot stand one question after another with no intimation of answer or direction. As a writer you need form, a limit which will force you to invention. Henry Ford did not say one day, "I think I will invent something great" and then build one of the first American motor cars. He was thinking about a form—a wheeled, self-propelled vehicle; and a purpose—faster travel on roads than was provided by horse-drawn carriages.

What is the right form of your piece of writing? There is no manual in which you may look up the answer. Like all good questions, this one cannot be answered simply. If you remember that a good piece of writing is composed partly through plan and partly through accident which the writer keeps himself ever ready to exploit, you may guess that a good form involves both discipline and freedom for the writer and the reader. It gives the reader a feeling that he can see the path at times, at other times that he has to work hard to open it up. Occasionally it will lead him astray on exciting side trips. Give the reader a small sense of direction for the journey, but don't keep nudging him in the elbow—This way! No! Over there! Now back again!

Professional writers are often mystified by the way they put together writing. They know it has a form but they seldom know its origin. They are afraid of outlining because they want things to happen to them as they write. Nevertheless their final draft usually possesses sure form, a movement that gives power to the events they have written about. Some emphasize freedom to discover. Some emphasize the need for plan. James Thurber said of Elliott Nugent, with whom he wrote the play *The Male Animal*:

> He could plot the thing from back to front—what was going to happen here, what sort of situation would end the first-act curtain, and so forth. I can't work that way. Nugent would say, "Well, Thurber, we've got our problem, we've got all these people in the living room. Now what are we going to do with them?" I'd say that I didn't know and couldn't tell him until I'd sat down at the typewriter and found out. I don't believe the writer should know too much where he's going. If he does, he runs into old man blueprint —old man propaganda.

Because Thurber wrote this passage doesn't mean that he never paid attention to the shape of his writing. He rewrote his stories dozens of times until he got them moving right.

Probably the reason professionals are so unsure in discussing form is that good form always comes out of the materials of a particular piece of writing. As he gains experience, the writer comes unconsciously to a sense of form for his materials. Always he holds in mind a few simple, fundamental forms that will limit him wisely and give his reader a sense of certainty among all the surprises he encounters.

> *A plot is a thousand times more unsettling than an argument, which may be answered. It is not a pattern imposed; it is inward emotion acted out. It is arbitrary, indeed, but not artificial. It is possibly so odd that it might be called a vision, but it is organic to its material: it is a working vision, then.*
>
> EUDORA WELTY

Here are a few such fundamental forms or patterns of movement. They may be useful if you do not let them bind you. Allow one to dominate your complete piece of writing and at the same time introduce several of the others to shape small pieces of the same work if you wish.

(a) *Simple Comparison.* X is different from B. You may show how X's arms differ from B's, then the legs of both, the shoes, etc. Or you may describe X completely and then B completely. As you make your observations and as you write, keep thinking: So what?

(b) *Before and After.* It was *this* way once. Now it is *that* way. You may emphasize the difference. You may ask why the difference. You may tell how the difference came about.

(c) *The Journey.* I (he, or it) started here and went through this experience or that country and came out there. Chronologically. First this happened, then that.

You may present the whole matter as story, or occasionally interrupt to explain significance. Show. Give the story. Tell. Explain why or discuss the significance of an act. But don't interrupt a story to tell or comment unless you do so frequently and regularly.

The Journey pattern is useful in writing about ideas (as well as events) which are apt to become confusing to the reader unless controlled. If it is your idea, you may show where it came from, how you took it on, and what you did with it over the years or days. If it means a good deal to you, the tale of your journey with it should be exciting, for the truth is that the journey was full of surprises—traps, bogs, a mountain with a view.

(d) *David and Goliath*. David has only a slingshot and courage against a gigantic warrior armed with spear and shield and wearing a coat weighing as five thousand shekels of brass. Any little or deprived or disadvantaged person against great forces. Who will win?

(e) *Will It Work?* An idea, a plan, an invention new and untried, or old but now standing against the established order—a variation of the David and Goliath story. The odds are against it because it is not now the accepted thing. Will it win through?

In deciding upon a form, a writer constantly juggles

1. the needs of his materials (they may cry out for a certain treatment),
2. the weight of his purpose,
3. the limitations and potentialities of his medium (is it a letter, an article in a picture magazine, a paper to be read aloud or silently in class?),
4. the knowledge and needs of his audience.

The professional knows he is writing to other human beings, who can be bored, who are often insulted by gimmicks, who have normal human needs for rising excitement, for hoping that every trip they take will pay off.

THE HOOK

A good device to remember is the fishhook. It rises slowly and then hooks back, so it will dig in and stick. It is barbed. Its curve points back to its beginning, to remind itself and the reader where it came from.

In the light of these comments on form and movement, consider some of the writings in this book. For example, "Reed" in Chapter 7, is a Journey. A girl feels faint while playing her clarinet at a competition. Step by step she leads the reader through her travails, over to the judge's desk, to a chair for rest, and back to the performance where she takes up where she had stopped. She is much like the hero of the *Odyssey*, apparently modest yet actually prodigious. Visitors wander into the room as she starts playing the unfinished half of her piece. They come in like foreigners, and the judge, like Jove, must explain what is happening. The Hook is that the innocent, fainting girl changes into a successful performer and the dignified authoritative judge into a human being who "collapsed in a chair." Surprise.

Tension. It creates life. When it is not present, no movement—death. You know the person, old or young, who spills his story in great oceans of tedious and irrelevant detail. "Stop! stop!" you say to yourself. "You began telling me about how you fell out of the tree at Aunt Louise's but now you're listing the names of all the trees in her woods!" A good writer knows more than he presents. But he gives the reader only the intersection points where X and Y spark. Or where After is a surprise in relation to Before. Don't tell the reader that John or Algernon is a man unless the other one is a bear with long claws on all four feet.

So there are no sure-fire formulas for shaping a piece of writing. But the strong writer keeps the pressure of form upon himself. He keeps asking:

Where is this going?

Does it arrive somewhere?

Does it add up?

Is something happening between things here?

Have I made clear, directly or indirectly, why I wanted to write this?

What did I want to say? Did I get it said?

WRITING ELEVEN: Choose one of your free writings you like and shape it more powerfully. You may have to expand or contract it radically. Does it already follow one of the patterns discussed in this chapter? Can you improve it with a Hook?

WRITING TWELVE: Look over your story in which you remembered childhood and your case-history. Can you improve them with a firmer pattern of development?

In subsequent longer papers you write as you work through this book, try early to find a form that belongs to your materials, your purposes, your audience.

Life is not free from its forms.

WALLACE STEVENS

. . . childhood word-play, adolescent
slang and double-talk, often derivative,
but natural and exciting. In general the
schools have made it their business to
kill this kind of playful interest, and
they have had the backing of society in
this effort . . . most professionals with
highly developed skills are fond of play-
ing with those skills.

W. NELSON FRANCIS

chapter 14

playing
with
words

Too OFTEN we act as if we were put on
this earth to die. In conversation we paralyze each other with inter-
minable repetitions, clichés, tedious details. Then we write down our
dullness so it will live beyond the moment.

We could act as if we were put on this earth to live, to carry ourselves buoyantly.

Take phrases you have heard before and twist them to see what
happens. Maybe nothing. Maybe something. Silly, like the words
of a disc jockey on radio station WBBM Chicago?

> Mostly fair in the morning followed by mostly cloudy in
> the afternoon followed by mostly evening.

Like most quick-minded word play, this statement started with no
point and ended sharp. Not only does the twist "followed by mostly
evening" delight because it surprises, but taken as a whole, it joshes
weather reports, their dullness, their heavy repetitiveness.

Americans are taught in school to groan when they hear a pun. Yet all the brightest writers love puns.

ROMEO: I dreamt a dream tonight.
MERCUTIO: And so did I.
ROMEO: Well, what was yours?
MERCUTIO: That dreamers often lie.
ROMEO: In bed asleep, while they do dream things true.

The most intelligent persons play with words, seriously. Intelligent readers and listeners laugh with them.

BOOK TITLE: *Up the Down Staircase*

PLAY TITLE: *Who's Afraid of Virginia Woolf?*

TV COMMERCIAL: Who said you can't teach an old dog food new tricks?

TV COMMERCIAL: Certs has the best taste I ever ate.

NEWSPAPER ADVERTISEMENT: Where does Lazy Maple Bacon gets its remarkable taste and aroma? From some sap in Vermont.

BUSINESSMAN IN CONVERSATION: You've buttered your bread. Now lie in it.

The word player takes the old and turns it. Like this:

Join the Navy and see Norfolk.

Or this:

He's three-square.

Or this:

Life is just a bowl of pits.

These three twists on tired aphorisms and slogans were written by a beginner in writing. Probably she heard the first one from a sailor but the other two are hers. She took the mealy old paste of these expressions and twisted them like pretzels. They came out crisp and salty.

The secret of productive play is simple: let yourself go. All great persons—artists, scientists, engineers, architects, cooks, designers—fool around. If their play produces something usable, they use it. If not, they feel no pain or guilt. You cannot feel guilty about play and become a creative person. In this game you must be loose with language. Sinful. Show no respect for the tried and blue. But do not expect all your play to produce chocolate gems. Many mudpies, much unsorted, unexciting sand and gravel.

More often than you will anticipate, you will stumble upon hidden wonders, both nonsensical and sensical. Note that the girl's twists on old sayings made sense, possessed point. Join the Navy and see the world. Often the promise of romantic travel in the Navy sours in the drabness of a stateside training center. He's four-square. Often a man expected to be solid and trustworthy turns out missing one side. Life is just a bowl of cherries. Not usually. So the twists led to truth, as well as to fun. When E. M. Forster decided to publish a book of essays showing some of the faults of democracy in Great Britain, he named his book *Two Cheers for Democracy*.

WRITING THIRTEEN: Try playing with words.
1. Twist a cliché. Here are some clichés.

(a) Everything is peaches and cream.
(b) It is both a pleasure and a privilege.
(c) It's raining cats and dogs.
(d) They worked long and hard.
(e) The woods was a white fairyland, covered with a blanket of snow.
(f) He danced with the greatest of ease.
(g) Please give me your undivided attention and keep a stiff upper lip.
(h) Make a concerted effort. Don't run around like a chicken with its head cut off.

Many writers attack a speaker's or writer's vague or pompous language through word play. It may be used to ridicule another person's narrow-minded complaints about people's language. Here the editors of *The New Republic* magazine satirize a judge's decision by playing with names in a way that complies with his decision but makes him appear foolish:

'S' VONDERFUL

A New York judge has turned down a request by a citizen to add "von" to his name. Petitioner Robert Paul Jama explained that he just wanted it to sound more German and less Slav, but Judge Maurice Wahl refused, because the Constitution says no title of nobility shall be granted by the United States.

Some of us thought you could call yourself anything you wanted to in this country, including King Cole, Count

Basie and Duke Ellington, to name a few. Hitting at as subtle a play for nobility as "von" suggests that both past and present celebrities are in for some editing. It's hard to imagine the late show featuring somebody called Erich Stroheim or an interview with that missile expert, Wernher Braun. An evening with TV should provide a whole new set of personalities.

One could start with a panel show featuring the ever popular Dorens: Charles, Mark and Mamie. Then a discussion of the Allen Belt, and at 11:30 the legendary Rip Winkle in a modern Hollywood version directed by Cecil Mille. Sponsored, of course, by the outstanding chemical corporation, Pont. It may sound democratic to say "Joe Maggio," but it doesn't swing, man. Besides, Richard Nixon has warned that the left-wing Du Bois Club, when pronounced with a Bronx accent, sounds suspiciously like The Boys Club, a right-thinking outfit. If you expunge the aristocratic prefix from the former, who indeed can tell them apart?

The matter can't be argued now before the late Justice Willis Van Devanter; anyway, he would have been obliged to disqualify himself or change his name to Willis Devanter. Or perhaps Vanter. Or should that be Willis Ter?

At first glance this editorial may seem a pointless bit of byplay, but not so. Without speaking directly, the editors are hinting that every citizen has a right to call himself what he will.

On August 22, 1966, when the largest American airplanes resumed flying after a mechanics' strike, Braniff International ran a full-page advertisement in *The New York Times* showing an airline hostess dressed in her high-fashion Turkish-looking uniform, sprawled tiredly on the floor, holding a sore foot. The copy read:

Welcome back, plain planes.
Your exteriors may not be covered with 7 different colors.
Your interiors may not be covered with Herman Miller fabrics.
Your hostesses may not be covered with Emilio Pucci outfits.
But, believe us, you've never looked so good.
While you were gone, we served sixteen thousand extra meals, poured twenty-five thousand extra cups of coffee and plumped nine thousand extra pillows.

You didn't come back a moment too soon.
Our Pucci's were just about pooped.

In this ad, one of the smaller airlines was telling how hard it worked while the major lines were on strike and at the same time implying that it was a luxury line and the others were plain. It was written by a man who spoke to a subtle point but did not take himself or his company too seriously.

Two days later, in the same newspaper, United Airlines demonstrated its ability to play on words by heading an advertisement "say where!" in gigantic letters. These two words make the reader think first of the familiar American phrase "say when," but then surprise him with their turn. Following the "say where!" in the ad, were the names of seventy-six American cities "served directly from New York." Then came a second line of gigantic type saying "say when!"

Think of seven more clichés and list them. Choose five from yours and those printed here and play with them. A student who felt worse than "something the cat dragged in" wrote "I felt like something that dragged in the cat." Henry Thoreau went beyond a cliché in this statement:

> If you have built castles in the air, your work need not be lost; that is where they should be. Now put the foundations under them.

And so did William Hazlitt:

> Miracles never cease, to be sure; but they are not to be had wholesale, or *to order*.

A college student twisted three tired expressions in this way:

> Home is where the garbage is.
>
> Love Is a Many Splintered Thing.
>
> I want a girl just like the girl that turned down dear old Dad.

2. Take figurative, metaphorical words and phrases literally. Look at some of your free writings, or begin a free writing and stop when you can twist a metaphor by reading it literally. Anne Haven Morgan was hearing "A bird in the hand is worth two in the bush" when she said this about bullfrogs in *The Field Book of Ponds and Streams*:

> The way to catch them by hand is to seize them very firmly by both hind legs, for a bullfrog "in the hand" is strong and apparently much larger than the same one in the pond.

The writer of the following television commercial for Hy-Grade Ball Park Franks put an old expression into a new setting with a double twist when he wrote:

> ADULT TO YOUNG BOY: Sir, would you say a couple of words about Hy-Grade Ball Park Franks?
> YOUNG BOY (smiling broadly): "Hot Dog!"

In the following passage, note how a beginning writer took literally the metaphorical word *outgoing* and the phrase *on her shoulders*:

> **A girl friend once told me that I wasn't outgoing enough. I thought she was very wise, always cracking books—a good head on her shoulders. So while I was out going to house council, sorority meetings, and working on committees, she stayed home and worked on my boy friend—another good head on her shoulders. Of course this put me out quite a bit and I decided some drastic steps should be taken. I told her that she wasn't outgoing enough herself, so she took my advice and stepped out, going with my boy friend.**

> SHARON BUTLER

Write a paragraph or two in which you twist words in this way.

The word player is not so much playing chess as just playing around. He may decide to put the play to practical use, but he does not need to any more than he needs to publish his first three bad drafts of a piece of writing. The more you play with words, the more often you will find playful statements crossing over into serious expression. E. E. Cummings, an American poet, constantly sawed up his words and tacked pieces on them. He looked at the word *mankind* and decided to write it *manunkind.* Then he used that new word in the first line of a bitter poem about the evils man has committed in the name of progress. It begins:

> pity this busy monster,manunkind

This was not simply a trick by Mr. Cummings. For years he had written against war and man's cruelty to man.

WRITING FOURTEEN: Play with titles of articles or books, with titles for your own writings. First study newspaper and magazine article titles. Note the puns, the newly created words. Here are some examples:

(a) *How to Cheat on Personality Tests,* by William H. Whyte, Jr.
(b) *A Problem of Design: How to Kill People,* by George Nelson
(c) *Arms and the Boy,* by Wilfred Owen

"Arms and the Boy," a title of a poem, plays on the first line of Virgil's *Aeneid*, which begins: "Arms and the man I sing . . ." The poet Wilfred Owen is suggesting that the reader should remember that boys rather than men are often killed in war.

    (d) *The Beast in Me and Other Animals*, by James Thurber
    (e) *Bed of Neuroses*, by Wolcott Gibbs
    (f) *Golf Is a Four Letter Word*, by Richard Armour

The word play in all these titles is pointed. It makes a reader think twice and see significance. When Sidney Cox, a writing teacher at Dartmouth College, published a book of reflections and musings about writing—not a program of specifics for learning to write, he called it *Indirections: for Those Who Want to Write*. He was playing on the word *Directions*.

> . . . the light of magic suggestiveness
> may be brought to play for an evanescent
> instant over the commonplace surface of
> words: of the old, old words, worn thin,
> defaced by ages of careless usage.
>
> JOSEPH CONRAD

Try to write the truth in your language and at the same time let your words speak to each other. One day a student playing with words wrote:

> **November, and the cornfields are brown and broken and they rattle in the freshening wind. Meanwhile across the cornflakes heavy voices grumble the usual. A word of meaning drowns in a sea of crunch.**

When he handed this paragraph to a teacher, he appended this comment:

> I was just playing with words and sounds and pictures. Somehow it reminds me of T. S. Eliot's coffee spoons [in "The Love Song of J. Alfred Prufrock"]. Know what? I'll bet if the thing were printed, someone would analyze it.

Here the writer is dishonest. The passage is more than meaningless sounds and pictures. In his play he must have had in mind tension between the fresh wind in the cornfields and the stale breakfast table conversation. It is a delightful and valid statement which makes its point in a sidelong manner. If incorporated into a larger context, it might become the most powerful paragraph of a paper. What a writer says unconsciously may carry more meaning than what he plans meticulously.

Much of Lewis Carroll's writing about Alice is sense rather than nonsense. Playful sense. Before you tighten your belt, purse your lips, and dry out your throat in preparation for impressing your audience, consider speaking playfully and seriously at once. Do you see no virtue in writing lightly? Remember that the persons you write to can avoid your writing more easily than your speaking.

Lewis Carroll is making sense in *Through the Looking Glass* when he has Humpty Dumpty say:

> "they gave it me—for an unbirthday present."

Alice and he go on:

> "I beg your pardon?" Alice said with a puzzled air.
>
> "I am not offended," said Humpty Dumpty.
>
> "I mean, what *is* an unbirthday present?"
>
> "A present given when it isn't your birthday, of course."
>
> Alice considered a little. "I like birthday presents best," she said at last.
>
> "You don't know what you're talking about!" cried Humpty Dumpty. "How many days are there in a year?"
>
> "Three hundred and sixty-five," said Alice . . .
>
> ". . . that shows that there are three hundred and sixty-four days when you might get unbirthday presents—"

In the same book Lewis Carroll is apparently not making much sense in the first stanza of "Jabberwocky":

> 'Twas brillig, and the slithy toves
>   Did gyre and gimble in the wabe:
> All mimsy were the borogoves,
>   And the mome raths outgrabe.

Millions of persons have taken those non-words to their hearts. They like nonsense. What they don't like is nonsense written by persons who think they are writing sense. In "Jabberwocky," Lewis Carroll was making a kind of sense. In the later stanzas he plainly tells a satirical story of a Jabberwocky (dragon) being slain by a brave young knight. Lewis Carroll is making fun of pompously heroic knights. The hero becomes ridiculous as he takes

> ... his vorpal sword in hand:
> Long time the manxome foe he sought—
> So rested he by the Tumtum tree,
> And stood awhile in thought.

After that puncture of the knight's armor, the reader can see that the first stanza is a setting of the physical scene for this knight's encounter with the dragon. It was a brillig day, and the toves and borogoves were out there in the wabe.

You can write so persons will enjoy reading your words. Why not do that? Something sinful about enjoyment? You landed with the Mayflower? Wear a wide-brimmed tall black hat? Put on a fool's colors and be wise for fun.

WRITING FIFTEEN: Write for twenty to thirty minutes. Start on something or someone you are fond of or despise. Say anything. Describe. Give your opinions. Say what others have said of this person or thing. As you write, listen to your words. Before you begin, read these examples of word play and use any of the methods that appeal to you.

(a) In Samuel Butler's novel *The Way of All Flesh*, Ernest Pontifex's tyrannical father says to him:

> "I must insist on two things: firstly, that this new iron in the fire does not distract your attention from your Latin and Greek"—("They aren't mine," thought Ernest, "and never have been.")

(b) "Do you think it's going to rain?"
Tweedledum spread a large umbrella over himself and his brother, and looked up into it. "No, I don't think it is," he said; "at least—not under *here*. Nohow."
"But it may rain *outside*?"
"It may—if it chooses," said Tweedledee; "We've no objection. Contrariwise."

(c) "How to Fold a Newspaper," title of magazine article (*The Reporter*, January 16, 1964) about the closing down of a newspaper.

(d) I wish I was a wittle egg,
As wotten as can be.
I'd put myself upon a wimb
A way up in a twee.

And the first bonehead Senior
That yelled and screamed at me
I'd throw my wittle wotten self
And spwatter he with me.

(anonymous poem in *Wind-up*, newspaper of St. Joseph High School,
St. Joseph, Michigan, December 22, 1965).

(e) What's the best chocolate candy under the sun? Melt in your
mouth, not in your hands. M and M's.

One difference between all this word play and much of the humor
that we hear every day in conversation and on television is that it is
making a point. It is not gag-humor, like these statements:

My Uncle George reminds me of a rabbit. He has a hare-
less head.

We have a cow that never udders a word.

Sometimes a play on words may be clever and pointed but inappropriate to the occasion, to the subject being played with, or to the
writer. For example, in a magazine advertisement a chemical-plastics
company once depicted a room divider made of plastic cane, above
a line of type reading "It's cane . . . and it's able." This is a play on
Cain and Abel in the Bible, but as used here, it is all wrong. Those
two names conjure up the great tragic story of brother killing brother.
No reader wants to connect it with an industry merchandising its
wares, especially when the two-page full-color spread showed two
sophisticated couples lounging in a sumptuous room decorated with
expensive furniture and a large Oriental painting.

As the author of this book was writing this chapter on word play,
he was called to a bedroom to kiss goodnight a six-year-old girl and
her visiting stepbrother, five, who was for the first time sleeping in
the same room.

"It's pretty nice, isn't it," he said, "to have a big brother to sleep
in the same room with you?"

"Yes," she said, "but it's nice to have a sister, too."

"Everything's nice in life," he said.

"Yeah, except liver," she said.

"And going to war."

"Yeah."

"That's another bad thing, like falling in the lake from a rope
up in a tree."

"Or falling in love."

> *Motion or change and identity or rest*
> *are the first and second secrets of nature:*
> *Motion and Rest.*
>
> RALPH WALDO EMERSON

chapter 15
maintaining flow

ESTABLISHING CONNECTIONS

A PERSON IS not really writing until he learns to play the part of his reader as he writes. Then he achieves a flow of thought from sentence to sentence. As the philosopher George Herbert Mead observed, man talks or writes to other men, or even to himself, by playing in his mind the role of the other. He cannot sense *I* until he recognizes *Me*. A. A. Milne's Christopher Robin is right in saying:

> When I was Three
> I was hardly Me.

A writer must be honest with himself as well as his reader. He must stick by his own thoughts and feelings. But if he drives out all thoughts of a reader as he writes, he is as insane as an outfielder would be if he fielded a hit made with a man on second base and then threw the ball generally in the direction of the infield, ignoring the new positions his teammates had taken. When a ball is hit to the outfield, an infielder runs out toward the ball so that he can relay the throw (from the outfielder who is fielding it) to the infielder who is covering third base, toward which the runner is heading. Other infielders back up third base to stop the ball if the throw is missed. Still other infielders take new positions, ready to intercept the relay throw if they decide they have a better chance to throw the hitter out at second base than the runner out at third base. As George

Herbert Mead says, the player "must know what everyone else is going to do in order to carry out his own play. He has to take all of these roles."

Holding the reader's role in mind while writing is not as difficult as one might first imagine. Human beings often do two things at once. A mother looks at a television commercial and hears it while telling her daughter to go wash her hands more thoroughly. An ambassador speaks graciously to another ambassador while reading the hidden significances in the other man's tone.

To establish flow, a writer places ideas and happenings in their setting and connects the sentence he is writing to previous sentences. He remembers that his reader probably was not there in that place, and surely not there in the mind that perceived what is now on paper. Here is a passage that does not flow smoothly:

PRE-DATING

Dating does not exist "as such" (regular company keeping with one or more individuals of the opposite sex). A junior high student is expected to be at least "interested" in the opposite sex or there is concern for his "abnormality." This is very true as far as my experience goes. There was little actual dating (in fact that was considered by many at that time to be abnormal as most did not date) but mostly large gangs of girls and large gangs of boys who would engage in throwing cracks across the room at each other. A favorite pastime was purse snatching. A purse would be taken from a girl and tossed back and forth between them, shooting it into wastepaper baskets and sliding them down the halls. There were also water pistols and pea shooters, both of which were major nuisances to girls and nothing short of riotous fun for the boys. I can remember going without my purse more than with it. I did not go to a reform school, although I don't know how normal or abnormal these incidents are. I was greeted in the morning with several streams of water from several water pistols. All in all, anyone who did not do these things was considered "out of it" even though many times it was unpleasant being "in." Girls were rarely in love but specialized in secret crushes. Boys were the crushers. They crushed everything. This is the way each showed interest in the other, and it was, at my school, the expected thing to do.

"Pre-Dating" has a valuable insight to convey but it travels over a road full of ruts and small boulders which often jump its wheels across empty space. The writer needs to pave the road so the wheels touch continuously.

In her first sentence the writer forgets to say where dating does not exist. And she breaks her opening sentence with an unnecessary interrupting definition. Her fellow students know what dating is. In the second sentence she mentions the place she should have cited in the first sentence—junior high school. Throughout the passage she puts words into quotation marks that she is not using in a new or strange sense, again insulting her readers.

The assertion in the second sentence comes surprisingly upon the heels of the first sentence—no dating, yet the student is supposed to be interested in the other sex. Ordinarily a writer should prepare a reader for such an unexpected turn, with signal words like *however*, *in contrast*, *but*, etc. This writer would have achieved more flow had she written her opening like this:

> In junior high school, dating as such does not exist. But a
> student is expected to be at least interested in the opposite
> sex . . .

The next statement ("or there is concern for his 'abnormality' ") forgets to specify who is concerned. And the next sentence ("This is very true as far as my experience goes") fails to specify what "this" and "my experience" refer to. Does the writer mean to say she was accused of being abnormal? or merely that students at her school were expected to be interested in the other sex but not actually date? Probably she simply meant that what she said about junior high schools was true in her school. Frequently students feel the academic world pressuring them to make large generalizations, so they talk about junior high schools when they are reporting only their knowledge of John Deere Junior High School and about women when they are thinking only of Mother. The passage might be revised this way:

> In my junior high school, dating as such does not exist.
> But a student is expected to be at least interested in the
> opposite sex or administrators and parents are concerned
> for his abnormality.

In the next sentence the writer says "There was little actual dating," forgetting she has already said "dating as such does not exist." This contradiction could be done away with by beginning the paper in this way:

> In my junior high school, dating as such rarely takes place.

Soon the word *abnormal* appears again, but applied to a different act than it was earlier. To create flow, a writer must hear his own words speaking to each other as well as to his reader. This writer might better have written her next lines in this way:

> Those few students who dated were considered by almost everyone in school as abnormal as those who showed no interest at all in the other sex.
>
> Instead of dating, most boys and girls stood at opposite sides of a room in large gangs and threw cracks at each other.

In the next sentence ("A favorite pastime was purse snatching") again the writer forgets to say who was committing the act. Several sentences later, she says purse snatching was a "major nuisance" to the girls and "riotous fun" for the boys, remarks which suggest only boys were snatching purses. But the information comes too late for the reader. To establish flow, a writer must sense when a reader needs to know.

This close analysis of a passage that does not flow may suggest the whole matter is more difficult than it is. The newspaper reporter often tells his reader in the first paragraph—who, where, what, when, and why. We have all learned naturally in conversation to identify for our listener places, persons, and time. We can do this in writing also. Reading writing aloud often shows a writer whether or not he has achieved the flow necessary for his reader.

Later in "Pre-Dating," the writer talks about purse snatching, interrupts with a comment on water pistols and pea shooters, and then goes on to mention purses again, stopping to make a crack about reform school then coming back to water pistols. In these lines she again talks about abnormality, but does not connect the idea with her earlier mention of the word. The reader naturally expects a connection, but finds none—a bad break in flow. In the last four sentences the writer moves from the girls specializing in secret crushes to boys who are crushers. A clever play with the word *crush*, but one that needs pointing up for the reader, who is apt to think the boys are having crushes on the girls until he comes to the sentence "They crushed everything" and sees that *crush* is used with another meaning.

Here is a revised version of the whole passage, only one of the possible ways to make the writing flow more satisfactorily. Since the writer is looking back on junior high school, she will be safer to speak in the past tense throughout:

In my junior high school, dating as such did not exist.
But a student was expected to be at least interested in the
opposite sex, or administrators and parents were concerned
for his abnormality. Those few students who dated were
considered by almost everyone in school as abnormal as
those who showed no interest at all in the other sex.

Instead of dating, most boys and girls stood at opposite
sides of a room in large gangs and threw cracks at each
other. The boys' favorite pastime was purse snatching. They
would take a purse from a girl and toss it back and forth
between them, shooting it into a wastepaper basket or sliding it down the hall. Water pistols and pea shooters were
riotous fun for boys and major nuisances to girls. I did not
go to a reform school, but I can remember being without
my purse more than with it and being greeted in the morning with streams of water from pistols.

Yet anyone who didn't do these things was considered out
of it, although being in was often unpleasant. Girls were
rarely in love but specialized in secret crushes. The boys'
crushes were different: they crushed furniture, books, and
girls.

This is the way boys and girls in my school showed interest in each other. It was the expected thing to do.

The principle of creating flow is to make the stream of ideas easy
for the reader to follow unless you have good reason to snag him on
a branch. If the ideas and materials are so complex that you cannot
make your sentences always flow smoothly, do the best you can to help
the reader. If you find your writing is a rock-filled rapids or an
overwhelming flood, maybe you don't know what you are trying to
say and had better not spill it on the reader until you do.

Maintaining a flow within sentences is an art practiced by almost
all professional writers, not only by the most talented. All good prose
flows in some way. Here is part of a regular column, "Racing," written
by the editors of the magazine *Car and Driver* (September, 1966, p. 68):

NIGHTMARISH BELGIAN GP
FOUGHT BY SURTEES, RINDT

SPA-FRANCORCHAMPS, Belgium—"It was just like walking through a door. On one side it was as dry and safe as
you like; on the other side it was teeming with rain. We
all went into it about 130 mph, which just wasn't on in the

wet." That's how Jackie Stewart described his arrival at
Burnenville on the first lap of the Belgian Grand Prix at
Spa. He was describing it from his hospital bed in London,
grateful to be around to describe it at all. Stewart was lucky.

Burnenville is the most feared corner at Spa, which is,
in turn, the most feared circuit in the world. Burnenville
is a downhill right-hand corner, blind, but fast enough to
be negotiated at more than 140 mph. It's a vital corner
because exit speed here dictates a car's speed along the
downhill straight to Masta, the fastest part of the 8.75-mile
circuit. That someone wasn't killed there this year is almost
unbelievable. The leaders got through Burnenville on that
first lap—Surtees in front with Rindt just behind—by scraping around the outside edge of the veritable wall of water,
and so did Brabham behind them. Stewart and Bandini
also got by, but after that, all hell broke loose. Bonnier
spun his Cooper-Maserati, taking Spence (Lotus-BRM) with
him. As they spiralled down the road, those behind braked
and weaved about desperately trying to avoid the whirling
cars. Hulme ran up the back of Siffert and both the works
2.5 Brabham-Climax and the Walker Cooper-Maserati were
out. For the second time in two weeks (remember Indy?)
Graham Hill had to thread his way through a labyrinth of
spinning cars, and once again, he succeeded. Bondurant,
Ginther, Ligier and Gurney also survived this catastrophe
and sped away down the Masta straight. Surtees was leading, with Rindt right behind. Rindt reckoned that Surtees
was slowing a bit too much for the "kink"—a blind S-bend
at the fastest part of the circuit. He closed in on Surtees,
and suddenly his Cooper was spinning, and spinning, and
spinning. It spun right through the S-bend and on down
the straight at almost undiminishing velocity. "Every time
I faced back up the road I could see more cars spinning—
I recognized Jackie and Graham in the BRMs. I must have
spun something like nine times . . ."

Like Rindt, Stewart had hit a deep puddle while plowing
through the spray, and his 2-liter BRM had let loose. He
spun off the road and mowed down a telegraph pole, leaving the monocoque a twisted wreck with Stewart trapped,
injured, and soaked in gasoline. Hill's 2-liter BRM also
spun here but came to rest undamaged. Hill saw Jackie
below him in a ditch, vainly struggling to free himself.

Sprinting over to help his team-mate, he managed to turn off the master switch on the wrecked dash panel, and realized that he would have to remove the steering wheel to get Stewart out. Just then Bob Bondurant appeared. He too had spun at the kink, and ended up trapped beneath his inverted 2-liter BRM. He could hear fuel running out all around him, but couldn't reach the ignition. Spectators righted him, and he emerged with only a bleeding chin and a sore arm. Bondurant and Hill freed Stewart, who was in considerable pain from a dislocated shoulder and a fractured collar bone. He was carried to a barn. After a long wait for an ambulance, Hill drove to the pits.

When only 7 of the 15 starters came around on the first lap the crowd was aghast. Phil Hill, who had started at the back of the grid with an M-G-M camera car, finally returned with the news that "there were cars all over the place at Burnenville and Masta." Hill's arrival put more light on the incidents at Masta, but not until Hulme drove his bow-legged Brabham back to the pits did word go out that no one had been hurt at Burnenville. It seemed incredible that seven cars could come unstuck at Spa with no serious injuries. . . .

This is a remarkable piece of writing because it handles a great many complex actions and a number of names without losing suspense or confusing the reader. Key words and connector statements are some of the devices the writers used to make the writing flow:

That's how—Burnenville—Burnenville, feared corner—Burnenville—Stewart and Bandini also got by—Gurney also survived—spinning—spun—spinning—Like Rindt, Stewart—He too had spun—cars all over the place at Burnenville and Masta—incidents at Masta—no one hurt at Burnenville.

The repetition of key words often aids the flow of a sentence, but always the most valuable stratagem is to keep in mind what the reader has heard in the preceding sentences and therefore knows at the present.

This column on racing cars possesses more than flow to make it good reading. It uses short sentences to build up speed. It sounds manly in its language and yet is not ridiculously tough-guy in style. Many of its words have staccato or biting sounds: *scraping, spiralled, braked, weaved, survived, catastrophe, sped, Rindt right behind,*

Rindt reckoned, kink, deep puddle while plowing, the monocoque a twisted wreck, etc.

Some beginning writers with great aspirations believe they should write so others cannot understand them easily. They read a difficult author whose vocabulary is beyond them and conclude that all great writers are almost impossible to understand. Or they read an experimenting author and believe his unconventional style is easy to master. They forget that he probably began writing prose that flowed in a traditional way. Then he experimented with styles that demanded more and more of the reader. Any competent practitioner—in baseball, painting, boating, or missile design—begins by mastering the traditional fundamentals of his craft.

A writer must remember that he is not trying finally to achieve a flow of words but of meaning. He may use connective words and phrases like these:

also	consequently	another
too	therefore	an exception
further	although	in the first place
in addition	moreover	despite
similarly	nevertheless	on the contrary
as a result	now	not always
however	still	for instance
on the other hand		

He learns the niceties of using these words. For example, he does not ordinarily write "in the first place" unless he is also going to say later "in the second place." But these words are only surface connectors. Deeper in his mind the competent writer connects his ideas and creates a break or shift in them only when he wants to.

In 1859, when John Brown was tried for attacking a federal arsenal at Harper's Ferry, some persons said the old man was crazy, but in his speech before sentencing, he spoke with a clear flow of ideas. Here is part of that speech:

> This Court acknowledged too, as I suppose, the validity of the law of God. I see a book kissed here which I suppose to be the Bible, or at least the New Testament. That teaches me that all things "whatsoever I would men should do to me I should do even so to them." It teaches me, further, to "remember them that are in bonds as bonded with them." I endeavored to act up to these instructions. I say I am yet too young to understand that God is any respecter of persons. I believe that to have interfered as I

have done, in behalf of his despised poor, was no wrong,
but right. Now, if it is deemed necessary that I should
forfeit my life for the furtherance of the ends of justice,
and mingle my blood further with the blood of my children, and with the blood of the millions in this slave
country whose rights are disregarded by wicked, cruel, and
unjust enactments, I submit. So let it be done!

In this statement John Brown employed a few connector words, but
generally attained the unity of his thought by remembering his subject as he went along. In one place he seemed to interrupt his thought
or shift ground quickly: "I say I am yet too young to understand
that God is any respecter of persons." But actually the idea here is
flowing out of a previous statement. Of God, Brown was using the
phrase "no respecter of persons," which means that God does not
respect any one person more than another because he is rich or
intelligent, etc. That idea flows naturally from Brown's previous
allusion to the Biblical statement that man should "remember them
that are in bonds as bonded with them." All men belong to the
human race, slave or free, says the Bible. God respects no one of them
more than another.

BREAKING CONNECTIONS

One of the commonest ways a beginning writer breaks the flow
of writing is to shift persons carelessly. For example, he moves from
one to *he* to *I* to *you*. Frequently he says something like this:

When one faces the last week of school with tests and
graduation and parties, you begin to feel swamped.

The impersonal *one* should be used sparingly. Often beginning
writers associate it with scholarly authority and use it ridiculously:

When one goes to a baseball game, one likes hotdogs better
than popcorn.

This attempt to bring in the objective observer or authority sounds
foolish in the context of eating a hot dog at a ball park. And it is
dishonest. *One* stands for man in general, and no one [that *one* is
sound] can safely say that baseball fans like to eat hotdogs more than
popcorn.

Often a writer succumbs to this pressure of wanting to make his
statements sound true for all men and all time, and he reverts to

the word *you* when he really means *I*. Another unconsciously dishonest move. Note in the following excerpt from a student paper how the writer achieved a good flow except for his one interjection of the word *you* for *I* or *we*.

> We started out at 4:00 a.m. on Friday in Bill's new Sting Ray convertible. The car had a 375 horsepower fuel injected engine which enabled us to clip along at an average speed of 100 miles per hour. We had made very good time all day and were both tired. Our seats felt as though we had been sitting in one spot for a year and not just all day, but it was my turn to drive again at 10:00 that night. By 12:30 a.m. Saturday, I was in the high rugged Rockies of Montana. The roads were winding like a snake ready to strike and at the edge of some curves there was an easy drop into what looked like nothing, but I knew bottom was some one, two, three hundred feet down the rocky precipice. The fog was thick as my mother's home-made chicken soup. It looked as though you had run against a solid gray floating wall. I had reduced my speed to 30 miles per hour on those winding curves by 2:00 a.m. and Bill was sound asleep. All I could hear was the constant steady roar from the powerful engine as it labored up the never ending curves . . .

The *you* in "It looked as though you had run up against" suddenly forces the reader to enter the action and breaks the spell. Instead of bringing the reader excitingly into a story, a switch from the narrator's *I* to *you* often confuses the reader and pushes the writer into generalizations rather than the particular truth of his experience.

The good writer knows when to use the objective, generalized *one* (One eats, one breathes) and the more informal *you* (When you're in college you must budget your time). He considers the total context in which he writes—to paraphrase the social psychologist Harold Lasswell—"Who is saying what to whom through what medium and for what purpose." He considers all these communication elements also when he decides to maintain or break the flow of ideas. Note how Henry Thoreau makes his reader jump:

> Let a man take time enough for the most trivial deed though it be but the paring of his nails. The buds swell imperceptibly, without hurry or confusion, as if the short spring days were an eternity.

The jump from paring fingernails to buds swelling is a shock to the reader. He must back up and think what Thoreau has said in the first sentence before he can see how the second sentence belongs with it. But it does. It presents another example of "taking time," but one which belongs to nature, not man. The intelligent reader enjoys being asked occasionally by the writer to find the meaning in such puzzles.

Often the introduction of a metaphor will break the flow of words, if not of idea. Here is Norman Mailer writing of John F. Kennedy just before his nomination to the presidency:

> His personal quality had a subtle, not quite describable intensity, a suggestion of dry pent heat perhaps, his eyes large, the pupils grey, the whites prominent, almost shocking, his most forceful feature: he had the eyes of a mountaineer.

The metaphor "eyes of a mountaineer" breaks the flow of description by adjectives.

Another way of breaking flow is for the writer to interrupt himself. Some letter writers are entertaining because they often interrupt themselves gaily and unashamedly, jumping about from subject to subject with no respect for propriety.

If the writer is creating dialogue between persons, he may have one of them interrupt himself because that is what speakers do when they wander, or don't know what they're talking about, or find themselves at loss for words which will continue their flow.

> RENNY: What do you say? Should we go?
> JUNE: She said she doesn't believe in God. Yes. O.K. She's a—I wish I could remember what she said.

Readers of a science textbook do not permit the writer as much mad leaping as other writers. The more difficult the ideas and examples for the reader, the more steadily the writer must keep his sentences running. Yet *flow and break* are as fundamental a pair of opposites as *repeat and vary*. A writer could not produce a powerful break, stop, diversion, or shock if he had not first created a steady flow.

The principle of *flow and break* applies to paragraphs much as to sentences, except that the reader is readier for a break in thought when he begins a paragraph than when he begins a new sentence within a paragraph. Generally writers do not have difficulty paragraphing. They know their reader expects a paragraph to be dominated by one idea or subject, not wracked by three or four equally significant ideas fighting for first place. When the writer senses he is moving to a new point or aspect of a large question, he usually begins a new paragraph. Recently scholars have been making a great to-do about analyzing paragraphs, treating them with all the care and awe given to classifying an extensive insect collection. But the fact remains—editors and writers seldom struggle over paragraphing.

"Maybe break the long paragraph into two?" asks the editor.

"O.K.," says the writer after a quick look at the manuscript, "it's getting a little long."

Editor and writer make such decisions thinking of the reader. Does he need to be helped to see that the subject has been changed or a new point brought up? Does he need a visual rest, like a morning coffee break, from several pages of unindented material?

In *Finnegans Wake*, James Joyce pushed disconnections even further than most readers believe they can be pushed. And in *Ulysses*, his preceding book, he asked the reader to jump around a great deal to follow him. For example:

> Mild fire of wine kindles his veins. I wanted that badly. Felt so off colour. His eyes unhungrily saw shelves of tins, sardines, gaudy lobsters' claws. All the odd things people pick up for food. Out of shells, periwinkles with a pin, off trees, snails out of the ground the French eat, out of the sea with bait on a hook. Silly fish learn nothing in a thousand years. If you didn't know risky putting anything into your mouth. Poisonous berries. Johnny Magories. Roundness you think good. Gaudy colour warns you off. One fellow told another and so on. Try it on the dog first.

But even here James Joyce had a purpose beyond shaking the reader up. He was trying to present in this novel the words that make up the stream of consciousness in a man's head. The attempt was experimental, made by an experienced, skillful writer who had first learned the traditional way of creating flow between and within sentences. For example, here is the opening of his short story "The Dead" from his early book, *Dubliners*:

> Lily, the caretaker's daughter, was literally run off her feet. Hardly had she brought one gentleman into the little pantry behind the office on the ground floor and helped him off with his overcoat than the wheezy hall-door bell clanged again and she had to scamper along the bare hallway to let in another guest.

The reader of this text should keep in mind that highly complex analyses of writing, such as those presented in this chapter, were made after the fact of writing. The writers who produced the subtle flow and ebb in a passage may well have produced them unconsciously. The wise writer writes; he does not worry his typewriter with a thousand theoretical possibilities as he hits the keys. If you have learned from this chapter, you should put your learning to use in the late stages of revising, in the fourth or fifth draft, not when you are first putting ideas to paper. As you sharpen your writing by such revisions you may begin habits which will make your subsequent first drafts flow more smoothly.

Writing is like juggling. You must keep two of the balls in the air at all times, but you must not become overly conscious of how you are doing that.

REVISING TEN: Go over the Childhood Story you wrote and make it flow more forcefully. Do you want or need some breaks in the flow?

> *It is the task not only of the actor but of the artist as well to find the sort of expression that will arouse in others what is going on in himself.*
>
> GEORGE HERBERT MEAD

*Side-by-side comparisons are more re-
vealing than you could believe. All kinds
of flaws and virtues that pass unnoticed
when we test cars individually stand out
with shining clarity when we get them
together.*

Editors of *Car and Driver*

chapter 16

comparing

FIRST-HAND COMPARISONS

WHEN PAPERS are read in class, there's
George again, getting all the praise. "Now do you see what George
has done? I wish all of you would follow his example. His paper is
the only one that represents really deep thinking."

So you go home and say to yourself, "Think deeply. Think deeply."
But how? Grit your teeth and say, "I'm going to be profound"? You
grit them and write the same paper you wrote last time. "I wasn't
born with it," you say, and give profundity back to George. He never
hits home runs in softball, anyway.

But whether he knows what he's doing or not, George follows a
method. And you can, too. All good thinkers make comparisons in
depth. They study two things for intersection points—where do they
cross in difference or likeness? They find an obvious difference, then
a likeness within that difference. Then a difference within that likeness—and they are down there with George.

For example, when Constantin Stanislavsky, the Russian theater
director who had strongly influenced American actors, found himself
assigned to play the part of an old man, he spent several weeks
comparing how young and old men move. The most striking difference
was in the way an old man sits down in a chair. He does not balance
himself on his feet and lower his hips slowly and steadily into the
chair, because his hamstring muscles are weaker than a young man's.
Instead, he stands before the chair, puts his fingers on the seat of the

chair to brace himself, and lowers himself gradually. And his voice quavers. He does not speak or sing out in joyful exuberance. He is slowed down in tone and act—so Stanislavsky concluded after weeks of studying old men and young men on street cars, in public places, in homes.

After the play was over on opening night, a number of Stanislavsky's friends came backstage and one told him that Stanislavsky's old man was not convincing. He had spent all that time getting oldness right, but something was wrong. With the help of his friends and further observation he came to see that no old person is old in every action. Sometimes he becomes excited and forgets to ease his descent into a chair. And on the day his horse wins the race, he cries out with joy like a young man. Stanislavsky found a major difference between old and young men. The old man lacks spring and resiliency in his body. Stanislavsky found a likeness within that difference: sometimes, in unusual happiness, the old man talks or moves youthfully.

Stanislavsky could have carried the comparison down into successive levels. He might have asked how an individual old man would have reacted to plopping himself in a chair. The movement undoubtedly hurt him a little. How did he react to the pain? Did he say, "Oh, I'm old, and I'll never let myself act young again"? Or did he disguise the pain from others and preserve the joy of the moment?

> *You can't judge any chemical's action*
> *merely by putting it with more of itself.*
> *To know it, you have got to know its*
> *limits, both what it is and what it is not.*
> *What substances are harder or softer,*
> *what more resilient, what more compact.*
>
> EZRA POUND

To compare is to think. To compare well is to think deeply. You must put a thing against something else before its character is revealed. Note the verb *is revealed* in the last sentence. It suggests the thing does the revealing. Actually, you are the one who does the revealing by placing another thing next to it which helps you see better. The thing—what it really is—is always a combination of the present moment and context in which you observe, the past experience you bring with you, and the thing itself. If a man holds up the index fingers of his two hands, he may see that one curves more than the other. Holding up only one, he might not notice it is not straight. But the one on the right curves more than the other, so he is able to see curvature. Suddenly he remembers his mother telling him not to suck that finger when he was a little boy.

To compare in depth, begin with two things that are obviously, grossly different. Then look for likenesses between them. Or two persons alike. Then look for differences.

You never liked your two uncles on your father's side. Both you associate with pain. Likeness. But Uncle Ben, now that you reflect, used to torture you mentally—asking you to do arithmetic problems at the table when you were flunking math. Uncle Richard sat his two hundred pounds on you in what was supposed to be playing at wrestling, and he twisted your arm so hard once that your shoulder ached all summer when you played baseball. Difference.

> *Likeness*: Both caused you pain.
> *Difference*: Mental pain, physical pain.

Now ask about their intentions. Uncle Ben never realized what he was doing. Perhaps he ragged you about arithmetic because you had shown up his son Ricky at baseball, but if he did, he was acting unconsciously. Uncle Richard—that elephant wouldn't have hurt a mouse. He just played hard at everything. And if you had told him he had hurt your shoulder seriously, he would have felt terrible.

> *Likeness*: Neither one consciously intended to hurt.

How could you think that because you had shown up Ricky at baseball that Uncle Ben was getting back at you? You remember other instances of his small revenge. His spitefulness. Put them down on paper and ask whether Uncle Richard ever did things like that. You are getting deeper and deeper. Maybe Uncle Ben had a cutting edge in personal relationships—realized or unrealized—that was not present in Uncle Richard. Maybe you aren't sure, but your speculations are opening up life for you. Taking this course you will soon have more anecdotes and examples than you can use in a paper. Good. That means you can choose the strongest ones and discard all the rest. Then you will be writing professionally.

> . . . *no perfect Discovery can bee made*
> *upon a flat or a levell.*
>   BEN JONSON

Likenesses within differences. Differences within those likenesses. Likenesses within those differences . . . and so on.

Chinese and Japanese people are renowned for their ancient tradition of contemplation, for sitting down before one flower or one branch in a vase and looking at it for an hour. Yet even for a Chinese trying to give himself up for an hour to that flower means to be comparing what is there with what is somewhere else, with what is not there. And the Japanese tradition of Haiku poetry, which is so dependent on prolonged free contemplation (as opposed to rigorous systematic analysis) is based on comparisons of objects. For example, Kato Shuson sat looking at a fire and wrote:

> In the depths of the flames
> I saw how a peony
> Crumbles to pieces.

This is a precise description of the peony: it looks like a flame when it crumbles. A person who would describe a crumbling peony only in its own terms would be speechless. Each rock and plant and creature on earth is unique, different from every other individual. That is why we call it an individual. Although all the leaves on the red oak are like each other in being different from the leaves on the pin oak, every red oak leaf is slightly different from every other red oak leaf.

This principle of natural uniqueness forces upon human beings the task of writing and talking of one thing in terms of another. American students have made haiku-like comparisons; for example,

> Afternoon sunlight
> Splattering through swaying tree-
> tops, butters the ground.

TOM THAYER

WRITING SIXTEEN: Write quickly and freely about a person who delights, irks, or puzzles you. Call him A. Show him in action. Let the reader hear him talking. Keep going as long as you can. If you don't have time to finish during one session, take up the writing again later. Let the free writing cool for a day or more. Now think of another person, B, who is strikingly unlike A in some way. Write quickly how he differs from A, then go on to try to find likenesses within these differences. You may take each characteristic of A you have found and ask whether or not B possesses it. In doing that, you will probably see new characteristics of A. Now look over all you have written about A and B and decide which strong passages can be brought together to make a good paper. Perhaps you will want to confine your discussion to a description of A, never mentioning B, no matter how much he helped supply new material about A. If mentioning B is natural and helpful, bring him into the paper.

Example: Grandpa is such and such a man. You put down your knowledge of him, writing freely and fast. Then you compare him to your sister's new baby. The baby has no hair on his head. Neither does Grandpa. But how do they react to their baldness? What differences does it make in their lives? Perhaps this comparison of baldness leads to no significant discoveries. Then don't discuss baldness in your paper. Other comparisons may pay off: how is Grandpa childish? childlike? How is baby grandpa-ish?

> *Didn't Aristotle say that it is the mark of a poet to see resemblances between apparently incongruous things?*
>
> MARIANNE MOORE

In writing comparisons, you will find differences easier to perceive than similarities. The natural principle of uniqueness is working here. Anyone can see that a tree is different from water. But he who can probe the likenesses between two such dissimilar objects will make the most valuable discoveries. For example, he may see that the surface of water blown by wind is rough, like bark. Pursuing that likeness, he may find that the corrugations of bark indeed do flow like water, that their flow over the years changes in predictable directions. Then he may think how wind affects the leaves, as it does water, but not bark. But he may observe that the windward side of the tree exhibits a slightly different texture of bark, and so on and on until he has reached a great and fundamental likeness between water and tree—the flux and change of life. When he finds a truth like this, it comes with power to him and his reader because he has worked his way through to it. The way gives credibility and meaning to the discovery at the depths, at bottom. That is a good phrase for thinking and observing—for it is *at bottom* that he should be writing most of the time. Not at the top or surface of things. When you have gone a real journey to find something, your listeners and readers will be impressed to hear your tale.

WRITING SEVENTEEN: Visit one place you hate or love on different days, at different times of the days. Observe it over a period of a week or more. Make at least four visits. Take a few notes each time. Write freely about it. Tell a reader what intrigues you. Then compare it with another place you have a chance to visit several times during the same period. You need not do all the describing yourself. If you wish, you may interview other persons who know one or both of the places well. Quote their liveliest and most penetrating observations. Here is a professional writer using comparison to strengthen an article:

THERE'S NEVER A QUIET MOMENT ON W. 15TH ST.

by McCandlish Phillips

"VRRRRROOM?" said Mrs. Charles Gaines as she sat in her handsomely appointed apartment on West 15th Street. "VROOM, VROOM, VROOM, VROOM."

She was imitating the sound a huge tractor-trailer makes when it tries to start up a ramp over a dip in the street outside her living room window.

Mrs. Gaines is an expert. Her front windows look out on 42 truck berths at a block-long loading platform for one of the largest express depots in the world—the Railway Express Agency's Manhattan Assorting Terminal.

West 15th Street has a split personality. The south side of the street is zoned R-8 (residential). The north side is zoned M1-5 (industrial). The invisible dividing line runs down the middle of the street.

On the south side there are 22 apartment buildings three to six stories high. Across the street is the 14-story head-quarters of the Port Authority.

The truck platform is on the south side of the Port Authority building, between Eighth and Ninth Avenues. The authority rented it to the express agency late last year for a 24-hours-a-day, 7-days-a-week loading and unloading operation.

Tenants in all the apartments facing it are living in acute distress.

The "CHIFF-CHIFF" of hydraulic brakes (like steam escaping from a narrow fissure), the scrunch of clashing gears, the thump of wooden boxes being unloaded, the blaring of a loudspeaker system, the growl of trucks being jockeyed in and out of position, the slamming shut of metal doors hardly ever stops.

"This was a window," Gerhardt Liebmann, an architect and artist, said in a small front bedroom of his seven-room apartment at 326 West 15th Street.

Now, instead of a window he can see out of, he almost has one he can't hear through. Over the glass he has installed two thicknesses of composition board, a wooden shutter and burlap curtains, "and it still doesn't keep all the noise out."

There has been a freight platform on that side of the building since it opened in 1932. But until last year it was used only from 8 A.M. to 6 P.M. on weekdays.

"You try and park a freight train—that's what these are, they come right off the tracks—in such a narrow street," a resident said, referring to the piggyback trailers.

The street is 36 feet wide. The big trailers are 42 feet long when detached from 9 foot driver cabs.

"The docking space recommended for trucks that long is 57 feet," Mr. Liebmann said. "If they had the docking space they needed, that would put them 16 feet into our bedrooms and right into our beds."

"There are two reverse gears, I've discovered," Mrs. Gaines, who lives at 320 West 15th Street, said with crisp authority. "The second one is the noisy one—but it's faster. They don't sneak out of here at night. VRRRR-ROOM! they gun the motors to get out, then CHUME! into gear, CHUME! into the next gear, then they slam on the brakes at the corner."

Mrs. Gaines, the wife of an actor, who complained about "swearing, shouting and yelling" outside her windows, said she was building up "a monstrous anger" that she did not think was good for her.

Miss Mattie Dechner has three rooms at 358 West 15th Street with five windows, all facing the street. She has a tape recording she made from 6:15 to 7:45 one day, which she calls, "A Quiet Sunday Afternoon."

Drivers sometimes have to bump over the curb onto the sidewalk to maneuver into position on the crowded street. They dent fences, crack stoops and make pedestrians shrink into doorways. Several weeks ago a distraught, rather elderly woman came out of the front door of her basement apartment and chased a driver down the block waving a hatchet, while people cheered from their windows. He got away.

Children can't play on the sidewalk, houses shudder, windows rattle, plaster cracks.

"You come home. You've worked all day, you're tired," Mr. Liebmann said. "Now's the time to sit in a chair, relax and have a beer. But the hell of it is, when you're through they're just beginning, and you know they're going to go all night."

"The terminal is a vital link in the service to the residents and the economy of New York City," a spokesman for Railway Express said. "This is part of the fabric of the absolutely necessary round-the-clock activity that supports the economic life of cities. Like the airlines, we're trying to do everything possible to ameliorate the noise, but we have to operate as we are operating to sort and dispatch inbound and outbound shipments to 50 states."

Hugh Graef, director of operations, addressed a letter to "All Drivers" last month that was handed to them with their pay, requesting that "each of you consider at all times the welfare of these residents."

"I can best sum it up," he wrote, "that we should treat these residents as we would want any of our relatives treated who might be faced with the requirement of living near a metropolitan truck terminal."

In this article, Mr. Phillips centered on one subject, the feelings of the residents living on the south side of West 15th Street. Then he compared the feelings of the truckers on the other side of the street. They are in almost total conflict—few likenesses. But as a good reporter, he quoted not only the lively statements of residents complaining about trucks, but the director of operations for Railway Express. He had his reasons for defending the operation, as the residents had theirs for attacking it. He was also human. He said,

. . . we should treat these residents as we would want any of our relatives treated who might be faced with the requirement of living near a metropolitan truck terminal.

Both sides were acting out of their vested interests.

WRITING EIGHTEEN: Comparisons need not always be analytical. Consider the following, written quickly as a free writing.

THE REAL THING

Sometimes I feel like I'm on a huge, barren desert. Not really a hot desert, just sandy and empty. I look straight ahead and see the mountains. They don't look so far away. So I trudge and work to get close to them—and the next time I look up, they seem farther away. I feel discouraged—but in the breast of man hope never dies—I heard that some place, I think—so I go on. There are a million mirages and false images I see. And at each one I stop. It seems I never learn to tell the difference. Just once it

would be nice to find the real thing. Not to fall flat on my
face and come up with my teeth gritting from the sand.
Each time I try to make water out of sand I fail. Maybe I
should stop—and just look for a cool, clean spring instead
of an ocean. There really aren't many oceans in the desert
anyway. In a spring I could be myself. I could be cooled
by the fresh water and my thirst would be quenched. The
mountains are getting closer now. Maybe when I reach
them I'll find my spring.

CHIP DUNPHY

In writing this passage, a girl compared her life to existence on a
desert. She let those two subjects speak to each other in productive
conversation.

Try two 10- or 20-minute free writings in which you play with a
comparison that points up some feeling or experience close to you
at the moment. Don't worry if your free comparing doesn't work out
well. The comparer always takes risks. Maybe he loses. He can always
try again. He need not show his misses to others. Maybe he discovers
a spring in the desert.

METAPHOR

Deep comparisons are only extended metaphors, one thing seen in
terms of another. Ring Lardner, the American short story writer,
wrote of a young boy observing a girl:

He give her a look you could have poured on a waffle.

When a comparison is hooked together by the words *like* or *as* it is
called a simile, as in these lines from the poet Henry Vaughan:

I saw eternity the other night,
Like a great ring of pure and endless light.

but the difference between metaphor (where one thing is directly said
to be something else, as in Samuel Butler's metaphor, "Evaporation
is an unseen heavenward waterfall") and simile is not as valuable to
learn as how to make good comparisons, whatever they are called.
Some metaphors and similes:

(a) Angus (speaking of Macbeth): Now does he feel
His secret murders sticking on his hands;
Now minutely revolts upbraid his faith-breach.
Those he commands move only in command,
Nothing in love. Now does he feel his title

Hang loose about him, like a giant's robe
Upon a dwarfish thief.

WILLIAM SHAKESPEARE

(b) . . . beyond him, one white sycamore straight as diving.

REYNOLDS PRICE

(c) A tree in spring is a double-barreled shot gun exploding.

FIFTH-GRADE CHILD

Comparisons like these may seem so remarkable to you that you cannot believe they would visit you. But that is what good metaphors usually do. They come to the writer; he does not manufacture them at will. They come to all persons, at all ages. Frequently they come most perfectly in fast, free writing, as they did to the girl who wrote this quick description:

> **I saw Chicago once. The heat *stood still* between walls formed by dirty *heaped-up buildings squeezed* tightly together. People walked under the "L" with greasy faces, not just white ones, but black and brown and yellowish-brown, eyes slanting up or down or straight across with lines fanning from the corners as they squinted. Even the hair piled high up on women's heads *escaped* in frizzy ringlets on the back of their bare necks. Children didn't hop on one foot or chase *fleeting* candy wrappers down the sidewalk, but walked *like grandfathers,* in order not to be *strangled* by the heat and soot. Red shirts and red dresses *stood out,* but everything else was grey, light grey or dark or dirty white, and everybody was too close to somebody or something. But at the end of the street the wind *purred* gently under the open sky and the sun *smiled down* on the *green face* of the lake.**

Most of the comparisons in this passage consist of simple personification of inanimate objects: candy wrappers are fleeting; hair escapes. Nothing remarkable about these, but four of the comparisons—

> Children . . . *walked like grandfathers* . . . the wind *purred*
> gently under the open sky and the *sun smiled* down on
> the *green face* of the lake.

strike with power. The first—children walking like grandfathers—gains power from freshness, originality. But the three metaphors which close the passage are not unusual. They gain force from smooth, pleasant sound and from the contrast the writer has built between their pleasant connotations and the unpleasantness of preceding words like *squeezed, frizzy, soot, heat, dirty white.* As always in writing, a word finds its meaning and charge more from the words that have preceded and followed it than from any one meaning ascribed to it in a dictionary.

Because all words on a page carry latent sound, most metaphors gain from sound as well as from the comparison they state. Shakespeare had his Prince Hal say:

> Falstaff sweats to death and lards the lean earth as he walks
> along.

So much is working in that sentence: the great metaphor of the fat man larding the *lean* earth would be enough of an achievement but Shakespeare creates a fine sound effect by filling the sentences with "l" sounds. Count them.

David Jones, the beginning writer who created the following comparison, also controlled the sound of his words skillfully:

> **With dawn come the ducks. You aim at the first one flying
> by and shoot . . . and watch him fly away. You missed be-
> cause you forgot to lead the duck. When shooting ducks
> you don't aim where they are; you aim where they will be.
> You must lead ducks just the way a quarterback leads an
> end. He doesn't throw the ball at the end; he throws it over
> his head or in front of the end and if it is properly thrown,
> the ball and the end meet at the same spot.**

In this passage, the segments of sentences rock back and forth in even lengths and then join *football* and *end* suddenly and finally with the words "at the same spot." *Spot* ends the passage with an explosive sound that echoes *shot.*

Beginning writers often shy away from figurative language, afraid they will fall on their faces with it. And they often do, because they make up metaphors and similes outside their experience. To find your metaphors and similes, look to your own life, what you know well. When you are moving through the everyday world and are arrested by a piece of cellophane tape plastered on the broken pair of glasses on your friend's nose, consider why it strikes you. And record in a notebook a precise description of what it looked like and what meaning it carried for you. Perhaps the tape looked dirty and ragged on an expensive pair of glasses. Then when you need a metaphor,

this comparison may come to you with all the freshness of its par-
ticularity.

> *Falstaff to Prince Hal: Thou hast the*
> *most unsavory similes, and art indeed*
> *the most comparative, rascalliest, sweet*
> *young prince.*
>
> WILLIAM SHAKESPEARE

WRITING NINETEEN: Record five sensory observations that strike
you vividly and that you might use as comparisons at some later date.
Do not choose what you think will impress others. Choose what hits
your senses and holds you, for whatever reasons.

In a sense all language is metaphorical, stands for something else.
The river runs. She smiles sweetly. The river is personified. Her
smile is compared to sugar. As a writer you should become aware of
the dead metaphor in language so you can exploit it. In *Walden*,
Thoreau began writing this sentence,

> We meet at meals three times a day, and give each other
> a new taste

and he remembered the metaphor in the word *taste*. Because he did
not allow the word to become abstract in his mind, he was able to
finish the sentence in this way:

> of that old musty cheese that we are.

You can do this, too. Suppose you say that

> Aunt Helen was a plain woman,

Get on that word *plain*. If Grandmother was hard but exciting, you
might continue your sentence this way:

> but Grandmother was the Rocky Mountains.

When you forget the dead and hidden metaphors in the language
you may compose foolish sentences. For example:

> Changing the course of a fast, deep river would normally
> be a lost cause, but this is one cause the North High family
> cannot afford to lose hold of.

This is a metaphor used by a student editor to ask others to help him
reform the school newspaper. In it, he forgets what he is saying and
asks the readers to keep hold of a river. He should remember that
water is impossible to grasp.

Here is an excerpt from a paint company's directions for using artists' colors:

> Where very thin glazes are desired, Liquitex colors mixed with the Medium may be quickly and lightly rubbed over the surface with fingers and thumb in the manner of oil glazes. On the other hand, unwanted color or glaze may be wiped off.

The writer committed a blooper in using the phrase "On the other hand." He forgot its dead metaphor. Just before that he is talking about literal fingers and thumb. Like a thousand other phrases in everyday language, "on the other hand" was once a brilliant metaphor. Now men use it so unconsciously they need to be jogged with the vaudeville gag: "On the other hand—she had a wart."

WRITING TWENTY: Write two 10- to 20-minute free writings in which you talk of things you love. Let yourself describe them in metaphor and simile that come from your deepest knowledge about objects or processes or occupations. Don't be satisfied with simple, brief metaphors: "His face was like a sunny day." Develop a metaphor, let its parts speak to each other and create new and continuing comparisons, as this beginning writer did:

> **When I think of barnacles I laugh because if they were attached to my bottom I'd feel important—like the Queen Mary. Maybe I ought to think like this when I take a bath and slide across the porcelain ocean at the end of a narrow day.**

> Alice didn't dare to argue the point, but went on: "And I thought I'd try and find my way to the top of that hill—"
>
> "When you say 'hill,'" the Queen interrupted, "I could show you hills in comparison with which you'd call that a valley."
>
> "No, I shouldn't," said Alice, surprised into contradicting her at last: "a hill can't be a valley, you know. That would be nonsense—"
>
> The Red Queen shook her head. "You may call it 'nonsense,' if you like," she said, "but I've heard nonsense compared with which that would be as sensible as a dictionary!"
>
> LEWIS CARROLL

chapter 17 keeping a journal

MOST PERSONS write notes to themselves
(Get Kleenex and catsup. "I saw a rhinusahorus at the zoo"—Timmy's
report at dinner, which should be forwarded in next letter to Grandma) and each spring they wish they had a note from last year telling
when they first saw blossoms on the lilac bush. But they lose the
notes, which are written on torn bits of paper, the backs of laundry
slips, or the flyleaves of books.

An old cigar box will not do, because not enough of the notes
get put in there, and those that do are difficult to consult: one must
riffle through all of them to find one.

The answer is a journal instead of a box, a bound ruled book in
which to make instant and permanent entries. Many professional
writers keep one.

WRITING TWENTY-ONE: Try keeping a journal for a week. You
may not be the journal kind of person—maybe you have a photo-
graphic memory or an aversion to recording anything you feel has
not been polished like a gem. But try keeping a journal for a week
and see. Here's a day from one of Henry Thoreau's journals:

Dec. 5, 1856. Clear, cold winter weather. What a contrast between this week and last, when I talked of setting out apple trees!

P.M.—Walked over the Hill.

The Indians have at length got a regular load of wood. It is odd to see a pile of good wood beside their thin cotton tents in the snow, the wood-pile which is to be burnt within is so much more substantial than the house. Yet they do not appear to mind the cold, though one side the tent is partly open, and all are flapping in the wind, and there is a sick child in one. The children play in the snow in front, as before more substantial houses.

The river is well skimmed over in most places, though it will not bear,—wherever there is least current, as in broad places, or where there is least wind, as by the bridges. The ice trap was sprung last night.

As I walk along the side of the Hill, a pair of nuthatches flit by toward a walnut, flying low in mid-course and then ascending to the tree. I hear one's faint *tut tut* or *gnah gnah*—no doubt heard a good way by its mate now flown into the next tree—as it is ascending the trunk or branch of a walnut in a zigzag manner, hitching along; prying into the crevices of the bark; and now it has found a savory morsel, which it pauses to devour, then flits to a new bough. It is a chubby bird, white, slate-color, and black.

It is a perfectly cloudless and simple winter sky. A white moon, half full, in the pale or dull blue heaven and a whiteness like the reflection of the snow, extending up from the horizon all around a quarter the way up to the zenith. I can imagine that I see it shooting up like an aurora. This is at 4 P. M. About the sun it is only whiter than elsewhere, or there is only the faintest possible tinge of yellow there.

There are a great many walnuts on the trees, seen black against the sky, and the wind has scattered many over the snow-crust. It would be easier gathering them now than ever.

The johnswort and the larger pinweed are conspicuous above the snow. Some fine straw-colored grasses, as delicate as the down on a young man's cheek, still rise above this crusted snow, and even a recess is melted around them, so gently has it been deposited.

The sun goes down and leaves not a blush in the sky . . .

My themes shall not be far-fetched. I will tell of homely
every-day phenomena and adventures. Friends! Society! It
seems to me that I have an abundance of it, there is so
much that I rejoice and sympathize with, and men, too,
that I never speak to but only know and think of. What you
call bareness and poverty is to me simplicity. God could
not be unkind to me if he should try. I love the winter,
with its imprisonment and its cold, for it compels the
prisoner to try new fields and resources. I love to have the
river closed up for a season and a pause put to my boating,
to be obliged to get my boat in. I shall launch it again this
spring with so much more pleasure. This is an advantage in
point of abstinence and moderation compared with the
seaside boating, where the boat ever lies on the shore. I
love best to have each thing in its season only, and enjoy
doing without it at all other times. It is the greatest of all
advantages to enjoy no advantage at all. I find it invariably
true, the poorer I am, the richer I am. What you consider
my disadvantage, I consider my advantage. While you are
pleased to get knowledge and culture in many ways, I am
delighted to think that I am getting rid of them. I have
never got over my surprise that I should have been born
into the most estimable place in all the world, and in the
very nick of time, too.

A day's record of observations and thoughts, from a journal which
ran into several thousand printed pages. From these pages Thoreau
put together several books, including *Walden*, a classic statement of
the joys of self-reliant living which has been read for more than a
hundred years in all parts of the world.

> *If a writer will go on the principle of
> stopping everywhere and anywhere to
> put down his notes, as the true painter
> will stop anywhere and everywhere to
> sketch, he will be able to cut down his
> works liberally. He will become prodigal
> not of writing—any fool can be this—but
> of omission. You become brief because
> you have more things to say than time to
> say them in.*
>
> SAMUEL BUTLER

Thoreau's entry for December 5, 1856 contained his usual miscellany of writing: simple notes of facts to mark the record of the year, observations of nature and men, thoughts. In your journal put down whatever strikes you. Think of it at once as private and public. You may be showing it or parts of it to others. If you find yourself recording such intimate secrets that you do not want them revealed, you can keep them in the book and copy out only those you want to show to others. The possibilities for entries are endless, as the following statement by Dorothy Lambert shows:

WHAT IS A JOURNAL?

Though a journal may be many things—a treasury, a storehouse, a jewelry box, a laboratory, a drafting board, a collector's cabinet, a snapshot album, a history, a travelogue, a religious exercise, a letter to oneself—it has some definable characteristics. It is a record, an entry-book, kept regularly, though not necessarily daily. Invariably some entries will be scrawled on the backs of ice cream wrappers, envelopes, paper bags, or programs, whatever blank surface available at the moment. Some will be nearly illegible, written in the dark in the middle of the night. These entries can be recopied, pasted in, or dated and kept loose in the rear of the journal, but they are part of it; inspiration settles on one at the most awkward moments, not necessarily as one sits down to write with clean page, sharpened pencil, and open mind.

It is a record kept for oneself. As such, it is fragmentary, allusive, disjointed, uneven in quality. Nor should it be polished and unified; then it would be a collection of essays. What matters is the one entry in ten which sparkles, ready to be set in the ring of an essay or story or poem or letter.

Not only is it a record for oneself, but of oneself. Every memorable journal, any successful journal, is honest. Nothing sham, phoney, false. Who is there to kid? Yet euphemism, the word which hides the fact, is so much a part of the world; to break through the euphemistic mold of thought to honesty is very difficult. A journal need not be a confession, or a psychoanalyst's couch, however. Honesty lies in observing undeceived what lies about, not necessarily what lies within.

Finally, a journal is a place to fail. That is, a place to try, experiment, test one's wings. For the moment, judgment, criticism, evaluation are suspended; what matters is the attempt, not the success of the attempt. In a journal one practices the lines before going onstage.

A journal may be all gems, or all logs, or all plans and blueprints, or all test tubes, or all confession, or all collections of oddments—or it may be a marvelous hodgepodge of the old-fashioned general store. What follows are some ways of seeing, of thinking of a journal, and some suggestions of what to do with it. You may follow one suggestion consistently, or try all, or none. At least you will become aware of what is possible.

1. Think of your journal as a treasury, a jewelry box for gems and gold nuggets, for quotes (others' or/and yours), pithy ideas, epigrams, turns of phrase, insights, analogies, puns, aphorisms, nutshell wisdom. You will write little, but think much.

2. Think of your journal as a storehouse into which you pack canned goods (others' ideas), fresh fruit, nuts, corn, string, straw, K-rations—almost anything edible and useful, in preparation for a rainy day, when you can browse through your storehouse with delight and constant amazement at what is there. Like a pack-rat or the Collier brothers, don't stop to be discriminatory in your salvaging and collecting.

3. Think of your journal as a collector's cabinet in which you place or mount butterflies and moths, or glass figurines, or . . . What will you collect? salt and pepper shakers? stamps? model ships in bottles? oddments, little ironic quirks of life? Do you collect for others to see, or just to have?

4. Think of your journal as a snapshot album and you a roving photographer clicking a shutter on life. Light and dark contrasts, color, texture, angles and circles, portraits, landscapes: what will you photograph? Steichen chose faces and hands; Ansel Adams chose the Sierras. See life through a lens, telescopic, microscopic, or wide-angle, but a lens. In focus.

5. Think of your journal as a laboratory for experiments, blank pages waiting to be tried. Dissect. See what the insides are like, how it runs, how it's put together. Examine

minutely; see with a microscope. Mix test-tubes. Weigh.
Trace patterns; fix laws. Ask questions and set about to
find answers.

6. Think of your journal as a giant wardrobe which you
can step into and try on marvelous clothes. Put on others'
styles, look in the mirror, see and feel how they fit. Wear
what you like; change with the seasons; try on 49 hats and
buy none. Be Parisian, Ethiopian, or Hindi: experiment,
experiment. Even poetry, though by phrases, not rhymes.

7. Think of your journal as a drafting board. Blank
pages will become blueprints, plans for a house to live in.
Or are you drafting just window sills, or a whole cathedral?
Accuracy, careful detail, sharp lines, no smudges on the
pages. If you are an idea-person, what will you build?
Watch your idea-house grow, as you add on bedrooms for
the birth of new thoughts.

8. Think of your journal as a psychoanalyst's couch, a
confession. Lie down, and talk, talk, talk. Ramble on about
irrelevancies, or else list in order your sins. Repeat, go over
and over as you peel away each layer of onion skin to the
core. Explore your depths. Dreams, Fantasies, Truths.

9. Think of your journal as a tape recorder attached
directly to your brain. Record your stream-of-conscious-
ness, your associational thoughts. Don't fuss for words;
write as fast as you think. Use dashes, dots, skip lines and
spaces for "punctuation." Replay: can you find a coherence
in your thoughts? Emphasize and clarify such associational
leaps.

10. Think of your journal as a continuous but unmailed
letter to a specific, real person. Preferably of the opposite
sex, highly interested in you. Make every entry a love
letter, every entry an act of love. Or choose to write to a
close confidant. Or to your mother. Or possibly to your yet
unborn children. What would you tell them? no moralizing,
no mush.

11. Think of your journal as a letter to yourself. What
would you have yourself know? Or remember ten years from
now? Which self of your many selves will you choose to
write to? Or yourself as you *were*, say, at ten? Or yourself
as you will be? Will your other self/selves answer back?
Turn your journal into a dialogue or triologue with yourself. Argue, debate, reconcile.

12. Think of your journal as a history—memoirs—and you as a VIP: the average citizen. Write for an extra-terrestrial reader, or a terrestrial one of the 22nd Century. Let them know how we really lived and thought. Or else record the current world events, as filtered through your eyes, your consciousness, your concern. Record how history touches you.

13. Think of your journal as a travelogue, even though you may travel only through tunnels from dorm to class, like an underground man. See afresh, as if you were born yesterday, or recently distilled from another planet. Record the quaint customs, lore, folkways, speech patterns, super-stitions, magic, and miraculous sights of the local terrain. Be Livingstone, Margaret Mead. Or be Magellan; chart the unknown; fill in the map of your world.

14. Think of your journal as a religious exercise, one which might lead to a religious experience, or religious insight. Write it as a letter to God. A dialogue? Follow St. Ignatius' meditative methods: application of the senses; composition of scene. But write it down. Become all tongue, all eyeball, all nose; only hands; the world's ear. Be at the place, fly back to the time. Put yourself in other's feet; especially try those you can't stand, those who seem foreign to you. Use these meditative principles in areas not consid-ered religious; meditate on the secular. Write prayers, per-sonal prayers; write litany; write secular prayers, secular litany. Search for metaphors, new metaphors, for the in-effable, the wordless, the inexpressible. Reach out into the void, reach down, reach up, to find ways of telling others what you believe.

Mrs. Lambert's essay on journals is not a map, merely suggestions. Take one, take several, as you wish.

The great journal keepers have always distrusted their memories. When an idea strikes them for a piece of writing, they write it down even though it is only an idea, so far without the materials to give it body. Samuel Butler, whose published *Note-Books* are widely quoted, made such notes for writing he hoped to do some day. Here are three out of a long list:

1. Tracts for Children, warning them against the virtues of their elders.

2. Family Prayers: A series of perfectly plain and sensible ones asking for what people really do want without any kind of humbug.
3. The Sense of Touch: An essay showing that all the senses resolve themselves ultimately into a sense of touch, and that eating is touch carried to the bitter end. So there is but one sense—touch—and the amoeba has it. When I look upon the foraminifera I look upon myself.

If you are aware of the fabulous quality of reality, your notebook is bound to be exciting reading in spots. Here are excerpts from a number of student notebooks:

1

Mom to three-year-old: "Mary Jane, get out of your Coke!"

2

I have drained six cartons of lemonade and twelve glasses of tap water since this afternoon, and two quarts of milk. I have a fever but am on my feet, slushing off to class—reading, writing, and I get paid today.

3

My seven-year-old sister at a birthday party: "Oh, Momma, my feet went to sleep. It feels like salt and pepper mixed."

4

One of the salesman at Sears absent-mindedly wore to work one shoe and one bedroom slipper. He didn't have time to go home to change, so he developed a limp for the day.

5

A white-haired old woman scooped up spilled dry oatmeal from a busy intersection after the bottom of her grocery bag had burst. She explained to one honking motorist that she didn't want to waste the oatmeal—she would take it home to her ducks.

6

My sister celebrated her sixteenth birthday yesterday. Her boy friend surprised her with a beautiful heart necklace. Later, a strange man surprised her at an intersection by pulling out in front of her car, and she rammed his car

with hers, cutting her forehead, nose, and mouth. One scar under her chin is heart-shaped.

7

Last week I saw two guys walking down Western Avenue carrying on a conversation ten feet apart. I even walked between them. Interpersonal relationships are growing less personal but this was too much almost to believe. One of them, I suppose, had determined to assert himself, keep his pace and have the other come up to him. The other probably determined the opposite, so they walked along, making fools of themselves.

8

Charlie came home on leave today after eight weeks of basic training. He learned to kill.

My Uncle was gassed in the First World War and when I knew him he sat in a chair watching television all day and talked in a hesitating manner.

9

On the corner of a parking lot on Rose Street, a mailman stopped at the mailbox, unlocked it, opened the front, took the mail out, and sat down inside the mailbox while he sorted the letters.

10

It's the first day of school. It seems so empty. Oh, there's lots of things to do, but there is something missing. There is no one older. When we were sophomores and juniors there was always the big seniors. Now there is no one left. We're seniors, last year of high school. Is it really the fact that we're as big as we will get? Hard to say what's missing. It's lonely here.

In writing journal entries a person should begin by concentrating on what he says rather than how he says it. Entry 10 is carelessly written. The expression *there is* appears too often. Twice it led the writer to use a singular verb with a plural subject ("there's lots," which says in reverse "lots is"; and "there was . . . the big seniors" which says in reverse "seniors was"). But the writer put her finger on why high school students sometimes feel lost at the beginning of their last year. Since she solved that puzzle, she should not have said, "Hard to say what's missing." If she wants to publish the statement more widely, she should omit that sentence and improve the verbs throughout. If you look at your journal entries some time after you wrote them and find them in need of revision, you might cross out words and make changes for practice, but you do not need to. A journal is personal. If a teacher or someone else can talk you into publishing some of your journal entries, fine; but you should not allow your journal to be graded.

Here are some more journal entries:

11

I hate that sand dune. It looked down at me. I felt small. It seemed to be laughing at me as the wind from the lake blew over it. I hated it even more. I began to run up the side. The sand, like wet cardboard, under my feet. Heat. I could feel it conquer my throat. It was steep. Bushes and fallen tree branches served as handles. My legs were aching. Made me go faster. I fell. Made me feel like a dog crawling on all fours. I went on. The laughter got louder as the wind blew harder. Just kept running. Panting, until I found myself standing on the top of it. The lake and beach below looked so small. And the sand dune. Now that it was under me, it didn't seem so big either. My turn to laugh. Felt like God.

12

Moved. Just like that. She moved. I had known her for a long time. She had thick, curly eyelashes, long. Envied. Lise always grew her nails long, too. It was sort of awesome to look at them sometimes. They were curved and filed into a fine oval. No one at school said anything about it. No teachers. They didn't say anything. It's different now. Lise moved. She went to Grand Rapids. The nuns there were different. Strict. Scary. Lise was in typing. The nun said to trim the nails by the next weekend. She didn't. The nun wasn't to be ignored. Up to the desk. Lise had to cut off all her finger nails. Right then. Right there. It's too bad she moved.

When you write in a journal, keep your sense of a reader. That reader may be no one else but you, but so much later in time that he needs to be spoken to fully, to be put there. The writer of Entry 13 chose an incident involving deep feeling and wrote strong sentences, but she held back a little too much.

13

> We went to the funeral and afterwards his grandpa asked
> me to go out to the house with all the other people. I did,
> and everybody ignored me. I think Kent did because after
> we went to the cemetery and the minister said the last
> words underneath the tent, Kent went over and sat in one
> of the limousines, leaving the door open, perhaps so I could
> come and say a kind word or pat him on the hand. I didn't
> want to. I lowered my eyes and walked right by him. I
> think he even said my name.

The value of a journal lies in its being a place. One place, not
four score. The writer can return to it to see what in the past he
has found and perhaps forgotten. In your journal you may write your
imitations of other writers and someday trace the development of
your own style, as Robert Louis Stevenson says he did in his journals.
That work helped him write *Treasure Island* and *A Child's Garden
of Verses.*

> All through my boyhood and youth, I was known and
> pointed out for the pattern of an idler; and yet I was
> always busy on my own private end, which was to learn
> to write. I kept always two books in my pocket, one to
> read, one to write in. As I walked, my mind was busy
> fitting what I saw with appropriate words; when I sat by
> the roadside, I would either read, or a pencil and a penny
> version-book would be in my hand, to note down the fea-
> tures of the scene or commemorate some halting stanzas.
> Thus I lived with words. And what I thus wrote was for
> no ulterior use, it was written consciously for practice.
> It was not so much that I wished to be an author (though
> I wished that too) as that I had vowed that I would learn
> to write. That was a proficiency that tempted me; and
> I practised to acquire it, as men learn to whittle, in a
> wager with myself. Description was the principal field of
> my exercise; for to any one with senses there is always some-
> thing worth describing, and town and country are but one
> continuous subject. But I worked in other ways also; often
> accompanied my walks with dramatic dialogues, in which
> I played many parts; and often exercised myself in writing
> down conversations from memory.

This was all excellent, no doubt; so were the diaries I sometimes tried to keep, but always and very speedily discarded, finding them a school of posturing and melancholy self-deception. And yet this was not the most efficient part of my training. Good though it was, it only taught me (so far as I have learned them at all) the lower and less intellectual elements of the art, the choice of the essential note and the right word: things that to a happier constitution had perhaps come by nature. And regarded as training, it had one grave defect; for it set me no standard of achievement. So that there was perhaps more profit, as there was certainly more effort, in my secret labors at home. Whenever I read a book or a passage that particularly pleased me, in which a thing was said or an effect rendered with propriety, in which there was either some conspicuous force or some happy distinction in the style, I must sit down at once and set myself to ape that quality. I was unsuccessful, and I knew it; and tried again, and was again unsuccessful and always unsuccessful; but at least in these vain bouts, I got some practice in rhythm, in harmony, in construction and the co-ordination of parts.

. . . That, like it or not, is the way to learn to write; whether I have profited or not, that is the way. It was so Keats learned, and there was never a finer temperament for literature that Keats's; it was so, if we could trace it out, that all men have learned; and that is why a revival of letters is always accompanied or heralded by a cast back to earlier and fresher models. Perhaps I hear some one cry out: But this is not the way to be original! It is not; nor is there any way but to be born so. Nor yet, if you are born original, is there anything in this training that shall clip the wings of your originality. There can be none more original that Montaigne, neither could any be more unlike Cicero; yet no craftsman can fail to see how much the one must have tried in his time to imitate the other. Burns is the very type of a prime force in letters: he was of all men the most imitative. Shakespeare himself, the imperial, proceeds directly from a school. It is only from a school that we can expect to have good writers; it is almost invariably from a school that great writers, these lawless exceptions, issue. Nor is there anything here that should astonish the considerate. Before he can tell what cadences he truly prefers, the student should have tried all that are possible; before he can choose and preserve a fitting key of words, he should long have practised the literary scales; and it is only after years of such gymnastic that he can sit down at last, legions of words swarming to his call, dozens of turns of phrase simultaneously bidding for his choice, and he himself knowing what he wants to do and (within the narrow limits of a man's ability) able to do it.

And it is the great point of these limitations that there still shines beyond the student's reach his inimitable model. Let him try as he please, he is still sure of failure; and it is a very old and a very true saying that failure is the only high-road to success. I must have had some disposition to learn; for I clear-sightedly condemned my own performances. I liked doing them indeed; but when they were done, I could see they were rubbish. In consequence, I very rarely showed them even to my friends; and such friends as I chose to be my confidants I must have chosen well, for they had the friendliness to be quite plain with me. "Padding," said one. Another wrote: "I cannot understand why you do lyrics so badly." No more could I! Thrice I put myself in the way of a more authoritative rebuff, by sending a paper to a maga-zine. These were returned; and I was not surprised nor even pained. If they had not been looked at, as (like all ama-teurs) I suspected was the case, there was no good in repeat-ing the experiment; if they had been looked at—well, then I had not yet learned to write, and I must keep on learning and living. . . .

The imitating which Stevenson speaks of is common to writers. How else would writers learn the fundamentals of good style? Benjamin Franklin tells in his *Autobiography* how he employed a slightly different form of imitation. He read and studied a passage of writing he admired, wrote down "short Hints of the Sentiment in each Sentence," and then several days later tried to reproduce the passage. Almost every professional writer has learned fundamentals in this way before developing his own style. No surprise here: long ball hitters have learned from imitating Harmon Killebrew and Hank Aaron, painters have learned from imitating Leonardo da Vinci and Van Gogh.

A good writer never plagiarizes from another writer, but he borrows obviously and he builds on what another writer has said.

When E. E. Cummings wrote his great line "pity this busy mon-ster,manunkind," discussed in Chapter 14, he may have got the notion of playing with *man* and *unkind* from Thoreau's lines in *A Week on the Concord and Merrimack Rivers*:

> I love man—kind, but I hate the institutions of the dead unkind. Men execute nothing so faithfully as the wills of the dead, to the last codicil and letter. *They* rule this world, and the living are but their executors.

When Thoreau wrote in "Walking":

> Any man can stop a hole to keep the wind away, but no other man could serve so rare a use as the author of this illustration did.

he was clearly alluding to lines Shakespeare gave to Hamlet:

> Imperious Caesar, dead and turned to clay,
> Might stop a hole to keep the wind away.

although he did not mention *Hamlet*. These two writers did not steal from Thoreau and Shakespeare. Cummings pushed further a word play of Thoreau—if he borrowed at all; and Thoreau turned a phrase of Shakespeare into half of a neat compliment to him.

All men must borrow from those who have gone before, but they should understand what constitutes stealing from the printed page, however difficult that act is to define. One does not always have to use quotation marks. All men are created equal—the reader recognizes the source. One can give the wise reader a hint that he is borrowing, as Thoreau did when he borrowed from Hamlet. But one should not take a series of words—say more than seven—from another writer when they are distinctive and valuable in style or message, and allow the reader to believe they are his own.

Student term papers often abound in such plagiarism. Speaking in the most obviously alien voices, students write stolen sentences like this:

> The nugatory effect of the prolix discussion was that the
> Treaty of Rackham was forever doomed.

This is calculated imposture, in writing called *plagiarism*. The most responsible way to borrow is immediately to acknowledge indebted-ness, not by footnote or quotation marks (although they are fre-quently helpful), but by naming the source:

> Burke said that . . .

IMITATING TWO: Try Franklin's method. Find a paragraph or short passage you admire. Copy it into your journal. Take brief notes of what it says. Then tomorrow attempt to reproduce the passage without looking at it.

IMITATING THREE: Write your own thoughts or observations into the same sentence patterns in the passage you copied down for IMITATING TWO.

IMITATING FOUR: Listen to a conversation between yourself and another person or between two other persons. Take notes if you can do so unobtrusively. Then try to reproduce the conversation accurately. Can a reader tell from your dialogue that two persons are talking in different styles or manners or moods? Have you heard the uniqueness in their words? Do they sound real enough to be believable?

WRITING TWENTY-TWO: After keeping a journal for a week, stop for a week and then go back to its pages. Choose the entry which most moves you, and work it up or cut it down until you have produced a small piece of writing whole and satisfying to you.

WRITING TWENTY-THREE: After one week's respite from journal writing, begin your journal again and make a daily entry or two for two weeks. Choose an object, a place, a person that interests you, and note it each weekday for two weeks—include weekends if possible. Observe it daily. You will see it in different lights because the weather has changed, the time of the day, the weather inside you. Write in your journal what it looks like and what it makes you feel, on at least ten different days.

Maybe you will find yourself writing a long description one day and only a word or phrase on another day. Ask other persons who have a chance to know this thing well, or to observe it frequently, how it looks to them and makes them feel. Record the best answers you get.

After all that looking and listening, put together from your best journal entries a piece of writing about that thing. It may be several pages long or a few compact lines of prose or poetry.

chapter 18
writing second-hand

WEASEL WORDS

IF YOU HAVE learned to write live words about your own experience, you need not write dead ones because you write about what you have read in books.

Here are four good writers writing about what they have read. The critic Mary McCarthy opens up a discussion of Shakespeare's *Macbeth* in this way:

> He is a general and has just won a battle; he enters the scene making a remark about the weather. "So fair and foul a day I have not seen." On this flat note Macbeth's character tone is set. "Terrible weather we're having." "The sun can't seem to make up its mind." "Is it hot/cold/wet enough for you?" A commonplace man who talks in commonplaces, a golfer, one might guess, on the Scottish fairways, Macbeth is the only Shakespeare hero who corresponds to a bourgeois type: a murderous Babbitt, let us say.

Miss McCarthy's lines are funny, yet she is writing scholarship.

John Holt, a schoolteacher, reviews the book *Toward a Theory of Instruction* by Harvard professor Jerome Bruner:

> As academic writing goes, this book is not badly written; but why should Bruner write like an academic when he

knows how to write clear, strong English? On page 25 we have "heavy dentition." Why not "teeth"?

Mr. Holt speaks directly, without fuss.

In *The Spirit of the Age* (1825), William Hazlitt, the British critic, praises the writing of William Wordsworth, and then goes on to say that his long poem "The Excursion"

> . . . fell stillborn from the press. There was something abortive, and clumsy, and ill-judged in the attempt. It was long and laboured. The personages, for the most part, were low, the fare rustic; the plan raised expectations which were not fulfilled; and the effect was like being ushered into a stately hall and invited to sit down to a splendid banquet in the company of clowns, and with nothing but successive courses of apple-dumplings served up.

Mr. Hazlitt hits the reader with an extended humorous metaphor.

These are three vigorous statements about other persons' writing. That they are all negative in response does not mean that all good writing about writing need be hostile to be alive. Here is George Bernard Shaw agreeing with the ideas of the playwright Henrik Ibsen.

> If we have come to think that the nursery and the kitchen are the natural sphere of a woman, we have done so exactly as English children come to think that a cage is the natural sphere of a parrot: because they have never seen one anywhere else.

Ibsen gave women an equal place with men in the world, and Shaw approved. In his last clause above he delivers a characteristic Shaw punch. But you do not have to be a professional to make your writing about writing skillful. Here is an assertion from a beginning writer:

> **In all his villainy, Falstaff never makes that mistake [failing to see that principles can be flexible]. He has the ability to live in day-to-day situations, twisting them to his own advantage. His mind is always open. He lies, steals, and flatters, fitting misfortune to his needs. He can talk about being an honorable thief, and dishonor himself by chopping apart a corpse at Shrewsbury. Falstaff will sacrifice principles if the situation arises, while Shylock, consumed by an obsession, cannot.**
>
> DAVID STEEN

All of these writers, professionals and amateur, speak in voices that ring true and strike the ear hard. Not any ear, but the ear of an audience tired of the thick, pulpy language which we call *pedantic*. You hear it from teachers in classrooms; you read it in the paragraphs of second-rate scholars; you see it in the writing of high school and college students who have imitated what was too much around them. When Lareen Morgan realizes she is being interviewed for "Senior Portraits," the high school newspaper column, she shifts into pedantic gear and says:

> High school has encompassed many memorable, yet trying
> times.

You may have the urge to reply, "So has working in the fertilizer plant." The word *encompassed* sounds impressive at first but on second consideration the reader realizes it is so inflated it is about to pop in Lareen's face.

When the college professor is asked to write an article for a learned journal, he too often shifts into Pedantic and says:

> Unquestionably the textbook has played a very important
> role in the development of American schools—and I believe
> it will continue to play an important role.

You may have the urge here to say, "So have spitballs." The professor goes on:

> The need for textbooks has been established through many
> experiments. It is not necessary to consider these experi-
> ments but, in general, they have shown that when instruc-
> tion without textbooks has been tried by schools, the
> virtually unanimous result has been to go back to the use
> of textbooks. I believe too, that there is considerable evi-
> dence to indicate that the textbook has been, and is, a
> major factor in guiding teachers' instruction and in deter-
> mining the curriculum. And I don't think that either role
> for the textbook is necessarily bad.

The professor begins his statement with the weasel word *unquestion-ably*. The very point he is going to try to make in the paragraph he calls unquestionable before he starts. From then on he throws (*lobs* would be a better word; nothing has force in this paragraph) a bunch of dull generalizations in his reader's face. Something has played a *role* in the *development* of something. How many times have you heard that vague line? What role? An *important* role. What does that mean? What kind and rate of development? How did the schools develop as a result of the textbook? What a mishmash of educational language: "need established . . . many experiments . . . virtually unanimous result . . . considerable evidence . . . major factor." These are Weasel Words. They don't say anything for sure yet they keep insisting they are certain and unquestionable. The professor talks about impressive experiments but never mentions one. He doesn't think it is "necessary to consider these experiments" yet he employs them as the only evidence for his argument. Note his last sentence:

> And I don't think that either role for the textbook is necessarily bad.

That's the only possibly exciting sentence in the paragraph. Someone has apparently said that using a textbook to guide teachers' instruction or determine the curriculum is bad. Who said that? Why? The writer needs to say, but he isn't fixing to say anything for sure. He won't give the reader anything he can examine and be sure about. He's just talking through his weasel nose.

Every writer talks weaselry at times. This language is hard to see because it is so common.

> It was *sort of* a flop.
> He was *kind of* a hero to me.
> That, *incidentally*, is four fouls.
> Going through the weeds there was *almost* like walking in a swamp.
> His father, *by the way*, is a crook.

> *"I've got a sort of idea but I don't suppose it's a very good one."*
> *Winnie the Pooh (by A. A. Milne)*

In hurried conversation such weaselries should be forgiven, but not in writing, where the author has a chance to revise and tighten. The weakness of *sort of* and *kind of* is that they do not tell the reader whether the writer really thought "it" was a "flop" or "he" was a "hero." If the writer wanted to communicate that the play was not completely a flop but a failure only in the first act, he should have said so. If he wanted to say that "he" was a hero in one way but not in another, he should have told in what way. Otherwise, he should have simply said: "It was a flop" and "He was a hero to me." Usually *sort of* and *kind of* take the punch out of the words they precede. They lessen rather than increase meaning. If you scatter them throughout your writing, your reader will eventually suspect you don't mean anything you say. Note these weasel words:

> The *final* conclusions of the workshop.
>
> There is a *limited amount* of seating space.
>
> Throwing mud in her face wasn't *too* nice.
>
> Falling down the stairs isn't *exactly* fun.
>
> But being in that wreck was an *especially* devastating experience.
>
> Mary was a *remarkably* lovely queen.

Other words frequently used in weasel fashion are *relative, particular,* and *various.*

> This is a *relatively* minor matter and need not concern us long here.

If the reader doesn't know relative to what, he can't extract much meaning from *relatively.*

> This is a *particularly* fine example of social organization.

Fine already tells the reader the example is above ordinary. *Particularly* steals attention from *fine.*

> In his travels around the world, the captain has encountered many diseases in *various* countries and *various* environments.

This is straight cornmeal mush. Most readers would like it better fried crisp and served with hot syrup. If the writer wants to make his point with power, he should say "about two thousand diseases in fifty-six countries and in environments ranging from ice floes to tropical rain forests."

Most academic writing is loaded with weasel words and phrases; for scholars are taught to be cautious, to qualify. But there are times to be cautious and times to be bold. Watch this pedantic phrase weasel its ways into an otherwise straightforward sentence:

> Last week the world was contained in a blue plastic egg filled with jelly beans and a set of rabbit teeth—*at least it was* for five-year-old Jack.

The author doesn't really mean to hint that anyone else's world beside Jack's was filled with that bunch of jelly beans and set of rabbit teeth, but she heard a weasel squeal somewhere and echoes it in her sentence.

As I write this chapter warning others of weaseling, I remember that when I was writing another text, an editor pointed out that almost always when I used the words *in fact,* I followed them with an unsupported personal opinion. Frequently writers try to make up for weak opinions by introducing them with one of the following expressions:

indeed	surely	honestly
obviously	certainly	frankly
of course	needless to say	sincerely

The most dishonest man I ever knew constantly prefaced his remarks with the expression, "I would be less than candid if I did not say—."

Writers are often dishonest with themselves: they speak apologetically, defensively, pompously, or condescendingly when they do not feel apologetic, defensive, pompous, or condescending. A teacher who once submitted a poem to an editor of a magazine, hoping for publication, referred to her manuscript in her covering letter as "This bit of fluff, modeled after 'The Children's Hour.'" Her comment sounds like the introductory remarks many persons make before they speak in a group meeting: "Now I don't claim to be an expert in this subject and what I have to say probably isn't worth much . . ." Then they make a fifteen-minute speech. One is tempted to say to the teacher: "If you think your manuscript is fluff, don't send it to the magazine"; and to the apologetic speaker: "If you don't think you are qualified to speak, don't speak. Or if you are qualified, don't waste our time telling us you aren't."

Whether a word is weaseling or not depends upon its context. If a writer brings most of his sentences alive with verbs crammed full of meaning, with details that speak to all of the reader's senses, he then can afford to use some of the paler, emptier words in the language: in fact his readers may crave relief from lines bursting with life. For example, Lois Phillips Hudson, in her short memoir "When the Fields Are Fresh and Green" (which appears at the end of this chapter), writes:

> At any rate, something important happened in the town
> and Edith sang for it.

Important is usually a weak word; *at any rate* is vague and almost meaningless, and *something* frequently shows a writer's lack of thoroughness in investigation. But here all the words are acceptable because Mrs. Hudson is demonstrating her honesty. In this faraway remembering of childhood she cannot recall every event or object clearly. An event stood out for the townspeople. Mrs. Hudson cannot remember why or how, so she is justified in using the vague word *important* to describe it. She is not vague in other parts of her story. A good writer learns what words and phrases lead him often into poor communication, but he does not try to achieve an absolutely pure diction. A sparing use of conversational tags like *very* or *too much* or *particularly fine* will not wreck an otherwise vigorous piece of writing. Nor will a little unnecessary repetition.

> *"What do you know about this business?" the King said to Alice.*
>
> *"Nothing," said Alice.*
>
> *"Nothing whatever?" persisted the King.*
>
> *"Nothing whatever," said Alice.*
>
> *"That's very important," the King said, turning to the jury. They were just beginning to write this down on their slates, when the White Rabbit interrupted: "Unimportant, your Majesty means, of course," he said, in a very respectful tone, but frowning and making faces at him, as he spoke.*
>
> *"Unimportant, of course, I meant," the King hastily said, and went on to himself in an undertone, "important— unimportant — unimportant — important —" as if he were trying which word sounded best.*
>
> *Some of the jury wrote it down "important," and some "unimportant." Alice could see this, as she was near enough to look over their slates; "but it doesn't matter a bit," she thought to herself.*
>
> LEWIS CARROLL

How much the readers know about a subject should affect the writer's decisions about cutting down his sentences. Samuel Butler, a strong advocate of tightening writing, said that diffuseness "sometimes helps, as for instance, when the subject is hard; words that may be, strictly speaking, unnecessary will make things easier for the reader by giving him more time to master the thought while his eye is running over the verbiage."

Nevertheless, most writers need to develop more ruthlessness toward their writing as John Ciardi, poetry editor of *Saturday Review,* said. It is theirs. They must initially love it. Finally, though, they must see it for what it is and remember that their readers are busy persons, and human beings, who are easily irritated by writing which does not get a satisfactory mileage with its words.

The ways of being untruthful about the world and dishonest with oneself are legion. But the effort to tell the truth is so exacting that once seriously undertaken, it becomes a habit. And one truth breeds another.

Not everyone who uses weasel words is a weasel at heart. If you read well the writings you examine and retain your essential honesty, you will use these expressions so seldom that your readers will not notice them. Do not strive for absolute purity; every man is born with an ego which at times drags him into a weasel's hole. The surest way to reduce weaselry in your writing to a forgiveable amount is to know what you are writing about and to find something to say you believe in. As you have seen, surprises then begin to appear.

SHOWING WHY A WRITING AFFECTS YOU

WRITING TWENTY-FOUR: Choose a piece of writing (book, magazine article, story, editorial, play, poem—makes no difference whether you read it in school or out) which moved you so much that you might naturally talk to a friend or classmate about it. Maybe you love it, maybe you hate it, maybe you have mixed feelings. But it hit you hard. Write a paper showing why and how it hit you. Let your reader see what in your experience or thinking made you excited by the writing. And in so doing, tell enough about the writing that another person who has never read that writing will see what hit you. This is not a book report. Don't try to summarize what you read. Don't try to cover everything in it.

Here is an example of such a paper, written by a college senior:

1

When I read *In Cold Blood,* our house was empty. One small reading light shone in the blackness of my musty den. It was late in the evening and the occasional creaking of the floors was the only sound. I swore I wouldn't read it again. It was a story of two men who committed four murders. This was what Truman Capote wished to show us, in the most factual language possible in a novel. The results were horrifying. They were not simply two characters. Capote let me know these men slowly, detail by detail, until I felt comfortable on a first-name basis.

I had never met two men who had shot four people in the head. They were men not unlike many students at this school. True, they had idiosyncrasies that were brought out, but they probably drank beer, brushed their teeth, and wore T-shirts just like I do. By the end of the book I actually felt sorry for them. They were human beings and capable of error.

How many eligible Perrys and Hickocks are in the dorm or my classes? If I point a pistol at a girl's head I am stupid, careless, and unsafe. If I move my right index finger one quarter of an inch, I become a maniac. One quarter of an inch is the measure of a madman. How many of us do not have one split second of weakness, one moment of unconsciousness when we do something completely irrational?

"I don't know why I did it. I guess I just wasn't think-ing."

I believe that a man, any man, at the right place, at the right time, and with the right apparatus, will kill for no apparent reason. We are all capable.

This book scared me, bothered me, made me sick. I do not even know whether I liked it, but I know I'll read it again.

TIM SWEENEY

The best critics, those who communicate unforgettable and valu-able insights to many persons, hold their readers and intrigue them by divulging how and why the object of their criticism has affected them. For example, Edmund Wilson, who has written critical articles for *The New Yorker, The Nation,* and *The New Republic* magazines for almost fifty years, in writing about a book by Alva Johnston on Samuel Goldwyn, the movie producer, brought in his own opinion of American movies in the 1930's. He introduced the discussion with this sentence:

The other day, after long abstinence from the movies, the result of having seen nothing but bad films for a year, I went to one for the first time in months.

Then Mr. Wilson went on to itemize how Hollywood had ruined gifted actors and writers by creating movies designed only to please the largest number of people possible. He was not afraid to introduce his own experience and observation into a discussion of a book he was criticizing.

Sometimes academic critics condemn this method, calling it "subjective." They insist that critics should be "objective," centering on the object out there and removing themselves from the act of criticizing. No human being can do this. As this text says elsewhere, every act of human perception involves the object, the observer, his past experiences on which he bases the assumptions he brings to the observing, and the present situation. Yet striving for more objectivity or subjectivity may be useful to you, depending on your purpose. If a critic is reading a book that presents many acts and opinions he has often disapproved of, he may need to strive for more objectivity than usual so he will not let his prejudices distort what he is reading. A piece of writing by someone else is always partly what you make it, what you bring to it. But it is also, and in large measure, what its writer made it. In writing this response to a piece of writing, you should not confuse your opinions or interests with those of the author you are examining. If, for example, you read this passage in *In Cold Blood*:

> Nancy wore her dress of cherry-red velvet, her brother a
> bright plaid shirt; the parents were more sedately attired,
> Mr. Clutter in navy-blue flannel, his wife in navy-blue
> crepe . . .

and you are interested in fashion designing, you might consider only those passages in the book which describe clothes, and leave your reader with the notion that Truman Capote was writing a book about how to dress. He was not. He was writing about murder. Don't rewrite the book to suit yourself.

Writing this critical paper asks that you will (1) tell enough of some part or aspect of the work so that your reader, who may be unfamiliar with it, will see what affected you so strongly, (2) tell enough of your own experience or thought which intersects with something in the work, so your reader can put himself in your place, and (3) show that this intersection was significant to you. Both some part of you and some part of the writing you examined must come alive and start talking to each other.

Here is the first draft of another such paper, written by a high school student. Its materials could be clarified and polished, but the critic and the work both come alive and encounter each other at a surprising point.

2

I've watched dirty little brats get up at 7:00 in the morning and play outside all day by themselves. Their mother works and so she can't watch them. They walk the streets by themselves looking for something to do. Anything that interests them they play with. You always read about kids playing in old refrigerators and getting suffocated. Their mothers didn't pay any attention to them.

I always swore I'd never be that kind of a mother. My kids are going to be happy playing in the yard so I can watch them. Kids aren't happy when they're neglected all day.

I read about Ulysses in *The Human Comedy* by William Saroyan. He walked around and amused himself all day. When he waved at the black man on the train, he marveled at life. This man was friendly. If he had been in his own yard, he would have missed the black man and missed his singing.

Ulysses would never have seen the boys steal the green apricots from Mr. Henderson's apricot tree. Ulysses would never have known that it isn't a sin for little boys to steal apricots. He would never have met Big Chris because he got caught in a bear trap.

I wanted to deprive my children of a childhood. My Ulysses would never know my love and he would never grow to be a man. His older brother would never reach manhood by delivering telegrams at night. I don't suppose I would ever wait up silently every night just in case my son wanted to talk. Delivering death messages isn't easy, and maybe he wouldn't even feel like talking. I'd deprive my children of life.

Now, if I could choose my future, I'd be poor. I'd work all day and my children would explore the city by themselves. At night I would come home and they would tell me what they saw. When my oldest son dies in war, my middle son will tear the telegram and I will invite a soldier who knew my son into my house.

The first time you try a criticism like this, you will probably fail to give enough of the work or of your own experience. In the following paper, the writer showed a fine understanding of the spirit of Huckleberry Finn, but he needs to include a few examples of how Huck "did such a neat job" of running away. And he needs to say a little more about why and how in his own life "Everything has to be proper and formal."

3

Cam told me *Huckleberry Finn* was the only book he enjoyed reading this year. Isn't it the truth? Everybody tries to make more out of a story and ruins it. But the adventure and fun in this book are real. I've always been sort of a tomboy. So, I know what it's like to run off and enjoy the outdoors. Wouldn't it be exciting to go down a river on a raft? I love to be around water anyway. And there would be lots of camping, too. It makes you feel clean and healthy. Why didn't Huck run away sooner? That's not so important. It just seems like he did such a neat job of doing it, though. But something like a lot of blood and a mess would upset my parents too much. I would have to run away without mess. That's the trouble with our society today, though. Everything has to be proper and formal. It would be more fun if I could relax and be messy. How about running away tonight?

The following paper is an original and compelling comment on death. All it needs to be a great paper is a little more about how death appears in the novel.

4

On the Beach, by Nevil Shute, is a stimulating look at death with a touch of the feelings of people near the end.

This book comes to mind in this time because of life passing so quickly. As everyone would eventually die in *On the Beach,* so will everyone die in our world. The difference is in the cause. And in the time. Here during the past couple of days I have noticed a closer relationship between teacher and student. The way of the gatherings of classes is deeper. I have seen a teacher touch a student, me, when she doesn't ever touch anyone. Feelings are here now. They are open and my mind sees it. People will realize for a time that life is short and one must see every thing that one can. It's hard. Now it's doubly hard and very tense. But these people are closer.

The librarian scolded me for talking and ten minutes later she came by and patted me on the shoulder. I am sensitive and in the air the eyes see the human feelings reaching out toward each other to hold for a while because there may not be a tomorrow for this person. In a time it will all pass away again and people will scowl at other people and strike out with whipped tongues and I will shudder at the sight of it and think of the memory of silence.

I will watch and be wary and then my day will come.

JAN OKEMURA

Like a number of writings by beginners printed in this book, Paper 4 needs grammatical polishing. The pronoun *it* is several times inaccurately or confusingly used. But the paper communicates feeling with subtlety.

Paper 5 more fully brings alive both the book and the writer's experience which intersects with it; but it, too, could be strengthened with more examples. Try to write a paper which achieves balance. And remember that what makes these papers provocative is their honesty.

5

Fleabags and flophouses, burleyque gals and bloody buckets. Strange words to those unaware of Skid Row, U.S.A. There's one in almost every city.

Sara Harris went to a Skid Row. She interviewed some of its inhabitants—prostitutes, drunks, addicts, and madmen; and in her book, *Skid Row, U.S.A.* reveals by a series of dialogues the people and the life they live.

Until I read this book five years ago, I hadn't even heard the words "flophouse" and "fleabags." I wasn't even aware that such fantastic people existed. People who live in 25¢ a night rooms. A Ph. D. who wore a Phi Beta Kappa key drank liquid black shoe polish as a substitute for expensive liquor. The utter abandonment of themselves so bluntly presented in this book shocked me and I didn't really believe it. But I asked a teacher about it and of course he affirmed that Skid Row was a serious problem. This made me want to take a better look at other people around me. I asked Mom to drive to the sections of town that would be considered something like Skid Row. She didn't want to, so I sneaked out and walked through town to the bars and dumpy hotels. A few men passed me,

> dirty and messy. Women in sloppy clothes shuffled by.
> One woman had on spiked heels that clicked and wobbled
> when she walked. I glanced quickly at their faces. The
> woman was a mask of wrinkles and stringy hair, of red
> eyes and orange lips, and I only stayed a few minutes.

This writer made his knowledge come home.

All of the five papers are presented here in their first drafts. You can probably see a number of ways to polish them. In Paper 5, for example, the third sentence gives away the conclusion and should be omitted, so the reader will accompany the writer on his journey and share his discovery. The next to last sentence should precede the one that now comes before it.

WRITING TWENTY-FIVE: Now that you've written a paper about a writing that you chose because it hit you hard (maybe you need to write two or three like that until you produce a first-rate criticism), try writing that kind of paper about a piece of writing you did not choose—the following story by Lois Phillips Hudson. Again, relate something in your experience or thoughts that touches something in this story. Show why you respond to the story positively, negatively, or with mixed feelings.

> *Writing must be as immediate as life,*
> *or there are no juices, no chance to in-*
> *volve yourself or others in your vitality.*
>
> RAY BRADBURY

WHEN THE FIELDS ARE FRESH AND GREEN
Lois Phillips Hudson

> *The boy moves through his life,*
> *keeping a shy*
> *Watch on the man who now assumes*
> *his face.*
>
> —DOUGLAS NICHOLS
> *Johnny Appleseed*

While we are growing up, we become more surprised every year that we seem to other people to be changing, because to ourselves we seem always to be the same. And even while we exult in the higher mark on the closet door where we are measured every year, we feel an increasing apprehensiveness that a day will come when we will seem to have changed so much that nobody will remember who we are.

Thus, when we are still very young, we sense that our first memories of ourselves constitute the only reality by which we will always understand our existence. The problem is that nobody ever seems to see anything the same way we see it, and therefore the memories by which we place ourselves in time and space can never be verified by anybody else. This is the loneliness and the terror of childhood—not to see things the way anybody else sees them, not to understand why some things are "real" and some things are not.

My first hazy memories of myself were set nearly two thousand miles from the place where my second, verifiable memories of myself began. My father's business failed in 1931, and my family moved from Seattle back to a desolate half-section in North Dakota just before I was four years old. At that age, I would, in any case, have begun slipping from my first dreamy existence into my second "real" existence, but it was the drastic change of place that seemed to me, over the next few years, to have been the cause of all the changes in my existence. I had one possession that unequivocally connected me with all the parts of that first existence—all the parts I couldn't remember, all the parts everybody agreed I remembered, and all the parts I alone was sure I remembered. That possession was a doll with opening and closing eyes that I got for Christmas in Seattle the year before we moved. I took her with me wherever I went, and frequently she got left at the weather end of a long prairie trek when I had gone looking for something—gone out to watch in the haunted cloudless morning and found only beautiful emptiness. After a few years the poor doll's face grew pale under the prairie sun, and lined with the fine cracks of excellent crockery. But still she had the same delicate brows, the same private smile of a baby who knows she will never have to grow up.

I made a special point of taking her whenever my mother and I went to see Edith Bagley and Edith Bagley's mother, because when we went there I really needed company. Edith and her mother had a dark high parlor filled with dark high furniture that I had to climb up into but that I must never touch with my feet. After Edith and her mother and my mother had all watched me and my doll get settled without doing any damage, they left us to ourselves. Edith and my mother had gone all through school together and then

through college together in Jamestown. Then they had come
back home together and my mother had married my father
and Edith had not married anybody. But Edith was talented
in a number of ways. My mother always played the piano
for her when she sang a solo, and usually when we went
there it was so they could practice something.

In one corner of the parlor was a table that was covered,
when Edith was not using it for her work, with an ecru lace
tablecloth that hung down so that all you could see of the
table was its four massive clawed feet flexing themselves
over the roses on the carpet. The chair next to the table had
lions' heads at the ends of its arms, and the lions were roar-
ing without making any noise. It was clear to me that furniture like that could come alive at night when people were
asleep, and I always tried to act wide awake when I was in a
roomful of it. I wiggled and cleared my throat and did as
many things as I could without having somebody tell me to
sit still.

In another corner of the parlor sat old Mrs. Bagley, who
did not, like the furniture, look as though she might be
alive. The top part of her was gray and white with sweater
and hair and skin and cloudy spectacles. The bottom part
of her was gay in the way a new grave is gay—all covered
with spots of color woven from wilted flowers over a shockingly high mound. The mound of her under the festive
mosaic of her afghan was appalling because you couldn't
imagine a regular body under there, with a stomach and
hips and legs. What *could* have been under that afghan?
Only once did I see any part of a body. Hanging below the
multicolored yarn fringe was a brown cotton stocking that
bulged far out over the top of a black, high-heeled shoe tied
with tasseled laces.

The parlor smelled of a half-century of dust and cooking
and of about twenty years of Edith's painting. I would sit
in one of the great chairs, watching every minute to see
that I didn't touch any part of any wooden animals, and
try to think of something to say in case I was called upon to
admire Edith's painting. It seemed to me unclean to paint
flowers and thistles and twisting vines all over plates and
cups that people were supposed to eat from and drink out
of. I always felt a little sick when Edith answered the door
in her smock, because I knew the smock meant she was

painting dishes, and if she was painting dishes, I would have to say something.

Edith weighed almost three hundred pounds. That was what gave her wonderful volume when she sang. Her face was round like a plate, and it had a finger wave for a frame —just like the tendriled edgings on her plates. She had soft boneless hands, but they were facile and clever, as weak hands often are.

One day I watched them work for a long time. They were making artificial lilies for Easter Sunday in our church. The claw-footed table was heaped with piles of wire, stiff threads with yellow nodules at one end, fuzzy orange things shaped like tiny cattails, squares of green and white paper of the consistency of snakeskin, needles, thread, pliers, and instructions. Edith picked up one of the long wires in one of her limp hands. She twirled a strip of stretchy green paper around the wire. "See!" she said. "Now we have a stem!"

After hard study of her diagrams, Edith produced an Easter lily. It had long pointed petals of snaky white paper and enormous reproductive organs made of the threads with the yellow nodules at their ends. All the thread ends and all the petal ends were wired together at the center of the lily, and all the wires were neatly hidden in a calyx made from a little green wax cup. Then she made a calla lily, so she could try out the fuzzy orange pieces that looked like cattails. I don't know how many lilies she made before my mother came back from grocery shopping. All I know is that a sentence started repeating itself in my head. It was a simple imperative sentence, and one I had made a point of memorizing after reading the story it was in. "Stop, Little Pot, stop!" That was the magic command that nobody could remember for days and days after the obliging Little Pot got set off by some idiot who knew only the starting words and not the stopping words. The picture with the story showed the town's whole population eating pathways with teaspoons through the streets of waist-high mush.

Like the porridge nobody knew how to turn off, Edith's lilies inundated the little Community Methodist Church on Easter Sunday. Lilies jammed the vestibule, the aisles, the altar, the pulpit, the windowsills, the hymnal racks. Guarded by my mother on one side and my grandmother on the other, sitting in a safe church pew, I sank into that

familiar lonely terror: everybody else's eyes were seeing
something that mine could not see. To everybody else those
things of wire and resinous snakeskin paper were flowers.

The year of that Easter was the hardest my grandmother
and grandfather and all the other people on the prairie
could remember. It was colder and windier and drier and
hotter and dustier. When the meager harvest was in, Number 1 wheat sold for twenty-six cents a bushel. Finally a
bleak frigid December brought the long year to an end. My
mother told me not to expect much from Santa Claus. I'd
given up believing in Santa Claus long before, and I know
she must have known that. But it was less painful for both
of us to pretend that it was Santa Claus who was poor.

That was the first time I had ever done any pretending of
the kind that grownups did, and it gave me, oddly enough,
that same feeling of lonely terror I had when I realized that
I must be seeing something that nobody else saw—or that
everybody else must be seeing something I couldn't see. I
began to understand that most people simply decided on
what they wanted to see and then saw it. They decided on
what they wanted to believe and then believed it. And
everybody pretended to believe what everybody else pretended to believe so that they could talk to each other. Santa
Clauses ringing bells on the street in Jamestown did not believe in Santa Claus. Edith Bagley did not believe in her
snakeskin lilies. They were all trying to make reality better
for everybody else. And they were all trying to explain themselves to each other in order to try to make themselves more
real to each other, in order not to lose each other. But the
harder they tried to make the world real for each other, the
more hopelessly they separated themselves from each other.
It was even more lonely to be *deciding* what was real than it
was not to have any idea of what might be real and what
might not.

It made me feel very old—to believe in Santa Claus because I decided to believe. From then on, I would be responsible for what I saw and what I believed. I would make the
decisions that created my existence and the decisions that
created the world. The more I succeeded in believing what
everybody else believed, the less real anything would be,
because the things that are the most real are the ones that
surprise us the most, and when everything must be decided

upon and agreed upon, nothing can surprise us any more. We can never be surprised by the color of the grass or the color of the sky, and so they can never be quite so bright as they were in that first existence, when we were always being surprised.

And just at that time when I needed her the most, my dearest proof of that other existence, my faded cracked Baby Dimples, disappeared. I looked everywhere for her, but I did not admit to my mother that she was missing. I was afraid I had left her outside on the wrong afternoon and she had been buried under a five-foot snowdrift. If I asked about her, my mother might exclaim, "Oh, *dear!* You *didn't* leave her out on the day we got that awful blizzard, did you?"

There was also the possibility that my mother had allowed her to fall into the grubby eye-poking fingers of my little sister while I was away at school learning about reality. Then my doll would be like most of the other dolls I knew. At best she would have one eye stuck open and the other stuck shut. At worst, the whole mechanism would be turned over in her head and the only thing that would show through the eyeholes with their painted lashes would be a steel bar with rubber bands attached to two dull metal balls (the backs of the glass eyes) suspended in an empty china skull, rolling up and down, opening and shutting in hollow darkness. If she had suffered such an attack, and was now on some closet shelf until my father could find time to try to fix her, I didn't want to know about it.

I was pretty sure, though, that I must have left her outside. I spent a few dusky afternoons digging deep into the most likely snowbanks. I knew I wouldn't find her; I just wanted to show her or somebody that I felt as bad as she did about her being down there under the suffocating whiteness.

I still hadn't found her when Christmas came. That Christmas morning was the bleakest in my memory. There was no towering pungent tree like the ones from that other existence where Christmas trees grew on all the mountains, in all the parks, and beside all the houses. There was instead a tiny tree that had lost all its perfume while coming hundreds of miles from Wisconsin or Michigan. And under the tree, as gaily wrapped as if our decisions and our agree-

ments and our responsibilities could always be made as
beautiful as surprises, were sleepers and mittens and stock-
ings and underwear—things I had been doing without during the first part of that bitter winter so that I could get
them for Christmas. And, of course, because I needed them
and because I was growing up now, I pretended that they
mattered.

It seemed to me that our little family would suffocate
from pretending in our little house that was so crowded by
our little tree—like my doll under the snowbank. But my
mother gave me a portentous look, as if to say that she knew
you couldn't have Christmas without surprises and that nobody expected you to. She slipped out of the house and
came back with a bundle in her arms—a bundle just the size
of a new baby, swaddled in a precious furry pink blanket.
The Christmas surprise! The Surprise that creates a universe of surprises every time it is born. She lifted a corner
of the blanket so I could see the baby's face.

It was dead. It must have died while she left it out in the
car, waiting to surprise us. Its cheeks were purple, like the
cheeks of people found under snowbanks after blizzard
snows have melted. Even its closed eyelids were purple.

"It's Baby Dimples!" my mother cried happily. "Santa
Claus took her away and made her all new for you!"

I looked at the dead face again and saw around it the pen-
like scrolls of Edith Bagley's plates. On the delicate brow
and cheeks I recognized the dusty purple paste that Edith
Bagley managed to use, in one spot or another, on all the
dishes and cups she painted.

"Isn't she pretty now?" my mother pleaded. "You left her
outside and she got all cracked and faded. Now look at her
pretty red hair! Look at her healthy cheeks!"

I couldn't have said it to myself then, but I understand that
even the master artificer which, in my little world, Edith
Bagley was, could never bring surprise from one existence
to another. Shock (a word I didn't know then, though I
knew the feeling) no doubt was transferable; surprise was
not. The glad surprise of a very young child that morning
has come, that the grass is green and the sky is blue—and all
without any decisions made by the child—that glad surprise,
I have now come to understand, is what we beg our artificers
for, pay them enormously for, especially at Christmastime.

But they, being part of the grownup conspiracy to decide what is real, being, like the rest of us, helpless members of the second existence, no longer know, any more than the rest of us, what is real—what is surprising.

I say that I understood this, and the way I know I understood it is that I knew I was making a statement about my existence when I said to my waiting, heartbroken mother, "Yes, my baby is much prettier now."

I was careful, after that, to tuck my doll into her crib every night, and to do it when my mother was sure to see. Since I never took her out of the house with me again, it wasn't hard to find her to do the tucking in. There had been nights when even the long summer prairie evenings had caught me in the dark, with the panicked sounds of hard-pressed fecundity all about me and the weight of the heavy-leaved black boughs over me—there had been nights when I risked my life to search for her in the grove, so I could bring her safely home and put her to bed, grieving and promising never to forget her again. But in our second existence we don't grieve and promise with the same unqualified passion with which we grieve and promise in our first existence. We remember, in our second existence, how forgetful we are.

And so, now that my last proof of my first existence had been transformed into the first proof of my second existence, I no longer had to seek her or grieve for her or make promises to her. She was always there in her crib, with her purple cheeks.

Something important happened in the town that winter, not long after Christmas. Somebody got married or, more likely, somebody left for the West Coast and had a party in the town hall before they went. If a family was going to sell out, it was that time of year that would make them decide. Christmas and New Year's over. Nothing to look forward to but snow till April. No commitment to a crop planted. Winter feed for the stock about gone, because of the last summer's drought. Not much cream to sell and not much of a price for what cream there was. A time of year when the Pacific Coast temperatures, printed in the James-town *Sun*, seemed unbelievable. It didn't seem to matter where you were during these Depression years. After you'd been in one spot for a while, you decided things couldn't be quite so bad anywhere else, and so you moved. My own family had gone from North Dakota to Seattle and back, and we were destined to go again to Seattle in another couple of years.

At any rate, something important happened in the town and Edith sang for it. I still hated her so much that I could barely speak to her when we went to her upstairs house so she and my mother could practice the songs she sang. I sat in the chair with the lions carved on its arms and listened while they went over and over the songs, but only one of the songs said anything I could understand, and that's why I still haven't forgotten it.

Edith stood by the piano, her smock trembling over the vast regions where her emotions echoed and re-echoed themselves, until she herself must have lost track of them and could believe only what everybody believed—that she had, as compensation for her appalling obesity, for her appalling mother, for her appalling loneliness, a great voice.

Another thing I cannot forget (and this is one way you can distinguish your first existence from your second: never in your first existence do you wish you could forget anything) is the painful difference between herself and the girl she sang about, as she stood, wide as the piano, at the high-note end of the keyboard upon which my little mother played. The song she sang, the one I can't forget, had these words:

The roses all have left your cheek—
I've watched them fade away and die . . .

Oh! I will take you back, Kathleen,
To where your heart will feel no pain,
And when the fields are fresh and green,
I'll take you to your home again.

I know I understood that Kathleen was not ever going to see the fields again, because the song made me cry. It was the first time any song had affected me that way. I sat in the lion-headed chair where I had once watched Edith make the lilies with no perfume, holding my fists against my eyes, horrified at crying over something as silly as a song—especially the kind of song that Edith Bagley would sing—and even more horrified that somebody might catch me.

If anybody could go back, if Kathleen could have gone

back, then nobody would cry over the song, but almost everybody does. We cherish our griefs over those green fields because our griefs seem to prove that what we grieve over must once have existed. It is good that all of us have these griefs. They do not separate us as do our beliefs.

Now that I am grown, I have discovered that our second existence does bring us one surprise—love. Now that I have children of my own, I try, as my mother did, to save their first existences for them, even though I know it is impossible. All the generations of us will go on forever trying to save the green fields for each other and we will always fail, but because it is for love that we try to do what is impossible, we redeem our second existence.

And in a way none of us ever really leaves those fields that made us. It is from those lost fields that we go on shyly, silently calling to each other. It is from those fields, forever sealed against the trespasses of our grownup selves, forever splendid with light falling like trumpet salutes through the old heavy boughs of the world, that each of us keeps his long watch on the people who come to assume his face.

*. . . the crudest honest sentence is a
re-sounding of experience. Have you
heard a bright child describe an airplane
crash? Have you heard a returned soldier
describe his once-more-slept-in bed, at
home? Sentences resound when experience is comprehendingly relived.*

SIDNEY COX

chapter 19

controlling sound

WRITING APPEARS a soundless enterprise:
the pen slides quietly across the page. And reading appears a silent act:
"Where's John?"

"He's curled up on the porch reading. I haven't heard a sound out
of him all afternoon."

But one writer says of another writer, "He hasn't any ear," and he
means the most damning criticism. For one of the chief resources of
a writer is control over the sound of his sentences.

Scanning the printed page, most readers hear in their unconscious
ear the sentences sounding against the echoing memory of all the
words they have heard in conversation.

The following passage, written by a beginner, utilizes sound skillfully:

I COULDN'T STAY

I couldn't stay in the library with the rain pecking at its
windows. The blackness outside invited me to lose myself
in its depth. So I walked into it, letting the sharp spray
tingle my forehead and tangle my hair. I walked slowly
until my coat was damp and heavy and my knee socks slid
around my ankles, making them itch. It was night and

nobody saw how the rain treated me. When I got to the room, I listened to water splattering under the wheels of cars and rinsing the stained sides of the brick buildings. I wanted to sleep through the night and wake up washed like the world on a new day.

SUE SMILTNECK

The girl who wrote this passage did not know how well she had used sound effects. Most writers don't consciously create all of their best sound effects. They write thinking of meaning, and their sensitive ear helps them select words that strike other ears significantly. In "I Couldn't Stay," note these sound effects:

rain pecking

*sh*arp *sp*ray *tingle* my forehead and *tangle* my hair

wa*ter* splat*ter*ing

*ri*n*s*ing the stain*ed* *s*i*d*es of the *bri*ck *building*s

*W*hen . . . *w*ater . . . *w*heels . . . *w*anted *to* . . . *w*ake up *w*ashed . . . *w*orld

It was a hard rain: the reader can hear it pecking and splattering. Rhythms are set up by the repetition of consonant sounds (*tingle, tangle,* etc.) in what is called *alliteration* and in the repetition of vowel sounds (*rinsing, brick, buildings*) in what is called *assonance.* Human beings like repetitions. They sense strength in the *repeat-and-vary* pattern. All persons employ sound skillfully without being taught. In a speech given to American teachers in 1966, Edmond Wright, a British schoolteacher, pointed out that under extreme emotional stress all persons speak in strong rhythm and often with alliteration.

David! You're a *d*irty, low-*d*own *d*og!

He told students to write down what persons at home said under stress: they found considerable alliteration. One student complained that he didn't hear any, so Mr. Wright suggested he go home and pour a glass of milk over his brother's head and then listen to his father. He did. He heard considerable alliteration.

Knocking around in every person's head are the sounds of his native language: spoken or muted echoes of what he has read, the lullabies his mother sang him, the rich cursing of men hunting or playing games, the formal rhythms of a trained voice reading in church or synagogue, the skip rope song, the hurried swallowed phrases of other children singing the "Star Spangled Banner" or chanting the "Gettysburg Address," the taunts they sang in the street:

Simpy Sam is a stupid old man!

Without trying, most persons can write rapidly such sound effects as these by a high school girl:

> I like to go fishing. But I don't like to touch worms or slippery, slimy fish. They wiggle. I went with Anne three years ago. That was fun until she broke her promise and made me take the fish off. Then it swallowed the hook. It was terrible. It wriggled and writhed in the bottom of the boat. Then it just lay there. Dead.

This is not an exceptional piece of writing. The seventh sentence suffers from It-ache. In the sixth, *it* refers to the fish; then suddenly *it* refers to the whole struggle of the fish with the hook. But in sound, the passage is strong. *Slippery* and *slimy* and *wriggled* and *writhed* alliterate with force and their sounds echo the sense of what they say. The last two sentences allow the record to run down appropriately, and *Dead* stands by itself, final—in its position, its shortness, and its two hard *d's*.

In the phrase "bottom of the boat," the writer has repeated the *b* sound skillfully. You may say that she did not mean to hit that sound hard and that it adds nothing to the passage because the *b* sound does not suggest *boat* or *bottom* as the *sl* sound in *slippery* and *slimy* suggests the squirming fish. True, but one of the marks of a strong writer is that through his sentences appears from time to time an occasional repetition of sound that gives his words a strength like the "bone" in spaghetti cooked not too soft by an expert Italian cook. Note this pattern of sound repetition in these next passages. The authors were probably not trying for any effects, but they achieved them nevertheless.

> Men are *h*orri*b*ly *t*edious *wh*en *th*ey are good *h*usbands and a*b*omina*b*ly conceited *wh*en *th*ey are not.

OSCAR WILDE

> It's like *wh*en you break up *w*ith a girl and you've explained all your reasons to her *wh*y. And *sh*e *s*ays, "I *s*till don't *s*ee *wh*y it *w*on't *w*ork." And you've *s*een *it* ou*t* and you've hi*t th*e *bl*ank har*d* col*d w*all of *s*oli*d* no*th*ing.

HIGH SCHOOL STUDENT WRITING FREELY

These passages get their bone from reepating consonant sounds. Vowel sounds also work their spell:

> These were *so*ftw*oo*ded trees, *po*plars, t*u*lip trees, *co*tton-w*oo*ds. There were fences ar*ou*nd *o*ne *or* tw*o* of the h*ou*ses, but mainly the yards ran into each *o*ther with *o*nly n*ow* and then a l*ow* hedge that wasn't d*o*ing very well. There were few g*oo*d friends am*o*ng the gr*ow*n people, and they were n*o*t p*oo*r en*ou*gh f*o*r the *o*ther s*o*rt *o*f intimate acquaint-ance . . .
>
>   JAMES AGEE

Here a highly skillful writer was trying to evoke the spirit of low-key joy felt by a small boy on summer nights. He did this partly by employing many variations of *o* sounds, and the *schwa* ("uh") sound that all the vowels take in certain words. Many American-English words carry with them a sound that supports the meaning they signify, as in this passage:

> **The door squeaked, then shrieked, and I felt my nerves frazzle once again, ragged nerves unraveled like the shattered end of the shoestring I couldn't get into the eyelet of my tennis shoe when I was a boy.**

Much academic writing suffers so from its empty abstract words that the reader never comes to the point of appreciating its repetitions of sound. For example:

> But besides these immediate practical advantages, important as they are, your membership in the Council enables you to function more effectively as a member of the English teaching profession. It does this by affiliating you with one of the most influential professional organizations for teach-ers . . .

Some bone of sound exists in that passage but no reader wants to hear once more together the tired words "function . . . effectively . . . affiliating . . . influential . . . professional." The above passage addressed to teachers may carry too many *f* sounds in too brief a space. Too frequent repetition of a sound may render a passage ridiculous. "Peter Piper picked a peck of pickled peppers" makes a funny tongue twister, but it will always tickle a reader with its little explosions rather than impress him with its meaning.

In the first place, certain sounds—the voiceless s, *for example—possess a* range of potential *suggestibility, rather than a fixed or single capability. Thus, a prominence of* ss *is capable of suggesting certain classes of natural sounds (rustling, hissing, sighing, whispering) but not other classes (booming, humming, hammering, or groaning).*

In the second place, this power of suggesting natural sounds or other qualities is relatively weak—*too weak to operate unsupported by meaning—and because of its range, is only* latent.

KARL SHAPIRO AND ROBERT BEUM

The following passage, written by a college girl, not only reveals an ear for sound that fits meaning but suggests in its overall rhythm the way a little girl talks:

Ugly dorm food! Thick chili and dry crackers make a pasty lump. I used to eat some soda crackers plain when I was little. In our backyard we made mud pies and ate crackers. It was heroic action to eat four in a row without taking a drink from the hose.

At my sixth birthday party we had to chew and swallow five crackers and then whistle to win a prize. Marlene Davis and I were the best. She had a big mouth and when she talked, white bubbles of spit came out of the corners. Naturally curly blonde hair kinked all over her head and dribbled down to her blue bug eyes. She was skinny, with scabby elbows.

We started eating crackers at the same time. Cramming them in was easy, but gagging them down hurt. Marlene had a head start with all that spit in her mouth. She won, so I called her "skinny bug-eyes" and made her cry. Then I opened my presents.

JUDY SMOLIK

This description of Marlene utilizes another major sound device used by professional writers: the quick ending sentence, the short punch that surprises. A short sentence after a number of longer sentences varies the rhythm of a passage. Rhythm is a device involving sound, a beat or lack of beat, sensed in the ear, not comprehended intellectually.

Parallel construction often creates sentences or parts of sentences of equal length and thus sets up rhythm that becomes powerful when controlled and occasionally varied. In the following excerpt from a meditation written by John Donne, Dean of St. Paul's Cathedral in London in 1624, listen for the equal and answering beat of parts of sentences following upon each other:

> Who casts not up his Eie to the Sunne when it rises?
> who takes off his Eie from a Comet when that breakes out?
> . . . No man is an Iland, intire of it selfe; every man is
> a peece of the Continent, a part of the maine . . .

Part of the power of Donne's meditation arises not from the sound of its syllables but from the formality of its language. If you read the following paraphrase of a part of Donne's meditation and then Donne's lines, you will hear the informal language of conversation and then the sonorous language of the cathedral:

> The death bell rings for anyone who thinks it is ringing
> for him, and even if it quits ringing for a while, its effect
> upon him brings him to God. Everyone looks at the sun
> when it comes up. And no one quits looking at a comet
> when it flashes. Everyone listens to bells everywhere. But
> no one could possibly stop listening to his own death bell.
> No man can live separately by himself. Every person is a
> bit of the whole world and if any little part of that world
> disappears, he is affected by its disappearance, just as he
> would be by the destruction of a friend's house or his own
> house. Because he is part of mankind. Don't ask whom the
> bell is ringing for. It's ringing for you.

That version swings in places, for example: "Don't ask whom the bell is ringing for. It's ringing for you." But it lacks the majesty of Donne's original. Listen to him toll the bell:

> The Bell doth toll for him that thinkes it doth; and though
> it intermit againe, yet from that minute, that that occasion
> wrought upon him, hee is united to God. Who casts not up
> his Eie to the Sunne when it rises? but who takes off his
> Eie from a Comet when that breakes out? Who bends not
> his eare to any bell, which upon any occasion rings? but
> who can remove it from that bell, which is passing a peece
> of himselfe out of this world? No man is an Iland, intire of
> it selfe; every man is a peece of the Continent, a part of the
> maine; if a Clod bee washed away by the Sea, Europe is the

lesse, as well as if a Promontorie were, as well as if a
Mannor of thy friends or of thine owne were; any mans
death diminishes me, because I am involved in mankinde;
And therefore never send to know for whom the bell tolls;
It tolls for thee.

Donne ends comment upon the bell with a short powerful statement:
"It tolls for thee." It gains its power from the long rolling statements
which precede it. You may employ this device. Let yourself—or some
character you're giving words to—get wound up and go on and on,
and then stop suddenly with a clincher.

Note how Ralph Waldo Emerson does this in a paragraph from
his essay "Self-Reliance." He gains further emphasis by shifting
from Elevated to Kitchen Language (a device which will be discussed in Chapter 20).

I have no churlish objection to the circumnavigation
of the globe for the purposes of art, of study, and benevo-
lence, so that the man is first domesticated, or does not go
abroad with the hope of finding somewhat greater than he
knows. He who travels to be amused, or to get somewhat
which he does not carry, travels away from himself, and
grows old even in youth among old things. In Thebes, in
Palmyra, his will and mind have become old and dilapi-
dated as they. He carries ruins to ruins.

These endings punch hard partly because of their meanings. If
what you say in an ending line is obvious and dull, it will not be
made impressive by being stated shortly. However, the reader may
be grateful even for a dull short sentence if all the preceding sentences were long. Just as professional writers learn to create flow in
their sentences—so they do not have to think consciously about it—
they learn to vary the length of their sentences. If a great many are
long, they habitually throw in a short one. And vice versa. They are
not afraid to throw in a piece of a sentence, a phrase, a single word;
and let it stand as a sentence. As they write, they hear the sound of
sentences as well as the sound of words.

Another way to create faithful and exciting sound in your writing
is to try to put down what you hear. The sound of a bullfrog? In
Walden, Thoreau calls it a *trump* and put it down *tr-r-r-oonk*! In his
Journals he describes the pigeon woodpecker's "whimsical ah-week
ah-week." In *The Field Book of Ponds and Streams,* Anne Haven
Morgan writes the American toad's call as "wheep."

When she heard the sound of traffic on a nearby street, a mother working in a beginning writers' course remembered her children's youth through sound:

HOME

At noon, traffic on Stadium transmits an even, steady sound, the passing of many cars blending together in a deep, harmonious hum. At two o'clock in the morning, a single car creates a gradual crescendo as it approaches, a diminuendo as it moves into the distance.

One car at night carries a lonesome, nostalgic sound. I am reminded of times I've lain awake waiting for teenagers to return. In the deep quiet of the country night I can hear the first faint sound of a car coming down the highway a quarter of a mile away, slowing down to turn the corner onto the gravel of our country road, the gradual increasing of sound as the car approaches; then a momentary lowering as it slows for the bump of the little bridge; an increasing again for the rise of the little hill where our house stood. I can remember lying tense and breathing lightly, waiting for the moment when the noise of the car would continue on past the house into the distance. Or— it would pause, diminishing abruptly as the driver pressed the brake and the car coasted with its own momentum into our driveway. I heard the final beat of the motor, the quick staccato of young feet, first on the porch steps, then on the stairs. Soon the hall light, always left on for the last one in, was snapped off.

My child was back under my roof again.

GERTRUDE ANDRESEN

Here the writer not only remembers sounds but evokes some of them by her choice of words and building of sentence rhythms. The statement

then a momentary lowering of sound as it slows for the bump of the little bridge

employs the word *bump* perfectly—a short word with a little burst and closure in it, coming in the middle of the statement so that it sounds exactly like what the writer is describing. Maybe *bump* was the only word that came to the writer's mind, luckily right in sound for her purposes. Maybe she also thought of saying *slight rise in the road, ripple,* or *protuberance,* and discarded them because they did not contribute anything in sound. Often a writer doesn't know how he achieved his good sound effects. Sometimes he doesn't hear them until a reader points them out. Yet they are there and he has a right to take credit for them.

You may train your ear by reading aloud good writing. Then when you read aloud your own writing you are more likely to hear skillful sounds. In reading a second or third draft you can change a word here or there.

To write fully, you must use all your senses. Remember how places and objects smell, the taste of the back of your hand, the touch of concrete, the sound of a laugh—an American's laugh, a Southerner's laugh, a Northerner's. Such variety.

The representation of sounds in words can become conventional and even trite—"bang!" "screech," "eek!" Here is a beginning writer recording sounds in fresh words:

> **I like the quiet crackling of root beer foam; the swish, then flap of the net as the basketball passes through . . . squeaky popcorn; slept-on mattress . . . moccasins treading soft sand, crisp as toasted linen; steel door weightlessly slammed shut; secret roar of sea shell; whirr of a movie reel; the ps-s-s-t of freshly opened coffee . . . whirr and buzz of the WALK signal; a Band-Aid coming off . . . creaky wicker chairs . . .**
>
> SISTER MARY LOIS GLONEK

IMITATING FIVE: Put down in words a page of sounds you like and dislike. Study the passage above by Sister Mary Lois. Note her accuracy and restraint. She avoided the obvious and conventional representations of loud sounds. You may follow her direction or others. Like all symbolizing of experience through words, the representation of sounds is complex and subtle. Sometimes it is almost a precise rendering of actual sound; sometimes a satirical conventionalization, as in the *Batman* series—"Zowie! Blat! Pow! Bam!"

The most significant sound in life is that of other voices. The best writers seem born with an ear's memory for the way a person speaks, and if they write down the conversations of a dozen persons in one story, all speak recognizably differently. Maybe this is a natural gift, not to be learned. But you may try, at least, to see whether you have it.

Few, if any, professional writers put down conversation that is absolutely and completely accurate in manner and extent; for it would be boring. Most of us talk dully a great deal of the time. But the skillful writer captures enough of the real tones and rhythms and dialect of his character in writing to make them sound authentic. Consider this passage from the first chapter of *Huckleberry Finn*. Mark Twain varied the length of his sentences, the repetitions of sounds within words, and the word patterns of a rural uneducated boy from Missouri:

> Her sister, Miss Watson, a tolerable slim old maid, with goggles on, had just come to live with her, and took a set at me now with a spelling-book. She worked me middling hard for about an hour, and then the widow made her ease up. I couldn't stood it much longer. Then for an hour it was deadly dull, and I was fidgety. Miss Watson would say, "Don't put your feet up there, Huckleberry;" and "don't scrunch up like that, Huckleberry—set up straight;" and pretty soon she would say, "Don't gap and stretch like that, Huckleberry—why don't you try to behave?" Then she told me all about the bad place, and I said I wished I was there. She got mad then, but I didn't mean no harm. All I wanted was to go somewheres; all I wanted was a change. I warn't particular. She said it was wicked to say what I said; said she wouldn't say it for the whole world; *she* was going to live so as to go to the good place. Well, I couldn't see no advantage in going where she was going, so I made up my mind I wouldn't try for it. But I never said so, because it would only make trouble, and wouldn't do no good.
>
> Now she had got a start, and she went on and told me all about the good place. She said all a body would have to do there was to go around all day long with a harp and sing, forever and ever. So I didn't think much of it. But I never said so. I asked her if she reckoned Tom Sawyer would go there, and, she said, not by a considerable sight. I was glad about that, because I wanted him and me to be together.

The forty-year-old man who was writing this book spoke in the voice of a boy. At times, he used adult words that Huck would never have spoken, but he captured a youth's language in enough of the lines to establish Huck's authentic voice and make it immortal.

The following two statements by William Carlos Williams differ completely from each other in sound. They move differently—that is one of the effects a writer can achieve by controlling sound.

THE DANCE

In Breughel's great picture, The Kermess,
the dancers go round, they go round and
around, the squeal and the blare and the
tweedle of bagpipes, a bugle and fiddles
tipping their bellies (round as the thick-
sided glasses whose wash they impound)
their hips and their bellies off balance
to turn them. Kicking and rolling about
the Fair Grounds, swinging their butts, those
shanks must be sound to bear up under such
rollicking measures, prance as they dance
in Breughel's great picture, The Kermess.

POEM

As the cat
climbed over
the top of

the jamcloset
first the right
forefoot

carefully
then the hind
stepped down

into the pit of
the empty
flowerpot

Dr. Williams' mastery of sound should come as no surprise to readers who know he was a poet. A practicing M.D., he wrote poems in his office in between seeing patients or on the way to visit them in their homes.

In "The Dance," Dr. Williams writes only two sentences, listing again and again a few nouns joined by prepositions, or a verb form ending in *-ing*. Once he says they go round and round, his parts of sentences repeat and repeat and thus go round and round themselves:

the squeal and the blare and the tweedle
a bugle and fiddles
their hips and their bellies

One way he gets the parts of sentences to swing is to join them with *and,* a word he uses six times.

Read aloud, the poem almost flies off the page, because Dr. Williams has employed so many sound effects—alliteration and assonance, the repetition of *ound* in *round, around, impound, Grounds, sound.*

Dr. Williams' second sentence is not actually a sentence but a jamming together of the parts of several sentences which do not keep straight their subjects and verbs. For example, the shanks are not "swinging their butts"; the dancers are. Dr. Williams knows what a sentence is, but here he deliberately violates grammar in order to increase the feeling that the speaker is himself breathlessly swinging around and around rather than reciting a carefully composed statement at a speaker's podium.

In the second poem about the cat, Dr. Williams has arranged his words to slow down the reader as he speaks the lines. Instead of the constant repetition of words ending in *-ing,* he uses many words ending in sounds that stop rather than prolong sound: the word *top* not a word like *new,* the word *jamcloset* not a word like *see.* Also many of his words begin with hard sounds: *cat climbed, flowerpot.* In "The Dance," he wanted beer-drinking peasants to swing in circles; in "Poem" he wanted a cat to step precisely and carefully. The sound of words is the poet's business. He must be able to control it as a pitcher controls a curve.

You may hate poetry or fear it because you have been tossed too many knuckleballs, those slow and slower mushy pitches that take forever to reach home plate. Because of that possibility this textbook has not asked you to write poetry, although to learn to write some poetry is to learn to master language, and thus to write any sort of statement, whether a business letter or a novel, with power. If you have urges to write poetry, give in to them.

But know what contemporary poetry is before you try it. Not a bunch of vague private thoughts about reforming the world or feeling sorry for yourself because you're lonely. Like all good writing, good poetry puts you somewhere in reality—perhaps in the mind of a real person. It's alive. You can see what William Carlos Williams wrote about, a Flemish painting he liked and an American cat. He is a celebrated American poet. Edna St. Vincent Millay wrote about looking at advertisements posted in a subway train and thinking her lover might die; Theodore Roethke wrote about the accidental death of one of his college students; Philip Booth wrote about teaching his daughter how to swim.

Write about your experience. You don't have to try poetry; but if you do, remember it is first of all concentrated form of expression. Pack the word. Pack the meaning. Play with words. Make one phrase say three thoughts or feelings. Remember, sound should speak the feeling you wish to communicate. Use rhyme if you wish, but keep it alive, fresh, surprising. If it comes out blue, true; moon, June, swoon —give up. Poetry must have guts and bone, whether it is delicate or slambang. It must have all the attributes of good writing discussed in this book, only brought to their ultimate concentrated power. That way, underneath, it carries truth.

> *Poetry is a response to the daily necessity of getting the world right.*
>
> WALLACE STEVENS

Do you often say, "I'll take my chances"?
Or do you more often say, "I just want
to know what to expect"? Is what you
ask from life each day your chance? Or
is it certainty?

SIDNEY COX

chapter 20

writing
reports
and
columns

THE LIVE CORE

MOST PERSONS expect two out of three
lectures, reports, sermons, editorials, and presentations to bore them.
And they do. So when they are told to write a report, they produce
another boring piece of writing. They forget that one out of three
reports they have read was entertaining, surprising, or exciting, like
this encyclopedia entry on Davy Crockett, taken from *The Oxford
Companion to American Literature*, 1965:

CROCKETT, DAVY (David) (1786-1836), born in Tennessee, spent a shiftless youth until his political career began
(*c.* 1816) with his appointment as justice of the peace. He
boasted that none of his decisions was ever reversed, because
of his dependence on 'natural-born sense instead of law
learning.' After being twice elected to the state legislature,
he accepted a humorous proposal that he run for Congress,
and to his surprise was elected, serving from 1827 to 1831,

and again from 1833 to 1835. Because of his opposition to
Jackson, the Whigs adopted him as a convenient tool
through whom to draw the backwoods democracy to its
standard. Davy was soon turned by skilful politicians into
a frontier hero, whose picturesque eccentricities, backwoods humor, tall tales, shrewd native intelligence, and
lusty pioneer spirit were all aggrandized. Whig journalists
were soon at work, and in short order turned out such
books, attributed to Davy, as *Sketches and Eccentricities of
Col. David Crockett* (1833), *An Account of Col. Crockett's
Tour to the North and Down East* (1835), *The Life of
Martin Van Buren* (1835), and *Col. Crockett's Exploits and
Adventures in Texas* (1836). With the exception of the
last, which is posthumous, he may have had a hand in all
these works, and he gladly claimed the *Tour* and life of Van
Buren. Swallowing the Whig bait, he enjoyed his sudden
rise to fame, and was glad to aid in propagating the myth,
which, however, removed him from office, since his constituents would not tolerate his desertion of Democratic principles. Piqued, he left Tennessee to participate in the war for
Texan independence, and a few months later died in the
heroic defense of the Alamo, adding a final dramatic chapter to his career. *A Narrative of the Life of David Crockett,
of the State of Tennessee* (1834) passes as his autobiography,
although the claim has often been disputed. In any case the
book has the robust manner attributed to Crockett, and
contains fine examples of the farce and exaggeration of
the tall tale.

This report includes a great number of specific facts—dates, offices
held, political parties, names of books—encompassing a lifetime, and
yet told in less than 350 words. Although James D. Hart, the editor,
was writing a reference book, he did not present simply a collection
of facts about Davy Crockett. He wrote the article with an angle:
Here is Davy Crockett, who became an American hero celebrated in
folk song and story. How did that happen? Did his life merit the
myth that has arisen about him?

Remembering his audience of educated Americans, Mr. Hart
did not begin the article by saying Crockett is a famous backwoods
hero. He expected his audience to know that, and he got right down
to telling how Crockett became famous. He omitted many facts about
Crockett's life, partly because he had to save words (he was writing

an 888-page reference work which names and describes thousands of persons, books, newspapers, and places), and partly because he did not want to divert the reader with facts not critical to his angle.

Mr. Hart did not think he was "letting the facts speak for themselves." He knew that all facts take on meaning because of their setting. He made his judgment about Crockett and chose facts which bore upon it. He presented Crockett as a man who rode luck to fame, allowed himself to be used by politicians, permitted his name to be connected to books that were in large measure not written by him, and deserved his fame as a skillful teller of tall tales.

> *Even the reporting of pure physical research findings, to cite an extreme example, is not unbiased. It is biased in favor of revealing the findings. In recent years the practical import and responsibility of such a bias has been felt deeply by atomic scientists. The question is not whether a communication is biased. The question is: toward what value system is the communication biased?*
>
> GERHART WIEBE

To write this report, Mr. Hart had to know a great deal about Davy Crockett. If he had known less, he would not have been able to find so many facts which touched his angle. Like all good pieces of writing, this report sounds authoritative partly because it implies the writer knew more facts than he employed—the iceberg structure, as some critics have called it.

When you write a report, know your subject. If it is a book, or books, you are writing from, you may need to read it several times, compare it with other books, and see what other persons think of it. Most of all, you need to test it in some way—does its experience or theory ring true to your experience, to your learning? Such questions will help you see more clearly what the book is saying. If you are writing a report from direct observation, you may need to ask questions to see how others see the subject. Talking with other persons about a book you have read or an event you have witnessed usually helps you see more than you saw on your own.

> *... I always try to write on the principle of the iceberg. There is seven-eighths of it underwater for every part that shows.*

> *Anything you know you can eliminate
> and it only strengthens your iceberg. It
> is the part that doesn't show. If a writer
> omits something because he does not
> know it then there is a hole in the story.*
>
> ERNEST HEMINGWAY

You should write a report with an iceberg of facts available to you, and you should choose and shape the critical facts to appear as the ice above the water. The professional report writer doesn't start writing until he has a large iceberg. He learns to sense when he has a sufficient core of materials and he learns quick, efficient ways of getting that core. For example, many sportswriters have available to them a running record of a basketball game, which looks like this:

UNIVERSITY OF TOLEDO VS. SAN FRANCISCO STATE DECEMBER 19, 1960 SECOND HALF		
TOLEDO		**SAN FRANCISCO STATE**
TIME LEFT		
20:00	29	23
19:29		25 Williams jumper center of keyhole
18:46		27 Williams laid in set up
18:28 Lewis made layup	31	
17:43 Lewis one-hand jumper beyond key	33	
16:06		29 Caranica drove for layup
15:56 Jones jumper side of circle	35	
15:14 Galicki personal foul		Brown missed personal foul
15:03 Galicki laid in Jones' pass	37	
14:43 Lewis' jumper side of circle	39	
14:28 Pawlak personal foul		31 Caranica laid in setup Caranica missed free throw

This part of the game record shows only five minutes and thirty-two seconds of the action. An assistant or a representative of the teams may keep such a record, but the writer knows it will be available and he uses it. You may make a similar log of the activities you cover. Be prepared with whatever instruments you need to collect materials—notebook, tape recorder, 3 $\times$ 5 cards, camera. Gather whatever printed information is available—an agenda outlining the order of items in a meeting, lists of officers or speakers, minutes of last meeting, programs. Double-check all names for spelling. Learn as much as possible about the event before you go to it.

The writer who goes underwater and discovers the whole iceberg gives himself a chance to make the report fascinating to readers. He can discard the dull, the partially relevant, the tedious, and present only the bright, snowy peaks. Here is a report of a baseball game by Robert Lipsyte (*The New York Times*, August 5, 1966). Think of how many notes and records Mr. Lipsyte must have consulted while writing this story. His angle was not hard to find: the New York Mets (in ninth place) had beaten the San Francisco Giants (tied for first) while the Giants were using their star pitcher Juan Marichal. Lipsyte chose to tell his story concentrating on the relatively unknown Ron Swoboda, the Met who hit the winning home run, and to bring in the famous Marichal as his antagonist.

METS BEAT GIANTS 8-6, ON SWOBODA'S HOMER IN 9TH

Ron Swoboda, who won it in the ninth inning with a three-run pinch-hit home run, said: "It was a story-book game. Holy Cow!" And it was just that.

Most of the crowd of 41,038 at Shea Stadium sat stunned yesterday long after the Mets had beaten the Giants, 8-6. Swoboda's drive cleared the leftfield fence and the 22-year-old outfielder jogged around the bases in a mood he later described as "elation . . . the epitome . . . my greatest thrill!"

More than 24,000 in the crowd had bought their tickets just before gametime because the great Juan Marichal was starting for the Giants. For almost six innings they got what they paid for—perfection from Marichal and something less than perfection from the Mets.

The 27-year-old Dominican righthander, out of action recently because of a sore finger, had registered his 17th victory Tuesday night, by the official scorer's decision, after retiring the last four Mets. Yesterday, kicking high on a dusty mound, he retired the first 17 Mets.

3 OUTS ON 6 PITCHES

In the second inning, with six pitches, he put out the side so quickly that he had to wave his sleepy outfielders back to the dugout. In the third, facing Dennis Ribant, the busy little Met starter, he was worked for his first full count before Ribant lined out to Willie Mays, a well-hit ball that Mays had to hustle to catch and gave a few plaintive voices reason to holler, "Let's go Mets."

In the sixth, Ribant bounced one over Marichal's head for a single, and the crowd prepared to console itself with a brilliant one-hitter instead of a perfect game.

The Giants, meanwhile, were doing what was expected of a team that started the sunny afternoon game leading the National League and fresh from having beaten the Mets three times in a row. They scored a run in the fourth on Willie McCovey's 21st homer of the year, a run in the fifth on Marichal's double and Jim Davenport's single and a run in the sixth on Jim Hart's 24th homer.

GIANTS GAIN 5-0 LEAD

In the seventh, San Francisco made the score 5-0. Tito Fuentes drove one of Ribant's pitches into the leftfield corner. Larry Elliot dropped it in foul territory and examined it, apparently thinking the ball was foul, while Fuentes went to third, credited with a double. Ossie Virgil, who had replaced Davenport at third base, then singled and McCovey walked.

With the bases loaded, Darrell Sutherland replaced Ribant, and Mays singled home two runs.

In the last of the seventh, the Mets began to move at last. They needed three singles and a throwing error by Marichal to get one run. The people who had come to see at least a shutout went home.

Tom Haller hit a homer for the Giants in the eighth, making the score 6-1, but it was a wasted gesture. In the bottom of the eighth, the Mets charged.

Jerry Grote reached second on a two-base throwing error by Virgil, and John Stephenson, a 25-year-old catcher pinch-hitting for Dallas Green, the third Met pitcher, blasted his first homer of the season. Singles by Chuck Hiller, Al Luplow and Larry Elliot made the score 6-4.

In disbelief, the crowd froze.

HAMILTON IS VICTOR

Jack Hamilton, the winning pitcher, put out the Giants in the ninth. Then Marichal strolled back to the mound. He demanded that it be dampened because he was kicking dust into his own face. A little man with a green sprinkling can scurried out and dampened the mound.

Satisfied, baseball's best righthander pitched two balls and a strike to Ken Boyer. Boyer hit the fourth pitch over the fence for his 11th homer of the season, and Marichal was pulled out for some showering of his own.

"Let's go Mets." There was no plaintiveness now, no whine. There was hope.

Ed Bressoud, who had been playing an erratic shortstop for the injured Roy McMillan, singled to left. Ron Hunt, pinchhitting for Grote, bunted, forcing Bressoud at second. Stephenson, hero of the eighth inning, hit a wrong-field single to right. There was one out, two men on base, and the score was 6-5.

The roar was swelling now as Bill Henry, a left-hander, replaced Lindy McDaniel, a right-hander. The next scheduled batter, Chuck Hiller, was called back for a right-handed hitting replacement and Manager Wes Westrum said to Swoboda, "Get a bat."

Swoboda later admitted he was excited because "that's it, when everybody's relying on you." He kept telling himself to "stay loose" and he forgot that the last time Marichal had started against the Mets, on May 20, Swoboda had won the game with a tenth-inning homer against the same Bill Henry.

The first pitch was high; it would have been a ball if Swoboda, overanxious, hadn't swung and missed. The second was a ball, low and inside. The third, waist-high and fast, was thrown with the stuff that dreams are made on.

Although Mr. Lipsyte, the reporter, tells the outcome of the game in the second paragraph, 8–6, he then begins a story in which he builds tension: How and when did Swoboda do it? What was happening to the marvelous Marichal? How did the pinch hitter outshine the star? Frequently writers of reports build their story around such tension between two poles. A report of a laboratory experiment can be a suspense story: Will the scientist find the answer or won't he? Will his newly improvised piece of equipment work?

Mr. Lipsyte was writing a story of surprise, an upset. So he put the reader at the game, watching the expected happen: Marichal pitching a one-hit game for six innings. Thus he built tension for the Mets' rally. He could have provided many details about other Giants' players than the pitcher, but his angle made him present little individualizing details about Marichal, who was the Giant.

> In the second inning, with six pitches, he put out the side
> so quickly that he had to wave his sleepy outfielders back to
> the dugout.

Like all good writers, Mr. Lipsyte does not forget what he has said. He makes facts and words speak to each other. In the fourth paragraph, he shows how well Marichal was pitching:

> Yesterday, kicking high on a dusty mound, he retired the
> first 17 Mets.

In the fourteenth paragraph, remembering the dusty mound, he says that Marichal

> . . . demanded that it be dampened because he was kicking
> dust into his own face.

This is the great Marichal demanding. Mr. Lipsyte says:

> A little man with a green sprinkling can scurried out and
> dampened the mound.

Later, Mr. Lipsyte says

> . . . Marichal was pulled out for some showering of his own.

Dust, dampening, showering: the words speak to each other. In the last paragraph, Mr. Lipsyte says:

> The third, waist-high and fast, was thrown with the stuff
> that dreams are made on.

For Mr. Lipsyte, the comeback of the Mets was so great that it deserved an echo of Shakespeare's lines in *The Tempest* (IV, i.):

> We are such stuff
> As dreams are made on, and our little life
> Is rounded with a sleep.

The speaker is Prospero, a magician who commands the air and earth. Mr. Swoboda was a magician at Shea Stadium.

Here is an Associated Press record of the same game as presented in *The Kalamazoo Gazette* for August 5, 1966. Probably only part of the original wire-service report was used, for the account was printed in a roundup article including games of other teams. You can see how the extra space available to Mr. Lipsyte allowed him to bring alive the scene. His report in many respects is fresher and more dramatic than the AP account.

METS SHOCK GIANTS WITH SWOBODA'S PINCH HOMER

Ron Swoboda, unlike lightning, has struck twice in the same place, and Bill Henry has been left smoking.

Just two weeks ago, Swoboda flashed off the New York Mets' bench and jolted fireman Henry by slamming the veteran reliever for a ninth-inning homer that gave the Mets a 3–2 victory over the San Francisco Giants.

Thursday, the 22-year-old right-handed hitter reduced lefty Henry to ashes, again coming off the bench in the ninth with a crackling three-run clout that carried the Mets to an 8–6 triumph over the Giants.

"It was just like a fairy tale," said Swoboda, relegated to pinch hitting this season when the opposition starts a right-hander.

The earlier belt kept the Giants out of a virtual tie for the first place in the National League. This one dropped them into second place, two percentage points behind Pittsburgh, which hammered Los Angeles 8–1.

The Mets trailed 6–4 entering the ninth when Ken Boyer started the Mets' thunder with a homer off Juan Marichal, seeking his 18th victory. Lindy McDaniel, who took the loss, relieved and gave up singles to Ed Bressoud and John Stephenson. Then Henry entered and moments later Swoboda struck.

Marichal, who had beaten the Mets 17 times in his career without a loss and retired the first 17 hitters Thursday, thus managed to slip off the hook.

Willie McCovey, Jim Hart and Tom Haller homered for the Giants and Johnny Stephenson also connected for the Mets.

In this report, Mike Recht of the Associated Press achieved some style by using the metaphor of lightning throughout—"unlike lightning, has struck twice . . . flashed . . . reduced lefty Henry to ashes . . .

a crackling three-run clout . . . the Mets' thunder . . . Swoboda struck."
His angle was that Swoboda again homered against Henry. But in the
paragraphs printed by the *Kalamazoo Gazette* Mr. Recht's story does
not take on the excitement of Mr. Lipsyte's, which led up to a sus-
penseful last paragraph.

Readers expect more life from columns of opinion than reports of
events. But a column or short piece of opinion or comment on passing
events does not become strong simply because it exhibits more personal judgment and opinion than reports and other more objective
writings. It may easily be boring, flat, and without significance to
readers. Here is a discussion of happiness published in a school newspaper.

HAPPINESS

> There are many different kinds of happiness. The meaning
> of happiness can be defined according to a person, his en-
> vironment and his heredity.
>
> Let's narrow this word down to what happiness is to high
> school teenagers. To one teenager, happiness might be a set
> of "wheels," a "weed," and plenty of "petro."
>
> This person seems to think that in order to be happy, all
> he needs is a showy sports car, cigarettes and gasoline. Why
> would he think this way? He might live in a shabby house,
> not have much in the way of good clothes or property, so
> he wants something more than the normal teenager, some-
> thing he thinks he can be proud of and show off.
>
> Another teen might decide happiness would be a good
> education and a bright future. This person has most of the
> "flashy" comforts of life handed to him on a silver tray.
> What he really wants is to make his own future, the chance
> to prove himself.
>
> Is either opinion wrong? Happiness depends on the per-
> son. Two extremes were taken in this case, to try and define
> what happiness really is. It all points out that to gain hap-
> piness there must be a certain amount of discipline along
> with the desire. If the desire is great enough, this thing hap-
> piness, in any definition, can be obtained.

The point of this passage is defensible. Not everyone needs to strive for
the same kind of happiness. An old idea, though, and of little value or
interest to a reader unless brought alive with telling examples. This
writer seems not to have found an iceberg. She says that driving a

showy sports car may be a legitimate kind of happiness, but she doesn't reveal enough knowledge of what it's like to drive a sports car to convince a reader. Why did she pick this example? Perhaps because she just came back from an exhilarating ride in a car. If so, she should have taken the reader on the ride. If not, she has chosen a wrong example. If she has not talked to a young person who wants to "make his own future" and a chance "to prove himself," she should not use him as an example. If she has, she should reveal what he has done, what he hopes to do, how his aspirations and achievements make him impressive. If she doesn't know such a boy, why is she talking about persons who value a good education and look toward their future?

Most professional columnists write out of consuming interest in particular events, ideas, persons. They are given a regular space to fill each month or week or day because they write compellingly. They are good writers to study because they frequently write of matters that other persons make boring. Here is a column (of July 30, 1966), which is a weekly feature in *The New Republic* magazine, written by a man always identified simply as T.R.B.:

THE HOUND AND THE RABBIT

The most compelling phrase in the English language after "I do," is "three . . . two . . . one . . . ignition." Let's talk about both expressions.

We found ourself down at Cape Kennedy last week watching the Young-Collins space shot in a world wholly unfamiliar to us. People talked what sounded like English, but wasn't. It was like sending a Hottentot to cover Luci Johnson's wedding.

The shot itself, of course, was the main thing. We had never seen one before; television doesn't do it justice. There was that heart-stopping split-second after "ignition." Then a burst of smoke across the meadow, a mile-and-a-half away. Then a hot light. Seconds later a rumble of sound. This was the Agena 10—the target rabbit that Gemini 10, the hound of heaven, would chase and find. After 100 minutes' head start the countdown came for Gemini again. "Ignition."

SUMMER THUNDER

This time the puff of smoke was bigger and the white light at the side intensely bright, like an acetylene flame. The noise, when it got across the meadow, might have passed for

summer thunder but it had a rhythm in it, a kind of pulse.
Then the great silver needle rose in slow splendor, carrying
its forked flame behind it. It was unbelievable.

It was the Indian rope trick done with a freight car. What
was most impressive was the *deliberateness* of the rise with
a kind of regal assurance, straight up. Birds flapped wildly
around over the Florida sandflats. There was a great cloud
of condensation vapor as it hit the sky. In no time Messrs.
Collins and Young were on their way like a couple of gnats
riding a Roman candle.

Experts briefed the newsmen afterward with a vocabulary
of angstroms, azimuths, burns, ions, and glitches. The whole
space experiment would collapse if they couldn't use "um-
bilical." What impressed this aging reporter was the youth
of these brilliant technicians, also their mood. It was unmis-
takable. They were dancing up and down with excitement;
tests to measure the pressure of sunlight; finding out if a
satellite carries an atmosphere of earth dust; peeking at
stars outside the earth's curtain; testing whether microor-
ganisms can live in space (maybe that's how life got to
earth). The scientists are on the fringes of the universe;
they are looking over the fence. Here is the great laboratory
that is changing "don't know," into "dimly perceive."

FROM KITTY HAWK TO CAPE KENNEDY

As a young man TRB acompanied Orville Wright and an
official party in top hats down the Potomac to commemor-
ate the 25th anniversary of the first flight. The sand dunes
at Kittyhawk were unstable, but some local gaffers had
agreed to take oath that such and such a sliding hill was the
right one, and everyone made speeches about the amazing
progress of aviation since the silly old days of 1903. They
were still flying biplanes, then.

And shortly the US will be celebrating the 40th anniversary of Lindbergh's flight. Well, you need landmarks like
that to get perspective on Cape Kennedy. Today earth-
orbiting is so routine that the public says ho-hum. It takes
a sudden emergency like that of Collins and Young with the
noxious fumes to recall the perils that brave men accept so
matter-of-factly. Pursuit, rendezvous and union are as natural now as the ascent of the water moth in its nuptial
flight above a New England pond, till it meets its mate
beyond the sight of men.

What awed us at Cape Kennedy even more than Gemini's single flight was the production-line of space craft which are now operating.

We had never got the hang before of the three stages, in the $20 billion moon operation.

They all fit together. First were the one-man Mercurys. They are over now. Today the two-man Geminis are also almost phased out. They are being put up at six-week intervals with two more flights scheduled. Then comes stage three: Project Apollo.

This is simply stunning. The Cape doesn't wait to end Gemini to start Apollo. The hangar or "barn" for Apollo is all built, higher than the Statue of Liberty; in fact you could push the entire United Nations building into either door.

A stupendous mock-up Apollo points upward at its landing pad, speculatively eyeing the moon. It is as impressive as a pyramid. But this thing, or something like it, will make a lunar trip within the foreseeable future.

The cost is vast. Maybe unwise. Personally it makes us tingle. Man is a puny thing in a lot of ways but, let's face it, he is indomitable. What the Russians have up their sleeves we don't know, but since they launched their last manned space craft the US has put up half a dozen. At the Kennedy Space Center they are now running sight-seeing buses for the public to see the place. They charge $1.75, which seems outrageous, but at least it's public.

HERE COMES THE BRIDE

Earlier we mentioned "I do" as a phrase of equal potency with countdowns. Normally we don't read women's pages. But a chance dinner table encounter with a society editor tore a veil from our eyes—the absolutely frenzied world of Luci Johnson's wedding, August 6. Where have we been? Every woman in the whole country is talking about it. Brides always have their backs to the public.

Ah, but the expression of this one, clad in a gown which *Women's Wear Daily* has already been penalized for prematurely revealing, will be reported. Something about a peephole through the banked Cathedral's flowers, we believe, from which a pool correspondent will scurry back to give eyewitness details to "the gals" (society reporters are always "the gals"). "She smiled softly"; "her lips trembled," or—oh

rapture—"she dropped a tear." Somehow we sympathize
with Papa Lyndon till this ordeal is over.

T.R.B. uses the old-fashioned editorial "we," but writes with personal feeling. He communicates the thrill he felt. Like the author of
"Happiness" he is talking about a big subject, here the wisdom of man's
costly exploration of space. But unlike that author, he writes out of an
experience up to his idea.

THE ALTERNATING CURRENT

This column is lively because it employs most of the strategies discussed in this book plus another one: the Alternating Current. Like
James D. Hart and Robert Lipsyte, T.R.B. shifts back and forth from
a lowly to a bookish vocabulary, what might be called Kitchen and
Elevated language. When we are talking informally in the kitchen
with friends or relatives, most of us do not use the word *compelling*
(which appears in T.R.B.'s first sentence), *slow splendor, regal assurance, fringes of the universe,* or *dimly perceive.* We say *main thing,
doesn't do it justice, got across, a couple of gnats, looking over the
fence.* Using the Alternating Current, a writer moves back and forth
between these vocabularies, putting *regal assurance* near *flapped
wildly around.* This alternation keeps the reader awake, makes him
sense a tension in the language. Bad preachers do not use the Alternating Current. They drone on in an unrelieved elevated vocabulary. Bad
editorial writers do the same. They have no sense of the lightness that
can be achieved in a writing that discusses a solemn subject in sober
setting.

We hold these truths to be self-evident . . .

This statement from the Declaration of Independence would be spoken
by few persons in their kitchens, but

all men are created equal

might well be there. Speaking of King George III, the writers of the
Declaration said:

He has plundered our seas, ravaged our coasts

in language again not of the kitchen, but the rest of the sentence might
have been said there:

burnt our towns, and destroyed the lives of our people.

You may understandably say that no one could keep up Elevated language through a piece of writing. But some persons try. In a good part of her column on "Happiness" the writer spoke in a voice foreign to the kitchen:

> There are many different kinds of happiness. The meaning of happiness can be defined according to a person, his environment and his heredity . . . Happiness depends on the person. Two extremes were taken in this case, to try and define what happiness really is. It all points out that to gain happiness there must be a certain amount of discipline along with the desire. If the desire is great enough, this thing happiness, in any definition, can be obtained.

"To try and define what happiness really is" is a statement that might be said in the kitchen. But it is not used consciously as a contrast to the more elevated language of the first part of the sentence. Note the alternation of language in Robert Lipsyte's baseball article:

Kitchen	*Elevated*
they got what they paid for	perfection from Marichal
hustle to catch	plaintive voices
The people who had come to see at least a shutout went home	a wasted gesture
Marichal was pulled out	In disbelief
he was kicking dust into his own face	an erratic shortstop
There was one out, two men on base and the score was 6–5	The roar was swelling now

Elevated language is usually more precise than Kitchen language and comes to us trailing associations different from those carried by Kitchen language. In many ways it is superior as a vehicle of expression, but no one wants to hear it steadily throughout a lecture or a column. The ordinary speech of the common man is our anchor, and no good writer forgets it. Even a writer composing articles for a reference book remembers the value of alternating between these two languages—James D. Hart wrote his article on Davy Crockett largely in Elevated language but he saves it from dead levelness by the word *shiftless* in the first sentence and by quoting the vernacular employed by Davy:

> natural-born sense instead of law learning.

The rest of the article is filled with Elevated: *picturesque eccentricities, aggrandized, propagating, constituents, etc.* Mr. Hart uses an occasional Kitchen expression like "were soon at work" or "Swallowing the Whig bait." Quoting a statement in Kitchen language is a good stratagem for a writer who feels bound to maintain a sober, dignified style, and sometimes he may through quotation point out a surprising variation in the style spoken by one of the persons he is reporting. For example, Mr. Lipsyte quoted the Kitchen language of Ron Swoboda:

> "It was a story-book game. Holy Cow!"

and then revealed him using Elevated language in describing his mood:

> "Elation . . . the epitome . . ."

Sometimes writers make a whole column or report out of what others have said. As reporter Lane Wick showed in Chapter 12, a good reporter is on the lookout for strong remarks from the persons he interviews. He does not use the dull statements that are made to him. For example, here is part of a column in a school newspaper, "Is Your Spirit Dead?" A dangerous subject—more space has been wasted in school papers trying to stir up spirit in a student body than on any other subject. And this column begins with two obvious and dead quotations:

> **School spirit is "a desire, a wanting" to make a school great, according to Varsity cheerleader, Betty Uvan. "No one else can improve school spirit except the individual himself," she said.**
>
> **"I guess school spirit," explained junior Dave Mark, "could be defined as a feeling of pride or respect in all of the representative units of the school and a willingness to assume the responsibilities of citizenship at school."**

What these students say is old stuff and the manner in which they say it is flat. But the following article is loaded with sparkling quotations:

> LONG HAIR WARMS THE HEAD
>
> **Girls started a big mess and now the boys are going to finish it. What mess? Well, girls came out with short "Page-boys" and slacks. Now the boys are trying to put the barbershops out of business. Besides that they have now begun pouring themselves into the cloth straws called pants.**
>
> **How do people feel about this trend? Stay tuned to the next lines for the exciting results.**

Jan Pennold says, "I don't mind long hair that much. I think tight pants are cool as long as they're not too tight."

Dave Mark: "Well, if they're intent on becoming girls, it's okay."

Rod Senson quipped: "I think hair should be closely trimmed . . . about at the shoulders." About tight pants he said, "Fine, I like tight pants."

Helen Sals, very disgusted, said, "Boys ought to look like boys; tight pants are disgusting, too."

Hugh Rich: "Long hair looks good, but if it's not kept neat, it can start to look cruddy. I like tight pants as long as they don't go to extremes."

Mary Mann said, "For guys in a group long hair is okay because it's their gimmick, but guys not in a group with hair like that look weird; tight pants are okay."

Kit Pramm cheered for it but couldn't conjure up a flip for it as she said, "Oh! I think there's a certain extent that's okay, but past that long hair is unmasculine. Long hair's okay if it's clean." About tight pants she added, "Oh yeah! (but I don't think they should go to extremes.)"

Fred Lance said, "Some people look good and others look terrible. I think it depends on the way they wear long hair. Tight pants are okay if you don't split them."

Carol Laurens said, "I don't like long hair, I don't like tight pants; not that I like baggy pants, but real tight pants are terrible."

Andy Charles said, "I don't think long hair looks too good; tight pants are okay."

Sam Rich fondly remembered his freshman year and said, "Long hair is great when a biology bug collection is due." And then he gave us this tailor-made statement: "Tight pants? Well at least you don't have to have them taken in."

Pam Miller said, "Long hair is okay as long as it doesn't go to extremes. I think tight pants are repulsive."

You've heard what these jokers and serious minded riddlers have had to say, but the worst is yet to come! Would you believe second worst? Well, this reporter thinks that boys look best in "Crewcuts and Skirts."

> *. . . to have a full kit of auditory patterns curved to real emotions we do need to listen. We need to listen, with inside matching on our own part, to those*

*whose phrases fit their inner state. We
are lucky if we listen less to lecturers
and experts, more to farmers, mechanics,
truck drivers . . . laundresses, and children out of school. The lucky listen to
those who have fun when they talk, to
born mimics and storytellers, to those
whose words, literate or not, play with
the people that they talk with, and keep,
somehow, in play with the motion of
their hearers' minds.*

                                    SIDNEY COX

The Alternating Current is not difficult to turn on in your writing.
The secret lies in the genuineness of its juice, the speech you already
have in your unconscious memory. If you remember your native dialect—the language you learned at Mother's knee—and alternate that
with the language of writing you have picked up through reading and
listening to teachers in classrooms, you will find the current naturally
coursing through your prose. Finding it is again a matter of honesty.
What is your voice? Do you hear how you speak when you are not
thinking of your language? Listen to the country, the Kitchen, the
ball game, the streetcorner talk in your life. Introduce it sparingly into
your writing. At the same time you will find yourself varying the
length of your sentences, and that is another form of Alternating. You
often talk in shorter sentences than those written in books.

The Alternating Current flows in this quick piece of writing: rich,
full descriptions and then short iron, mannish sentences.

I used to hunt with Gramp. He didn't hunt like my
father. We would walk along the cramped, hollowed-out
cowpath. The bushes and weeds would push out at us from
both sides. I always walked behind. It led along the murk-
filled brown-greenness of the channel that connects his two
lakes. I would wait for something to break. He taught me
never to kill anything unless I was going to eat it. He helped
my brother shoot a pigeon once. He would have eaten it if
it had not smelled so much.

When the hunting was poor, we would go down by the
lake and shoot beer bottles that some ass had left behind.
There were always some there. Gramp would sit on a rotten
stump and remember. He used to shoot pickerel as they
pulled their heavy egg-filled bodies up the narrow channel.
He said that they would spawn near the roots of the silver-

gray pussy-willow trees. They're gone now; so are the pickerel. He would sit and laugh. And tell how the warden had chased him for two miles up to his slate-gray house. He had hid in the barn until he had left and then fried the warm fresh pickerel on the old black stove that was the heart of the house on a cold misty morning. We all learned something from him although he never taught us anything. I never knew it until he left. Tomorrow is never the same.

TOM CRONK

This is the way writers keep their writing alive. Tom Cronk may not have known that he was following an age-old tradition, but he was. Preachers use this method, poets, men who tell stories around pot-bellied stoves. If you open a book like *Ten Contemporary Thinkers*, a collection of modern essays edited by Victor Amend and Leo Hendrick, you will find that every third or fourth paragraph exhibits the Alternating Current. For example, E. M. Forster writes:

What about Force, though? While we are trying to be sensitive and advanced and affectionate and tolerant, an unpleasant question pops up: does not all society rest upon force? If a government cannot count upon the police and the army, how can it hope to rule? And if an individual gets knocked on the head or sent to a labour camp, of what significance are his opinions?

Don't think for a moment that Mr. Forster doesn't know "knocked on the head" comes from the barroom and "significant" from the library. In the same book, Archibald MacLeish, former Librarian of Congress and poet and dramatist, says:

The old words of freedom and revolution are still around, louder than ever, but somehow they are not the same. Revolution, which was once a word spoken with pride by every American who had the right to claim it, has become a word spoken with timidity and doubt and even loathing.

"Louder than ever" is Kitchen; "timidity" is Library, Elevated. Maybe "still around" is from the alley.

All of the ten contemporary thinkers in this book (including Robert Hutchins, George Orwell, Joseph Wood Krutch, Carl Becker, Walter Lippmann, C. S. Lewis, Julian Huxley, E. B. White) write part of their essays with the Alternating Current.

The lively writer creates tension in his sentences through many ways

—employing the Alternating Current; moving between the general and particular, the long and short sentence, the expected and the unexpected. By reading his work aloud to himself and to others, he trains his ear so that he writes with variety. He does not write half his work in Kitchen language and half in Elevated language, but rather continually alternates them. Always he thinks of his audience and his purpose. If he is writing a satire, probably he does not alternate his style: he may be taking on the voice of a pompous fool and needs to stick to it. In some writing, he cannot afford to vary his language or he will break a spell, a mood.

WRITING TWENTY-SIX: Write a report of a place, a person, or an event, maybe a short sketch of your grandfather modeled on the Davy Crockett article. Or a report of an event you know a certain group of readers would like to hear about. Find an angle, cram in the critical facts, keep the narrative alive with Alternating Current.

WRITING TWENTY-SEVEN: Write an editorial or column of opinion. Find an iceberg of fact on which to base what you present to the reader. No matter how lofty your thoughts, you can base them. You will do better, probably, to begin with the core of experience and let yourself earn the idea or opinion. Remember how the column "Happiness" suffered from lack of underpinnings. Note how this little essay grows out of experience:

OLD CREEPY DEATH

It's rainy and cool outside and we waded through too many ankle-deep puddles before getting back to the dorm. Now my feet are cold. But that's nothing new. They'll stay cold until I fall asleep and can't feel them anymore. I wonder what it would be like to go to sleep with warm feet? Even on recent warm nights they've been carefully smothered under layers of blankets and quilts that have been folded down to the end of the bunk. It would be fine if you could ignore them, but I never can. You're all warm and comfortable except for those two awful extremities. They ache cold. And though they seem to be separate from the rest of me, they are persistent in keeping me awake.

I once knew a girl who wore sleep socks. They were regular wool socks except they had felt faces on the soles of them. One was a woman's face with cute little bow lips and long eyelashes. She offered to let me wear them and I tried to. But I couldn't stand it. I kept thinking of those faces on the bottom of my feet and of how I had one male foot and one female foot. I didn't like the idea of the two of them being alone together down there, especially on my feet. It was no way to get my feet warm. Besides, I felt bad when I had to make a trip to the john and walked on their happy-go-lucky faces. I don't like the idea of socks, anyway. Even if they would work. My feet feel bound and too restricted. So, maybe I've chosen cold feet.

But what makes me so conscious of them is what the cold feels like. I've always thought that their kind of cold must be how death feels. Like poems have told me how death and coldness creep up on you until you're completely cold and completely dead. So every night I thrash my feet around to make sure the cold isn't creeping up my legs. When I think of me dying I think of dying in bed while I'm sleeping so I won't know about it. And I can't help but think that I'll most likely die the night that I can't keep the cold limited only to my feet. That's why I hate them the most, the pleasant thoughts that accompany them. I put off sleep for a while each night to make sure that the rest of me is staying warm. But then, I've probably got it figured all wrong. Death will probably play a trick and the cold will work its way from top to bottom. But that wouldn't really be so bad, to have your nice, warm, cozy tootsies be the last to go. Because as long as my feet are warm I can feel warm all over and I could ignore old creepy death.

LOIS BERG

When you write reports and columns of opinion, use the Alternating Current if it is appropriate. Just because you may be writing your own opinion doesn't mean you can forget your reader. He's alive. He wants to be kept awake while reading.

The Alternating Current is usually more appropriate to columns of opinions than to reports, but you saw at the beginning of this chapter how it gave texture to a report on Davy Crockett. Nevertheless, many reports call for a less attention-getting style. A business executive may ask an engineer or consultant to visit a plant and report on the efficiency of its operations. A scientist may have to report on the behavior of fish used in an experiment. Often their reports should be highly objective, keeping the observer out of the sentences as much as possible. However, those who write and read such reports should never forget that any human report is a product of an individual's perceptions.

irony. 2 a: *the use of words to express something other than and esp. the opposite of the literal meaning.*

Webster's Seventh New
Collegiate Dictionary

chapter 21
writing
indirectly

YOU DON'T HAVE to write in a straight line that runs right at your reader. You can shoot words off on a diagonal, a little off target, and expect the reader to see where the bull's-eye really is. Making a point indirectly gives it surprise.

You may turn upside down what you say. Exaggerate. You may say exactly the opposite of what you mean. Take up a serious subject lightly or a trivial subject heavily. A funeral is no place for jokes, but a writer can write humorously about funerals. Evelyn Waugh did and called his novel *The Loved One,* a story about an ostentatious burying park in California. You may joke about poverty. Jonathan Swift did and called his essay "A Modest Proposal for preventing the Children of Poor People from being a Burden to their Parents or the Country" (by roasting them as food for the rich).

Here are some of the ways a writer speaks indirectly:

(a) *A writer may play dumb,* pretend to be holding one opinion while tipping off the reader to his true, and often opposite, opinion.

In chapter seventeen of *Huckleberry Finn,* Samuel Clemens, talking through Huck, speaks so indirectly, yet with such a straight face, that many readers don't see what he is saying in this description of the Grangerford house and family:

> It was a mighty nice family, and a mighty nice house, too. I hadn't seen no house out in the country before that was so nice and had so much style. It didn't have an iron latch on

the front door, nor a wooden one with a buckskin string, but a brass knob to turn, the same as houses in a town. There warn't no bed in the parlor, not a sign of a bed; but heaps of parlors in towns has beds in them. There was a big fireplace that was bricked on the bottom, and the bricks was kept clean and red by pouring water on them and scrubbing them with another brick; sometimes they washed them over with red water-paint that they call Spanish-brown, same as they do in town. They had big brass dog-irons that could hold up a saw-log. There was a clock on the middle of the mantel-piece, with a picture of a town painted on the bottom half of the glass front, and a round place in the middle of it for the sun, and you could see the pendulum swing behind it. It was beautiful to hear that clock tick; and sometimes when one of these peddlers had been along and scoured her up and got her in good shape, she would start in and strike a hundred and fifty before she got tuckered out. They wouldn't took any money for her.

Well, there was a big outlandish parrot on each side of the clock, made out of something like chalk, and painted up gaudy. By one of the parrots was a cat made of crockery, and a crockery dog by the other; and when you pressed down on them they squeaked, but didn't open their mouths nor look different nor interested. They squeaked through underneath. There was a couple of big wild-turkey-wing fans spread out behind those things. On a table in the middle of the room was a kind of a lovely crockery basket that had apples and oranges and peaches and grapes piled up in it which was much redder and yellower and prettier than real ones is, but they warn't real because you could see where pieces had got chipped off and showed the white chalk or whatever it was, underneath.

This table had a cover made out of beautiful oil-cloth, with a red and blue spread-eagle painted on it, and a painted border all around. It come all the way from Philadelphia, they said. There was some books too, piled up perfectly exact, on each corner of the table. One was a big family Bible, full of pictures. One was "Pilgrim's Progress," about a man that left his family it didn't say why. I read considerable in it now and then. The statements was interesting, but tough. Another was "Friendship's Offering," full of beautiful stuff and poetry; but I didn't read the poetry.

Another was Henry Clay's Speeches, and another was Dr.
Gunn's Family Medicine, which told you all about what to
do if a body was sick or dead. There was a Hymn Book, and
a lot of other books. And there was nice split-bottom chairs,
and perfectly sound, too—not bagged down in the middle
and busted, like an old basket.

They had pictures hung on the walls—mainly Washing-
tons and Lafayettes, and battles, and Highland Mary, and
one called "Signing the Declaration." There was some that
they called crayons, which one of the daughters which was
dead made her own self when she was only fifteen years old.
They was different from many pictures I ever see before;
blacker, mostly, than is common. One was a woman in a slim
black dress, belted small under the arm-pits, with bulges like
a cabbage in the middle of the sleeves, and a large black
scoop-shovel bonnet with a black veil, and white slim ankles
crossed about with black tape, and very wee black slippers,
like a chisel, and she was leaning pensive on a tombstone on
her right elbow, under a weeping willow, and her other
hand hanging down her side holding a white handkerchief
and a reticule, and underneath the picture it said "Shall I
Never See Thee More Alas." Another one was a young lady
with her hair all combed up straight to the top of her head,
and knotted there in front of a comb like a chair-back, and
she was crying into a handkerchief and had a dead bird
laying on its back in her other hand with its heels up, and
underneath the picture it said "I Shall Never Hear Thy
Sweet Chirrup More Alas." There was one where a young
lady was at a window looking up at the moon, and tears
running down her cheeks; and she had an open letter in one
hand with black sealing-wax showing on one edge of it, and
she was mashing a locket with a chain to it against her
mouth, and underneath the picture it said "And Art Thou
Gone Yes Thou Art Gone Alas." These was all nice pictures,
I reckon, but I didn't somehow seem to take to them, because if ever I was down a little, they always give me the
fan-tods. Everybody was sorry she died, because she had laid
out a lot more of these pictures to do, and a body could see
by what she had done what they had lost. But I reckoned,
that with her disposition, she was having a better time in the
graveyard. She was at work on what they said was her greatest picture when she took sick, and every day and every

night it was her prayer to be allowed to live till she got it
done, but she never got the chance. It was a picture of a
young woman in a long white gown, standing on the rail of
a bridge all ready to jump off, with her hair all down her
back, and looking up to the moon, with the tears running
down her face, and she had two arms folded across her
breast, and two arms stretched out in front, and two more
reaching up towards the moon—and the idea was, to see
which pair would look best and then scratch out all the
other arms; but, as I was saying, she died before she got her
mind made up, and now they kept this picture over the head
of the bed in her room, and every time her birthday come
they hung flowers on it. Other times it was hid with a little
curtain. The young woman in the picture had a kind of a
nice sweet face, but there was so many arms it made her look
too spidery, seemed to me.

This young girl kept a scrap-book when she was alive, and
used to paste obituaries and accidents and cases of patient
suffering in it out of the *Presbyterian Observer*, and write
poetry after them out of her own head. It was very good
poetry. This is what she wrote about a boy by the name of
Stephen Dowling Bots that fell down a well and was
drownded:

ODE TO STEPHEN DOWLING BOTS, DEC'D.

And did young Stephen sicken,
  And did young Stephen die?
And did the sad hearts thicken,
  And did the mourners cry?

No; such was not the fate of
  Young Stephen Dowling Bots;
Though sad hearts round him thickened,
  'Twas not from sickness' shots.

No whooping-cough did rack his frame,
  Nor measles drear, with spots;
Not these impaired the sacred name
  Of Stephen Dowling Bots.

Despised love struck not with woe
  That head of curly knots,
Nor stomach troubles laid him low,
  Young Stephen Dowling Bots.

O no. Then list with tearful eye,
  Whilst I his fate do tell.
His soul did from this cold world fly,
  By falling down a well.

They got him out and emptied him;
  Alas it was too late;
His spirit was gone for to sport aloft
  In the realms of the good and great.

If Emmeline Grangerford could make poetry like that before she was fourteen, there ain't no telling what she could
a done by-and-by. Buck said she could rattle off poetry like
nothing. She didn't ever have to stop to think. He said she
would slap down a line, and if she couldn't find anything to
rhyme with it she would just scratch it out and slap down
another one, and go ahead. She warn't particular, she could
write about anything you choose to give her to write about,
just so it was sadful. Every time a man died, or a woman
died, or a child died, she would be on hand with her
"tribute" before he was cold. She called them tributes.
The neighbors said it was the doctor first, then Emmeline,
then the undertaker—the undertaker never got in ahead of
Emmeline but once, and then she hung fire on a rhyme for
the dead person's name, which was Whistler. She warn't ever
the same, after that; she never complained, but she kind of
pined away and did not live long.

What you have read is a mild satire of the décor of a house and
a strong satire of a sentimental little girl who wrote bad poetry. Obviously Huck thinks the house beautiful, but Clemens suggests with
small cues that he does not. He might admire artificial fruit, but when
he has Huck mention "where pieces had got chipped off and showed
the white chalk or whatever it was," you should begin to suspect his
intentions in this writing. Think of the whole picture: the mantel
a garish display of painted scene; crockery birds, dog, cat; and turkey
wings. On the table an oil-cloth spread displaying a spread eagle—
more wings. The books: standard family pieces, revealing no indi-
viduality of mind in their choice, all perfectly piled as if never used.
The pictures on the wall patriotic and sentimental. The room is as
gaudy as a souvenir shop at Niagara Falls, and Clemens wants the
reader to know this at the same time he wants him to see that Huck
Finn is completely inexperienced in judging such matters. The room
goes perfectly with Emmeline Grangerford's poetry, which Twain
hits more directly in hard satire.

Clemens' indirectness enables him to make three points at once. He scores the Grangerfords' lack of cultural independence, shows his hero limited in experience, and slyly criticizes the American middle-class for its use of pseudo art objects in its homes.

(b) *A writer may directly say he doesn't understand, when he does,* as this high school student did in a poem:

> I wonder if the mail has come
> (Not that I really care.)
> Our quarrel was really very dumb.
> I wonder if the mail has come!
> (I shouldn't have said that 'bout her hair.)
> Should I have written? Do I dare?
> I wonder if the mail has come.
> (Not that I really care.)
>
> KATHY CURRIER

(c) *A writer may take on another character's views,* perhaps his own when he was young, and pretend he doesn't know any more now than he did then, as did this girl in an account of her childhood:

TOMATOES

I was four when I had my first encounter with a tomato. We lived in Santa Barbara in a gray house separate from our neighbor by a garden of green and black stripes. The old man, Mr. Swift, fussed in his garden each dewy morning and worried his tomato plants into growing green and tall.

One early summer morning I was playing in the outskirts of the garden and happened to notice ladybugs crawling on Mr. Swift's prize plants. I didn't want them chewing up the fruits of my dear neighbor's labor so I decided to help him. I knew he would thank me when he found out I had gotten rid of the speckled pests for him. The only trouble was I was afraid to touch the bugs, so I had to break off each leaf that had an orange dot on it. I had gone through six rows when my mother called to me through the screened window that lunch was ready. Mr. Swift never knew that I tried to help him because I wasn't able to finish my job. A mysterious telephone call during lunch upset my mother and she spanked me right in the middle of a fried egg sandwich and wouldn't let me go outdoors the rest of the day.

It's a wonder that poor Mr. Swift's garden ever grew. One evening after supper my mother sent me out in the yard to break up a tea party that had been going all afternoon. Three of my dolls lay asleep on the ground around the orange crate tea table, and I feared they would be sick because it had turned very cold. I bundled them in my wagon and was pulling them to the back door when I noticed the garden.

Someone had played a mean trick on poor old Mr. Swift. Each of his tomato plants was hidden under a sawed-off milk carton. I knew they couldn't breathe inside there and would die if I didn't uncover them. It didn't take as long as getting rid of the bugs because I could just kick over each box with my foot. It was dark when I finished and got my dolls in the house. My mother scolded me for tracking in mud; I had been too late though, because next morning all the plants lay wilted on the ground. My neighbor didn't understand when I told him they died because they couldn't get their breath—he said, "The wind did it." I don't think he was a very smart farmer.

I don't know if Mr. Swift planted tomatoes again the next year because that winter we moved to Nebraska. We lived on the corner one block over and two blocks down from Grandma's house. In the spring Grandma gave me some seeds so I could plant a garden of my very own and learn responsibility. I decided I would have tomatoes because I already knew all about growing them. Besides, maybe I could send some to poor Mr. Swift. Daddy helped me. He spaded up the garden and planted the seeds, and then I watched them grow. My mother let me use my allowance to buy a sprinkling can from the dime store so I could water my garden. Daddy showed me which were the weeds and I tugged them out by the roots so they wouldn't choke my tomatoes. My garden grew and Daddy put a tall slender stake for each plant to climb. I watered my garden four times the first day and at least once a month after that. My garden grew as I played with the three boys next door, but I never got any tomatoes to send to my old neighbor. My mother told me that the odd blue flowers on my tomato plants were called four o'clocks, and I picked a bouquet for her.

CAROLINE SIEBLER

When you write indirectly, you must be consistent in style and viewpoint. You cannot use the Alternating Current without blowing the whole electric circuit. You must take a position or attitude or mood or role and stay in it throughout your writing. You are working on at least two levels. On the first, you must move authentically at all times. If your name is Alice and you are traveling through a Wonderland, you must believe in it all the time. You may have doubts and express amazement at what you see, but finally you must believe. And the Queens and Humpty Dumptys you encounter must be naïve and small-minded at all times on the first level, no matter how cleverly on the second level you manage to make them appear normal human beings.

In the story "Tomatoes," the author maintains the child's point of view beautifully except in a few spots, such as when she uses the word "outskirts" and the phrase "fruits of my dear neighbor's labor." Look for others. When you play another role than your own, you must stay in a voice that is right for that role.

> *Either stick to tradition or see that your inventions be consistent.*
>
> HORACE

(d) *A writer may make fun of pompous or pedantic persons or milksop and toadying persons by mimicking their language and pushing it to further excesses.* This exaggeration is often called burlesquing. For example:

IMPORTANT THINGS TO REMEMBER

Some things in this course will be more important than others. The most important thing to remember is that the War of the Tulips was fought before the Treaty of Pootrecht. Other important battles were the Alley Ambush of 1412 and the Small Slaughter of 1303. These are all important, but not as important as the date of the War of the Tulips.

(e) *A writer may blow up a trivial matter so large that it bursts.* For example:

The students who support the campaign to bring greasy and crumbly potato chips back to our cafeteria have completely rejected the traditions of Rich Central and are attempting to maliciously destroy the unity of our school

> ... They are undoubtedly using innocent potato chips as a
> guise for their plot to overthrow the Cafeteria Honor
> Committee and instill chaos, disunity, and trash through-
> out the school ...

This was the method Jonathan Swift used in *Gulliver's Travels*, a
cutting satire of the way adult human beings conduct themselves in
every department of life. In one part of the book he blew men up
and in another he reduced them.

(f) *A writer may exaggerate his case*, speaking excessively so that
what he attacks seems not simply deserving of criticism but absolutely ridiculous. This method is often used by an essayist, columnist,
or editorial writer. Here is Thoreau writing in *Walden*:

> And I am sure that I never read any memorable news in a
> newspaper. If we read of one man robbed, or murdered,
> or killed by accident, or one house burned, or one vessel
> wrecked, or one steamboat blown up, or one cow run over
> on the Western Railroad, or one mad dog killed, or one lot of
> grasshoppers in the winter,—we never need read of another.
> One is enough. If you are acquainted with the principle,
> what do you care for a myriad instances and applications?
> To a philosopher all *news*, as it is called, is gossip, and
> they who edit and read it are old women over their tea. Yet
> not a few are greedy after this gossip. There was such a
> rush, as I hear, the other day at one of the offices to learn
> the foreign news by the last arrival, that several large
> squares of plate glass belonging to the establishment were
> broken by the pressure,—news which I seriously think a
> ready wit might write a twelvemonth, or twelve years,
> beforehand with sufficient accuracy. As for Spain, for in-
> stance, if you know how to throw in Don Carlos and the
> Infanta, and Don Pedro and Seville and Granada, from
> time to time in the right proportions,—they may have
> changed the names a little since I saw the papers,—and
> serve up a bull-fight when other entertainments fail, it will
> be true to the letter, and give us as good an idea of the
> exact state or ruin of things in Spain as the most succinct
> and lucid reports under this head in the newspapers: and
> as for England, almost the last significant scrap of news
> from that quarter was the revolution of 1649; and if you
> have learned the history of her crops for an average year,
> you never need attend to that thing again, unless your

speculations are of a merely pecuniary character. If one may judge who rarely looks into the newspapers, nothing new does ever happen in foreign parts, a French revolution not excepted.

(g) *A writer may treat an act lightly that is ordinarily feared*, in order to reduce its power.

For example, Julie Beach, writing in a student newspaper, begins a column with these paragraphs:

> **For those students who have not yet reached the grand old age of eligibility for a driver's license, here are a few helpful hints to get them through the ordeal.**
>
> **First of all, get plenty of sleep the night before the test is going to be taken. It helps one get a passing grade if the road signs can be read clearly.**
>
> **When walking out to the parking lot with the policeman, try to remember where the car is parked. It doesn't pay to put him into a grouchy mood by walking around the lot for half an hour.**
>
> **After getting into the car, remember to unlock the door on the passenger's side. If a tapping noise is heard, don't be alarmed. It is only the officer knocking on the window, trying to get in.**
>
> **The key should now be placed in the ignition, then turned. If for some unknown reason it won't turn, take it out and flip it over; it was probably in upside down . . .**

(Reminder for persons working on tightening: in paragraph 2 the words "is going to be taken" could be omitted, and also the word "noise" in paragraph 4.)

(h) *A writer may turn upside down or outrageously distort the treatment of an event* in order to ridicule the straight, sober, or trite treatment it is usually given.

For example, sports writers frequently present a dull roundup of the year, in which they try to make every team's record look impressive. Steve Henson, sports editor for *The Torch* (newspaper of Rich Township High School Central Campus, Park Forest, Illinois, May 13, 1966), decided he had had enough of such trite stuff and wrote a spoof, part of which follows:

> **. . . You all remember Central's football team, better known as Bill Barz. Smashing through the season nearly undefeated (well, you can't win 'em all) Barz and his teammates beat up**

everybody (if not on the field then out in the parking lot after the game). Cinderella Quanstrom put on his helmet and glass slippers and really turned in a great season. We can't forget guys like Denny Zumbahlen and Larry Morris, who averaged 38 tackles per game—31 of them after the whistle had blown.

The Olympian Gridders were undefeated at home, using the advantage of the home field, the home refs, and Central's own Mr. Matheny running the scoreboard. It was simple—how else could you beat somebody 51–0? "Football Player of the Year" has to go to little 6'8", 295 lb. Bill Barz, to go along with his other awards of all-conference, all-area, all-suburban, all-state, and all-world . . .

The varsity cagers were a great team, though, and exciting to watch. Hundreds of records were set during the season. Hot Dog Madderom averaged about 40 points per game and set a game high record when he tossed in 68 points against T. F. South. Randy hit on an amazing 22 field goals in that game in only 97 shots from the field. His best performance was in the Oklahoma game. Randy really scored and made several fine passes. Ed Younker tied the world record of falling asleep during a game (17 times) and Bob Moyer hit the most number of free-throws without a miss by a manager: 2 (also a world record). Bob Ewing grew the longest beard by a 6-foot forward in the entire South Suburban area . . .

The Rich Central golf team has not been up to par this spring. Don Richmond, the "most consistent performer," really tore up the course at Olympia Fields last week, with a 67; in fact some fairways are still being repaired. He shot a Country Club record 58 last Saturday, with an eagle on the 5th hole, birdies on the 7th and 8th, and by forgetting to play the back nine . . .

One of Steve Henson's strategies in this column is to begin a statement in conventional manner and then end it with a kicker:

. . . who averaged 38 tackles per game—*31 of them after the whistle had blown.*
. . . He shot a Country Club record 58 last Saturday with an eagle on the 5th hole, birdies on the 7th and 8th, and *by forgetting to play the back nine.*

Another of his strategies is to present an actual fact and invent new facts which carry it to ridiculous heights:

> . . . to go along with his other awards of all-conference, all-area, all-suburban, all-state, and *all-world*.

The truth is that Rich Central teams had a good season; for example, the baseball team won the District Championship and the football team lost only one game. But the indirect writer does not speak pure and whole fact. He risks being misunderstood. Mr. Henson's spoofing is consistent enough to make most readers aware of his intent, but even though he said, "we remind you to not believe everything you read" one student complained in a letter, saying,

> You stated that *no* one ever went to *any* of the wrestling meets, and you did not even recognize the existence of a wrestling team.
>
> This proves you have never gone to a wrestling meet; regular, or any of their district, sectional, or state meets . . . So shape up, and apologize for the unjust insult you tossed to our boys, or don't call yourself a fair sports editor.

Answering that letter, Mr. Henson said:

> If you believed that I was not exaggerating when I said "nobody went to any of their meets" and that no wrestling team even existed, then you must have taken everything else in the column seriously too. You must have believed that I was not exaggerating when I said that Barz was 6'8" and 295 lb., or that Madderom scored 68 points against T. F. South, or that Zumbahlen and Morris tackled 31 men after the whistle, or that Ewing tossed the shot through the gyn wall into the little theatre.

He shows by his answer that he realizes that indirect writing cannot alternate between straight and indirect expression. It must be consistent in its attitude.

At times all of us speak indirectly naturally and with ease. To a girl falsely modest about her pretty new dress, we say, "You look horrible, Anne, absolutely rotten." In sarcasm we say to a person who has assigned us an unpleasant job, "Oh, this is lovely work—I wouldn't want to do anything else." A common line spoken by a soldier in World War II to another soldier digging a ditch was: "Whatya gripin' about? You're learnin' a trade." We mimic the way a teacher acts or talks. In dozens of ways, we speak with double tongue, knowing closely our audience and sensing how far we can go in indirection without losing them. As writers, we can learn to sustain and unify a piece of indirect communication which cuts and cuts down, astounds and delights, cajoles and teases.

WRITING TWENTY-EIGHT: Write quickly a piece of indirect writing about something or someone you know well and feel strongly about. Whatever your degree of factualness or exaggeration, make your statement ring true. Do not attack or ridicule someone for something he did not do or say and cannot have done or said. All must be true, at least in the sense of being representative. Play with ideas, approaches, words. Then reconstruct, make consistent, tighten, sharpen, polish.

> *You writers, choose a subject that is within your powers, and ponder long what your shoulders can and cannot bear. He who makes every effort to select his theme aright will be at no loss for choice of words or lucid arrangement. Unless I am mistaken, the force and charm of arrangement will be found in this: to say at once what ought at once to be said, deferring many points, and waiving them for the moment.*
>
> HORACE, 13 B.C.

"Of course you know your A B C?"
said the Red Queen.
"To be sure I do," said Alice.
"So do I," the White Queen whispered; "we'll often say it over together, dear. And I'll tell you a secret—I can read words of one letter! Isn't that grand? However, don't be discouraged. You'll come to it in time."

LEWIS CARROLL

chapter 22

para-
phrasing

HENRY THOREAU was right to say that we should wear old clothes for major enterprises. We should confront our severest tests feeling most ourselves, with patches at elbow and knee that remind us of work already done and years already lived. And so with words, we should own them by use. They should sound right to us because we have heard them in our own mouths.

And yet the day will come when we attend the President's ball or our own wedding and we cannot wear old clothes. Then we need to have practiced wearing a stiff collar or it will redden our neck and stiffen our behavior. And so with words, if we do not practice using words stiff to us, we will never make them supple and comfortable in our mouths.

The dilemma: how to enlarge our vocabularies so as to write more accurately and precisely and yet avoid speaking a phony language.

One way is to increase our reading vocabulary—to look up new words in dictionaries and fix their meanings so securely they become as familiar to us as friends' faces. Then to use them strategically in our writing, but sparingly. We are apt to use new words clumsily, so they do not quite fit the grooves in which we place them, so they bring to our readers' faces smiles of amusement rather than admiration.

We must learn all the ways of a word before introducing it to others
as ours. We can do this by studying good writers closely, *paraphrasing*
their words into our words while trying to retain their meanings—
all shades and connotations—exactly.

Often teachers say they never knew a subject until they began to
teach it. Often writers say they never knew what another writer was
saying until they tried to put it in their own words. Paraphrasing is
difficult. You must thoroughly understand a writer before you can
translate him into other words. And your words must not only make
as much sense as his—and the same sense—but they must be written
in American-English idiom, the way we Americans put such words
together.

Here are several lines from Walter Lippmann's *Public Opinion,*
a book written in 1922, still the most penetrating statement ever
made on the subject of stereotyping. Mr. Lippmann wrote:

LIPPMANN I

There is, of course, some connection between the scene outside and the mind through which we watch it, just as there
are some long-haired men and short-haired women in radi-
cal gatherings. But to the hurried observer a slight connection is enough. If there are two bobbed heads and four
beards in the audience, it will be a bobbed and bearded
audience to the reporter who knows beforehand that such
gatherings are composed of people with these tastes in the
management of their hair.

PARAPHRASE I

There is obviously some relation between the exterior situation and the mind with which we observe it, just as there
are some black-jacketed men and tight-slacked women at
drag raceways. But to the hasty perceiver a small relationship is sufficient. If there are two black jackets and four
pairs of tight slacks in the crowd, it will be a black-jacketed
and tight-slacked group to the reporter who believes ahead
of time that such crowds are made up of persons who dress
this way.

This paraphrase is valid. Its new phrases remain faithful to Lippmann's ideas. It uses specific examples of its own which reveal that
the paraphraser understands the point of Lippmann's examples.
And its phrasing remains true to American-English idiom, except in

the somewhat ridiculous hyphenated word involving the opposite notions of tight and slack.

One cannot make a a good paraphrase by automatically substituting a dictionary synonym for each word in the original text. He must understand that text and the precise meaning in that context of each word the author has used. Like a good translator of a foreign language, he must take the thought into his mind and speak it forth again in natural, idiomatic phrases. A trained reader can easily see when a paraphraser is just substituting words rather than understanding and translating. For example, here is another statement by Lippmann:

LIPPMANN II

In all these instances we must note particularly one common factor. It is the insertion between man and his environment of a pseudo-environment.

A student attempting to paraphrase those sentences wrote:

PARAPHRASE II

In every case we must underly one general fact. It's the entering of a false behavior of humans in their society.

He is not using American-English idiomatically. Americans do not say that a person "underlies a fact." The next sentence in the paraphrase is totally unidiomatic. It does not make sense at all. Who is entering a false behavior? Is a behavior ever entered? The paraphraser has not even seen the principal relationship of the elements in Lippmann's second sentence. On one side is man and on the other his environment. Between them is a pseudo or false environment.

man	false	environment
	environment	

At one time the paraphrase substituted the word *behavior* for *environment* and at another time *society* for *environment*. Society may be man's environment at times, but behavior never. The weakness of *society* as a synonym for *environment* is that it is not all-inclusive. Other things, such as air, land, and water, may also be man's environment. A sounder word for *environment* would be *surroundings*, which could include both man and nature. If the paraphraser could not come up with as apt a synonym as *surroundings* for *environment*, he would have done better simply to repeat the word *environment*. In para-

phrasing one cannot always find a precise and accurate substitute word
—yet precision and accuracy are the first requirements.

PARAPHRASING ONE: Write a paraphrase of the following passage
by Paul Goodman:

> Consider a likely useful job. A youth who is alert and will-
> ing but not "verbally intelligent"—perhaps he has quit high
> school at the eleventh grade (the median), as soon as he
> legally could—chooses for auto mechanic. That's a good
> job, familiar to him, he often watched them as a kid. It's
> careful and dirty at the same time. In a small garage it's
> sociable; one can talk to the customers (girls). You please
> people in trouble by fixing their cars, and a man is proud
> to see rolling out on its own the car that limped in behind
> the tow truck. The pay is as good as the next fellow's, who
> is respected.
>
> So our young man takes this first-rate job. But what when
> he then learns that the cars have a built-in obsolescence,
> that the manufacturers do not want them to be repaired or
> repairable? They have lobbied a law that requires them
> to provide spare parts for only five years (it used to be ten).
> Repairing the new cars is often a matter of cosmetics, not
> mechanics; and the repairs are pointlessly expensive—a tail
> fin might cost $150. The insurance rates therefore double
> and treble on old and new cars both. Gone are the days of
> keeping the jalopies in good shape, the artist-work, of a
> proud mechanic. But everybody is paying for foolishness,
> for in fact the new models are only trivially superior; the
> whole thing is a sell.

In paraphrasing this passage, use words in a manner that belongs
to you and other Americans you know. Don't paraphrase the first
sentence by saying, "Now bring to your own attention a possibly
efficacious livelihood possessing utility." Your voice may differ from
other Americans of your age, but you would probably do better to
begin, "Think about a possibly valuable employment." If *employment* sticks in your pen, repeat *job*. Take up the challenge: try to
restate all statements but if all other words you find distort Mr.
Goodman's meaning, repeat his word. When you finish the first draft
of your paraphrase, read it aloud—the surest way to discover whether
or not you are writing in the American idiom. And expect that you
will need a second draft for sandpapering the edges. Read your paraphrase to others who have tried the same task.

PARAPHRASING TWO: Write a paraphrase of the following passage by Walter Lippmann.

STEREOTYPES

The subtlest and most pervasive of all influences are those which create and maintain the repertory of stereotypes. We are told about the world before we see it. We imagine most things before we experience them. And those preconceptions, unless education has made us acutely aware, govern deeply the whole process of perception. They mark out certain objects as familiar or strange, emphasizing the difference, so that the slightly familiar is seen as very familiar, and the somewhat strange as sharply alien. They are aroused by small signs, which may vary from a true index to a vague analogy. Aroused, they flood fresh vision with older images, and project into the world what has been resurrected in memory. Were there no practical uniformities in the environment, there would be no economy and only error in the human habit of accepting foresight for sight. But there are uniformities sufficiently accurate, and the need of economizing attention is so inevitable, that the abandonment of all stereotypes for a wholly innocent approach to experience would impoverish human life.

What matters is the character of the stereotypes, and the gullibility with which we employ them. And these in the end depend upon those inclusive patterns which constitute our philosophy of life. If in that philosophy we assume that the world is codified according to a code which we possess, we are likely to make our reports of what is going on describe a world run by our code. But if our philosophy tells us that each man is only a small part of the world, that his intelligence catches at best only phases and aspects in a coarse net of ideas, then, when we use our stereotypes, we tend to know that they are only stereotypes, to hold them lightly, to modify them gladly. We tend, also, to realize more and more clearly when our ideas started, where they started, how they came to us, why we accepted them. All useful history is antiseptic in this fashion. It enables us to know what fairy tale, what school book, what tradition, what novel, play, picture, phrase, planted one preconception in this mind, another in that mind.

The purpose of this exercise is to sharpen your understanding and command of words, to present to you words new and old to you that carry new shades of meaning. You must get your clues as to the meaning of each word from the context in which it appears. What is Lippmann's main point? How does that point weigh upon his words to bend or press them toward one of their possible meanings rather than another? You must use a good dictionary constantly and never be content with the first meaning of a word you encounter until you have looked further. Study all possible meanings and try to guess which one Lippmann intends here. For example, in another place in his book Lippmann says:

> The alternative to the use of fictions is direct exposure to the ebb and flow of sensation. This is not a real alternative, for however refreshing it is to see at times with a perfectly innocent eye, innocence itself is not wisdom, though a source and corrective of wisdom.

Considering what you have read so far in these excerpts from *Public Opinion*, which of the following words do you think most accurately paraphrases *innocent* here?

honest	fresh	unprejudiced	naive
harmless	moral	clear-eyed	guiltless

None of these words expresses precisely what Lippmann means by *innocent* here. No dictionary can give every possible meaning which an accurate writer may build up for a word. Probably the words *unprejudiced* and *fresh* are nearest to Lippmann's meaning of *innocent* here. *Unprejudiced* in the sense that the eye and the mind attached to it were not overly influenced by what they perceived in the past, but were approaching a new experience relatively freshly, ready to see the object before them as well as to see it in terms of past views of somewhat similar objects.

From this example, you can see that there are no limits to the depths of subtlety you may descend to in paraphrasing a keen and sensitive writer's sentences.

PARAPHRASING THREE: Choose a passage of one to two hundred words which challenges you to new perceptions. Copy it down and then paraphrase it. If possible, persuade another person to paraphrase it and compare your version with his.

> *It is not all books that are as dull as their readers.*
>
> HENRY THOREAU

chapter 23

the
order
of
words

A CHILD OF SIX speaks as if he knew his meaning depends a great deal on word order. He wouldn't think of saying:

Of wouldn't he think saying.

And he wouldn't mess up the agreement signals in this sentence by using a word that signals twoness when it needs to signal oneness:

Johnny and Bill has his own bike.

And he wouldn't say:

It was nice of they.

because in the American grammatical system words like *he, she,* or *they* preceded by prepositions signal their relationship by changing to the object form (*him, her,* or *them*). Kids know this by the time they're six or eight. But sometimes they run into an adult—maybe a teacher—who is so worried about someone saying,

> You and me should go to the show.

that they say,

> She did not give it *to* you and *I*

when their unconscious and normal feeling for the signal would make them say,

> She did not give it *to* you and *me.*

J. D. Salinger made his hero Holden Caulfield, in *The Catcher in the Rye,* talk in this highly self-conscious ungrammatical way:

> I think I probably woke he and his wife up . . .

When Eudora Welty said that beginning and professional writers have the same troubles—not being serious or truthful—she might have added that they both have the same troubles with grammar. Most editors find little that is grammatically weak about the writing they edit, and when they do, the weaknesses are usually confined to a few troubles to be expected in the writing of anyone using the American grammatical system. Frequently they involve (1) confusing word order, (2) lack of clear signal by pronouns, and (3) verbs that do not signal which nouns they belong to.

In reading over the first draft of your writing, look first for these possible weak spots.

Word order signals meaning:

Original. When green I love the woods most of all.

Is that when I am green (sick at the stomach) (Young, like a green plant?), or when the woods are green? If the latter, the sentence should read:

Revision. I love the woods when green most of all.

or

Revision. I love the green woods most of all.

Thoreau opened Chapter Two of *Walden* with this sentence:

Original. At a certain season of our life we are accustomed to consider every spot as the possible site of a house.

His grammar would have been slightly confusing had he written:

Misrevision. We are accustomed to consider every spot at a certain season of our life as the possible site of a house.

Now *spot* and *season* are too close to each other. The phrase *at a certain season* should be close to *accustomed*.

In your writing, place next to each other those words which belong together in meaning. In the following sentence, the words in italics and in small capitals belong together in meaning but are separated from each other in position:

> This task, which George found highly agonizing, *grew*
> under the heat of the afternoon sun *soon* to be *unbearable*,
> and he QUIT working at it steadily EVENTUALLY.

When the words are rearranged (and a Whichery removed), the sentence is improved:

Revision. Under the heat of the afternoon sun, this agonizing task soon grew unbearable and George eventually quit working at it steadily.

The new order makes more sense, but it reveals the sloppy thought on the part of the writer. If the task "soon" grew unbearable, then why did George wait until "eventually" (whatever that means) to stop working at it? Either the "soon" or the "eventually" should be eliminated. Better yet, the writer might tell the reader what he means by "soon" or "eventually." How many hours or minutes?

Not every sentence changes its meaning with a change of word order. For example:

Original. Our minds thus grow in spots . . .

Revision. Thus our minds grow in spots . . .

Revision. Thus grow our minds in spots . . .

Revision. In spots thus grow our minds . . .

American-English grammar does not do all its signaling of meaning by word order.

REVISING ELEVEN: Examine your last two long pieces of writing for blunders and weaknesses in word order. Write down on a separate sheet of paper your weak sentences and your revision of them. Reading aloud will help you in this task.

All writers and speakers occasionally let one of the segments of their sentence dangle out on a limb where it can fall off the tree. The most distinguished example is probably a sentence in Thomas Jefferson's First Inaugural Address:

> About to enter, fellow citizens, on the exercise of duties
> which comprehend everything dear and valuable to you,
> it is proper that you should understand what I deem the es-
> sential principles of our government, and consequently
> those which ought to shape its administration.

What is "about to enter" is Jefferson, not "you," who are fellow citizens,
or "it," which here is one of those vague words which can't enter anything. A dangling construction fails to make clear who is doing what.

> While walking back from my English class, a squirrel
> came up and stepped on my foot.

Squirrels returning from English classes will upset anyone.
   More examples of dangling constructions:

> Not finishing dinner until 8:30, another problem was in
> the making.
> By subtly mentioning to one set of parents that it would
> be nice if we could all be together, they usually take the
> hint and invite others.

But enough of these sinful errors. The good writer masters grammar
in order to control his words, and meaning is his target. In a given
paragraph, he may use an expression that is technically a dangling
construction but nevertheless communicates his meaning clearly. For
example, here is the masterful English writer William Hazlitt beginning the third paragraph of his essay on Sir James Mackintosh:

> To consider him in the last point of view first. As a poli-
> tical partisan, he is rather the lecturer than the advocate.

The first sentence does not show clearly who is doing the considering,
and the whole group of words is not really a sentence at all. But it
works, and an editor would be a fool to change it.
   The commonest word-order change made in manuscripts by editors
is to bring together subjects and verbs which have been thoroughly
separated.

Original. *Professor Rending,* in approaching his subject, stumbled in
circles, like a drunk.

Revision. In approaching his subject, *Professor Rending* stumbled
in circles, like a drunk.

The method here is to pull out the segment of a sentence which is
properly introductory, such as

When he was altogether prepared,

from the sentence in which it occurs:

> President Wilson, when he was altogether prepared, presented his plan to the League of Nations.

and put it at the beginning.

Revision. When he was altogether prepared, President Wilson presented his plan to the League of Nations.

Often, such rearrangement allows the writer to eliminate a wasted expression such as a Whooery:

Original. Queen Gertrude is a weak person, who is, in spite of her faults, held in high regard by the three men in her life.

Revised. In spite of her faults, Queen Gertrude is held in high regard by the three men in her life.

All writers slip occasionally in making clear the reference between pronouns and their antecedents and the agreement between subject and verb. Therefore editors routinely check for these slips and find them frequently:

> Sol and his buddy Georgie, who is his uncle's favorite baseball player, often *tries* to eat more than he can hold.

Revised. Sol and his buddy Georgie—his uncle's favorite baseball player—often *try* to eat more than they can hold.

> The haggling and the bickering and the many hours of long drawn-out close reading I had to do when I was tired— it was all too much for me.

Revised. The haggling and the bickering and the many hours of long drawn-out close reading I had to do when I was so tired were all too much for me.

Note that most slips in pronoun reference and noun-verb agreement occur in long sentences which interrupt themselves with qualifications and side-trips. Editors examine such sentences closely, expecting meaning may have slid into a ditch.

Commonly professional writers use *which* and *that* to refer to the the word immediately preceding:

> I like HAMBURGERS *which* are well done but not dry.

But increasingly these days, they are using *which* or *that* to refer to a whole action described in a number of preceding words:

> Renny approves of making changes now, which is all right with me.

You will do well to stay with the conservative practice of including a clear referent word immediately preceding *which* or *that* as in HAM-BURGERS *which*. If you ignore this practice and create a sentence that cannot be misunderstood by your reader, let it stand; but the odds are against you. Note that if the example contained three more words,

> Renny approves of making changes now in the plan, which is all right with me.

the reader couldn't be sure whether what is "all right with me" is the whole plan or the changes. The reader's understandable interpretation of the sentence is probably that *which* refers to *plan*, the word immediately preceding it.

These little matters of reference and agreement are the higgledy-piggledy of grammar. More crucial matters exist. When you think of word order—the way words come together in phrases and clauses (pieces, hunks, segments, absolutes, whatever you call them at the moment)—think of how you may control it to bring your writing alive.

Try telescoping three or four sentences into one, so that the first reaches out and grabs part of those that follow. Here are three sentences too closely related to stand separately:

Original. Immediately Juliet sees the only solution to her problem. That solution is suicide. This is a highly illogical choice.

You can tack on to the first sentence the essential elements of the second and third sentences:

Revision. Immediately Juliet sees the only solution to her problem—suicide, a highly illogical choice.

Such tacking-on must be done with care. If the sentences preceding those above have suggested that the author is judging Juliet's behavior, this revision may be clear. But if not, the reader might take the sentence to say that Juliet sees suicide as a highly illogical choice, a meaning which would jar against the notion embodied in "only solution."

Study the Tack-On sentences of good writers. You will see they frequently write down a subject and verb (and sometimes an object of the verb) and then simply add nouns or prepositional phrases, or phrases beginning with verb forms ending in *-ing* or *-ed*:

(a) *It would become a sorcery,*
              a magic.

ARCHIBALD MAC LEISH

(b) *There is a pulpit at the head of the hall,*
        occupied by a handsome gray-haired judge
            with a faculty of appearing pleasant and impartial
                to the disinterested spectator,
                            and
                        prejudiced and frosty
                to the last degree
            to the prisoner at the bar.

MARK TWAIN

(c) *Each of us lives and works on a small part of the earth's surface,*
                moves in a small circle,
                        and
    of these acquaintances
                knows only a few intimately.

WALTER LIPPMANN

(d) *There were several ladies on board,*
        quite remarkably beautiful or good-looking,
        most of them, alas,
                now dead.

IVAN TURGENEV

(e) *Let us arrange the contents of the heap into a line,* with
        the works that convey pure information at one end, and
        the works that create pure atmosphere at the other end, and
        the works that do both in their intermediate positions,
                the whole line being graded so that we pass from
                one attitude to another.

E. M. FORSTER

Occasionally an author uses the Tack-On method at the beginning
of his sentence:

(f) Approaching Concord, doing forty, doing forty-five, doing fifty,
        the steering wheel held snug in my palms,
        the highway held grimly in my vision,
        the crown of the road now serving me (on the righthand curves),
                now defeating me (on the lefthand curves),
    I began to rouse myself from the stupefaction which
            a day's motor journey induces.

E. B. WHITE

Most beginning writers need to nudge themselves into Tacking-
On more often but the habit comes naturally to many persons. These
statements were written by high school students not coached to
Tack-On:

It is the great American tradition to shed your
anxieties and slothfully recline at the rim of a pond,
        resting and
        letting your unattended pole slip in the motionless wet.

While playing tennis I feel a sense
of freedom,
of being able to release the pent-up emotions from
        hours, days.

Man, who could have been so useful, is now dead,
not physically,
but emotionally and mentally.

Another way of exploiting the force of word-order in American-English is to place a word in an unusual or dominant position in the sentence.

> *[Ask] How many words out of their usual place, and whether this alteration makes the statement in any way more interesting or more energetic.*
>
> **EZRA POUND**

In many sentences the position of most weight for a word is the end. Frequently you can punch a word by putting it last in a sentence.

> **I went up to get a friend to go to class with. While waiting for her to get ready, I glanced around the dorm room. There were clothes, hairdryers, curlers, pressers, strewn all around the six-girl room. On the desk sat a book entitled *Social Disorganization*.**

Note how the power of the statement would be lessened had the last sentence been written:

> A book entitled *Social Disorganization* sat on the desk.

Of Sir Walter Scott, William Hazlitt wrote:

> The old world is to him a crowded map; the new one a dull, hateful blank.

Had he placed his words in normal order, he would have written less forcefully:

> The old world is a crowded map to him; the new one a dull, hateful blank.

Hazlitt's version forces the essential words to the end of each word group, where they gather power and achieve parallelism. To move a word out of normal position is to surprise the reader.

Normal Order. He was a lost man.

Unusual Order. He was a man lost.

A writer must develop an ear for normal word order and respect that order. If he continually scrambles it, he will confuse his reader rather than surprise him. The principle involved here is the old one mentioned in Chapter 8: repeat and vary. Vary the normal pattern, but sparingly. And don't forget to create a pattern of expectation in the first place.

REVISING TWELVE: Take two of your past writings, one free writing and one a planned longer work, and go over each word and sentence to see where you can change word order and improve the clarity or force of your statements. Write in the changes on the original so you and others can see what difference they make in the writing.

"He has got no good red blood in his body," said Sir James.

"No. Somebody put a drop under a magnifying-glass, and it was all semi-colons and parentheses," said Mrs. Cadwallader.

GEORGE ELIOT

chapter 24
observing conventions

FROM THE AGE OF FIVE onward most Americans know and practice the social conventions of their region and economic class. They say "thank you" and "you're welcome" and they eat with or without napkins or finger bowls or whatever is proper to the persons they associate with. Their ego is involved. They want to be liked, to feel right in the social circle they choose for themselves.

But most Americans don't know the publishing conventions of the educated world. They have been taught commas and semicolons as they have been taught "please" and "May I introduce my brother—" but each year in school they learn them for a test and forget them the following day. Why? Because they never expect to have their writing published, or even dittoed and passed around the class. Their ego is not involved.

But the torture of being required each year to learn again what they never learned and aren't going to remember once again this year is slow and unbearable. *Semicolon* becomes a dirty word. Like Mrs. Malaprop, they confuse *apostrophe* with *parenthesis* and *hypothesis* and *apotheosis*.

What should they do if they're sixteen or sixty and haven't learned the American conventional system for aiding readers in understanding the meaning of printed rather than spoken sentences? About the only chance they have is to study sentences in print and deduce for themselves the system. If they look to a textbook for rules, they will forget them again quickly and painfully.

If you're in this unhappy group of persons laden with guilt about commas and italics, begin observing. Construct generalizations which explain why certain mechanical conventions of print are used in the right-hand column of sentences below. For your convenience the left-hand column presents sentences naked and innocent of most punctuation or other signaling devices. Look at them first. Make your guess at what they need in the way of signals. Then study the signals printed in the right-hand column, which follow the normal conventions of writing published in most magazines or books. Note that they do not follow newspaper conventions, which are different from those of books.

DIALOGUE

Well, if we went to Raleigh we could get Mr. Isaacs Christmas candy. Before she could answer Mamas footsteps passed in the hall overhead so she said Don't you reckon we ought to stay closer-by than Raleigh? He turned to her. Look—are you sticking with me or not? She looked and said Yes. Let's go then. She scraped their dishes and left them in the sink and said I'll get my coat. Where from. My room. All right but come straight back.

"Well, if we went to Raleigh, we could get Mr. Isaac's Christmas candy."

Before she could answer, Mama's footsteps passed in the hall overhead so she said, "Don't you reckon we ought to stay closer-by than Raleigh?"

He turned to her. "Look—are you sticking with me or not?"

She looked and said "Yes."

"Let's go then."

She scraped their dishes and left them in the sink and said, "I'll get my coat."

"Where from?"

"My room."

"All right, but come straight back."

REYNOLDS PRICE

SEMICOLONS, COMMAS, PERIODS, DASHES, COLONS

Learn these marks in this order if you want to master punctuation quickly. The semicolon has only four or five major uses, the comma dozens. If you know a semicolon is not called for, you can bet wisely that what you need is a comma.

UNPUNCTUATED

1. Well I agree you could say the atom bomb doesn't go boom

CONVENTIONALLY PUNCTUATED

Well, I agree. You could say the atom bomb doesn't go boom;

it just obliterates a few hundred thousand people.

2. The world needs a little loosening of discipline and the schools need a little tightening of self-discipline.

3. He was no good for he had fallen apart at both the seams and the cuffs.

4. Renny a boy without guts was my enemy but Pedro a boy without guts was my friend.

5. I like Jackson Michigan Michigan City Indiana and Indianapolis Indiana.

6. It was a large city however I walked its streets without fear.

7. She was however a girl one could get along beautifully without.

8. Those days when Grandpa was a boy are long gone now the snows are deep and my Jaguar won't start.

9. In the last analysis Bertram doesn't measure up to the job.

10. Although a writer can lie about facts he should never lie about feelings.

11. When the moon comes over the woodshed behind the university library it feels out of place because Robert Frost is not there.

it just obliterates a few hundred thousand people.
(or):
Well, I agree you could say the atom bomb doesn't go boom. It just obliterates a few hundred thousand people.

The world needs a little loosening of discipline, and the schools need a little tightening of self-discipline.

He was no good, for he had fallen apart at both the seams and the cuffs.

Renny, a boy without guts, was my enemy; but Pedro, a boy without guts, was my friend.

I like Jackson, Michigan; Michigan City, Indiana; and Indianapolis, Indiana.

It was a large city; however I walked its streets without fear.
(or):
It was a large city; however, I walked its streets without fear.

She was, however, a girl one could get along beautifully without.

Those days when Grandpa was a boy are long gone; now the snows are deep and my Jaguar won't start.

In the last analysis, Bertram doesn't measure up to the job.
(or):
In the last analysis Bertram doesn't measure up to the job.

Although a writer can lie about facts, he should never lie about feelings.

When the moon comes over the woodshed behind the university library, it feels out of place because Robert Frost is not there.

What a sight it is, to see Writers committed together by the eares, for Cere-
monies, Syllables, Points, Colons, Com-

*ma's, Hyphens, and the like? fighting,
as for their fires, and their Altars; and
angry that none are frightened at their
noyses, and loud brayings under their
asses skins?*

BEN JONSON

12. I liked working there in the city next to the subway with its rattle its earth jar its grimy dirt that settled in the whorls of the ear and transferred itself from my sweating neck to my white collar by nine each morning.

I liked working there in the city next to the subway with its rattle, its earth jar, its grimy dirt that settled in the whorls of the ear and transferred itself from my sweating neck to my white collar by nine each morning.
(or):
I like working there in the city next to the subway—with its rattle, its earth jar . . .

13. She is sweet notwithstanding her sour tongue and pretty as cottage cheese.

She is sweet, notwithstanding her sour tongue, and pretty as cottage cheese.

14. I always found Archie that sad bag of a man worth his weight in tin.

I always found Archie—that sad bag of a man—worth his weight in tin.

15. We walked across the square a place deserted by everyone but the familiar urchins who were dipping their feet in the fountain as if it were a cold day in February.

We walked across the square— a place deserted by everyone but the familiar urchins, who were dipping their feet in the fountain—as if it were a cold day in February.

16. She was a beautiful plump hen of a woman whose legs were properly pipe-stems ending with gigantic feet and I loved her clucking and pecking her squawking and fluttering.

She was a beautiful plump hen of a woman whose legs were properly pipe-stems ending with gigantic feet; and I loved her clucking and pecking, her squawking and fluttering.

17. The Alsatians were losing the Martian war quickly they had no missiles or orbiting vehicles.

The Alsatians were losing the Martian war quickly; they had no missiles or orbiting vehicles.
(or):
The Alsatians were losing the Martian war quickly: they had no missiles or orbiting vehicles.

18. The General Velocipedes car was a beauty stinking heater buckling back wheels and valves that needed regrinding after a turn around the block.

The General Velocipedes car was a beauty: stinking heater, buckling back wheels, and valves that needed regrinding after a turn around the block.

SIGNALS FOR EMPHASIS

Conventionally, book and magazine writers and editors emphasize words with italics and quotation marks. When they use a word as an example of a word rather than as a regular part of a sentence, they usually put it in italics, which are indicated in handwriting or type-script by a single underline. (A double underline indicates small capitals; triple underline, capitals.)

19. The use of and is more difficult than most beginning writers realize.	The use of *and* is more difficult than most beginning writers realize.
20. Phrases like in terms of and with respect to can kill off an otherwise good speech.	Phrases like "in terms of" and "with respect to" can kill off an otherwise good speech.

More often than not, the words *say, call, refer to as* are followed by quoted words.

21. Those are what Mr. Wick calls "critical elements."

Frightened by Mrs. Clutched, their old third-grade teacher, many beginning writers use quotation marks around any word that would seem unusual in the sterile air of Mrs. Clutched's classroom. They say:

We had a "bunch" of good pitchers on our team and they used to "bug" each other constantly.

Nothing looks more square to an experienced editor or reader than this overuse of quotation marks. It implies either that the writer is a phony and won't admit that the words he's quoting belong in his vo-cabulary, or that the words *bunch* and *bug* are absolutely new to his readers in the use he has put them to. If they are slang, he should decide whether or not he wants to employ slang. If it is inappropriate to the subject and situation, he should not use it. If it is customarily set in italics—and there you can see the principle behind italics and quotation marks: to help the reader when he needs help, to inform him of what he is not apt to see on his own when he is reading in a healthy state of perception—then he should use italics or quotation marks.

NUMERALS

Unless numerals are being used in an article or book constantly, the professional writer conventionally writes in words those numbers that can be written in two words or one, and all others in numerals. He never begins a sentence with a numeral; for without an opening capital letter, a sentence looks as if it is part of the preceding sentence.

22. We counted twenty-four eggs within one hundred feet but there were 142 in the whole area.

If a sentence requires a number like 136 (written in numerals because it cannot be written in two words) and several other numbers, they are all written in numerals, for the sake of consistency:

23. ALWAYS: Three thousand and eighty-four men were ready; they each had 136 ounces of food, 32 feet of rope, 2 cans of suppressed napalm, and 12 rounds of ammunition.

NEVER: In the cages were rabbits in groups of 4, 3, and 6. 7 of them were kept in the barn in a larger enclosure, and 413 in all the buildings combined.

TITLES

Quotation marks are not used around words that appear above a piece of writing as its title. That would be like writing,

My name is "John."

Exception: When the title consists of, or in part of, words borrowed from another source, those borrowed words may be enclosed in quotation marks. Even then, if the borrowed word or phrase is well-known, it need not be quoted:

To Be or Not to Be a Ham

Writers citing names of other published works are careful to follow a consistent signaling system. Usually they *italicize* (or *underline*) names of whole works—a novel, history, encyclopedia, anthology, play, magazine, newspaper. They *put in quotation marks* smaller parts of those whole works: a chapter, article, poem, newspaper report (its title is its headline).

24. Jerry Kobrins Why Gleason Got the Headlines is another star-centered article in TV Guide but Up at Yale by Neil Hickey seriously looks at what college students are writing that could raise the level of television drama.

Jerry Kobrin's "Why Gleason Got the Headlines" is another star-centered article in *TV Guide*, but "Up at Yale" by Neil Hickey seriously looks at what college students are writing that could raise the level of television drama.

25. The Old which is the first chapter of Renfrew's latest book The Gnu and the Auld is a masterpiece of humor.

"The Old," which is the first chapter of Renfrew's latest book, *The Gnu and the Auld,* is a masterpiece of humor.

SIGNALING POSSESSION

The apostrophe to signal possession is the hardest conventional sign to remember because it is slowly fading away in use. In formal names printed in capital letters, it is no longer used:

VETERANS ADMINISTRATION.

In the days before dictionaries began to establish conventions firmly (Dr. Samuel Johnson's *Dictionary* of 1755 solidified spelling and other writing conventions in England, and Noah Webster's *Dictionary* of 1828 did the same in America), writers often used the apostrophe to indicate plurals, as did Ben Jonson in 1640 in the line quoted in this chapter:

... Points, Colons, Comma's

(Capital letters were conventionally used in England and American then for most major nouns in a sentence), and in Chaucer's day (1400), possession was signaled by an *-es* ending on words:

As dide Demociones doghter deere . . .
That lordes doghtres han in governaunce . . .

Chaucer used no apostrophes for possession, although here the daughters in both lines belong to the fathers mentioned. Writing about two hundred years later, Shakespeare commonly used an *-s* ending to signal possession, but still without an apostrophe:

It was a Lordings daughter, the fairest one of three . . .
A womans nay doth stand for nought . . .

Conventions in publishing change like conventions in ladies' dresses but not as fast. At the moment, most printed books and magazines in the United States are employing the apostrophe to signal possession, even though it is no more necessary in most instances than in Shakespeare's day.

26. I got my moneys worth when all the ladies cakes were left in my car.

I got my money's worth when all the ladies' cakes were left in my car.

27. A womans nay doth stand for nought.

A woman's nay doth stand for nought.

28. Jamess trouble was not the Worthingtons trouble.

James's trouble was not the Worthingtons' trouble.

SCHOLARLY WRITING

Two common miswritings in scholarly work are the abbreviation for *page* or *pages* and the signal for paragraph indention.

WRONG: pg (pgs)   RIGHT: p. (pp.)

P   ¶

Pg. may be some lazy person's abbreviation for *pig*, but it is not the conventional abbreviation for *page*. Understandably persons make the sign of a double-stemmed capital P to indicate *paragraph*, but the proper sign has nothing to do with the letter P. It is a sign used in illuminated manuscripts before 1440, then without such long stems, and still in use today.

Footnotes are a pain to writers, readers, editors, and printers; but some scholarly tasks require them so that scholar-readers may trace easily the steps through which a writer made his case. Like all conventions, footnotes are being constantly changed in form, usually in the direction of simplicity.

In footnotes, *Ibid.* means "the same as above." The following set of footnotes reveals a standard pattern. Why do some *Ibid.* entries include page numbers and some not?

1 Fred M. Oliver, *Love Problems of High School* (New York, 1939), pp. 33-34.
2 *Ibid.*
3 *Ibid.*, p. 101.
4 Karl Heimson, "The Courting Pattern," *New Ways in Education* (Englewood Cliffs, Texas, 1956), p. 555.
5 Oliver, p. 101.
6 Heimson, p. 420.
7 *Ibid.*, pp. 419-425.
8 William G. Looney and James Brass Smith, editors, *Thinking and Talking* (New York, 1965), p. 13.
9 George Walker, "Sex," *The Teacher's Magazine*, vol. 14 (June, 1967), pp. 13-14.

Text of paper employing above footnotes:

> Fred M. Oliver, psychologist at Nendy High School, Oak Pond, New York, cites the informal conversation of students. Jane, a senior, says "I'm mad for you, John," meaning in the new dialect of her group that she has decided to take John's part in his quarrel with his girl friend Susan.[1] This new game, played at several high schools in the area,[2] represents a clever playing with words—taking old slang or in-group expressions and giving them their literal rather than traditional meaning. "Cool it" to these students means to open the windows or turn down the thermostat.[3]
>
> Conventional students in a Kansas high school do just the opposite. They develop a new language for love and dating which consists of giving new double meanings to the

commonest expressions, like "Wash the linoleum" or "Is it cold out?"[4]

Oliver[5] and Heimson,[6] however, both state explicitly that they admire high school students' ability to invent new language. Heimson presents six pages of new expressions created by students in a high school of only one-hundred students.[7] Thirteen out of the twenty-five articles in a recent anthology on language center on the speech of American teenagers.[8] Parallels with these American developments have been found in Hungary by George Walker.[9]

This passage is footnoted in conventional form, but it is ridiculously overfootnoted. The reader couldn't stand that many footnotes in that short a space. The writer of these paragraphs is so overwhelmed by his sources that he has lost command of his own expression and line of development. If you are required to use footnotes, reserve them for documenting ideas or facts either so unusual and controversial or so detailed that they need to be credited to a writer. Footnote what readers are likely to want to check further.

A list of books, which occurs at the end of a paper, an article, a chapter, or a book, usually contains fuller information about the books: the publisher, number of volumes in a set, etc. In footnotes, names of authors are arranged in normal order: first name first. In a bibliography, they are arranged last name first, so that the order of the books in the list will be useful, easy to consult because arranged by author's last names alphabetically:

BIBLIOGRAPHY

1. Heimson, Karl. "The Courting Pattern," *New Ways in Education* (Englewood Cliffs, Texas, Pinetree Press, 1956), 158 pp.

The "158 pp." indicates that the volume contains 158 numbered pages, a way to show the reader how extensive the book is.

BIBLIOGRAPHY

2. Looney, William G. and James Brass Smith, editors, *Thinking and Talking* (New York, Mouth Press, 1965), 450 pp.
3. Oliver, Fred M. *Love Problems of High School* (New York, Kissinger Co., 1939), 413 pp.

In short papers documenting notes make more sense at the end of the paper than as footnotes at the foot of each page. Footnotes are hard to type at the bottom of the page—the writer can't gauge how much room he needs. And they are hard to set in type—the printer can't gauge the room either, and he must shift to smaller type as well. An intelligent alternative to footnotes used frequently in scientific publications employs parenthetical references: (2: 33-34), which means that the book referred to is number 2 in the bibliography and the references are to pages 33 and 34 in it. Part of the above text would then be written this way, referring to the piece of bibliography given above, which would be printed at the end of the paper or article. The paper would contain no footnotes:

> This new game, played at several high schools in the area (2: 33-34), represents a clever playing with words—taking old slang or in-group expressions and giving them their literal rather than traditional meaning. "Cool it" to these students means to open the window or turn down the thermostat (3: 101):

The wise writer and editor adopt a pattern of documentation of sources that fits the purposes of the writer and, as much as possible, of the reader. If the place of publication and publisher are not apt to be significant to the reader, the writer omits them from footnotes and supplies them only in bibliography. Almost always he gives page references and dates of publication because they are useful to the reader in locating material and in assessing the up-to-dateness of assertions and facts. All conventions need the help of common sense: the man who speaks outside in February with his head bare in order to observe a convention may find others soon observing his funeral.

Here are a few more models of conventional footnotes: For a book:

[1] George M. George. *The Georgeness of the World* (New York, George Book Company, 1918), pp. 33-34.

For a magazine:

[2] Margaret Mead, "Trends in Personal Life," *The New Republic* (September 23, 1946), 115: 348.

For a newspaper article:

[3] "College Dating Changes Pattern," *The New York Recorder*, June 2, 1952, p. 13.
[4] George Kriver, "Bronx Hospital Planned," *The Bronx Bomber*, June 3, 1967, p. 1.

For a government document:

[5] *Dating Problems in Urban High Schools*, United States Health Service Publication 1090 (Washington, 1953), p. 7.

For an encyclopedia:

[6] "Harvard University," *The Encyclopedia Britannica*, 14th edition.

For an excerpt from a book not read in the original but seen reproduced in part in another book:

7 Francis E. Merrill, *Courtship and Marriage* (New York, 1949), in Edwin R. Clapp and others, eds., *The College Quad* (New York, 1951), p. 74.

For a personal interview or conversation arranged by the author:

8 Interview with John Rogers, Dean of Men, Northside High School, Chicago, Illinois, April 4, 1967.

BORROWING WORDS

Conventionally the professional writer commands his words and those of others, but he never implies he owns the words of others. He inserts borrowed words naturally into his own sentences.

Wasting Borrowed Words:	*Commanding Borrowed Words*:
His dearest relative described him as "He was a great guy, full of fun, but gentle."	His dearest relative described him as "a great guy, full of fun, but gentle."

The professional writer does not refer to a statement he is quoting as a *quote*, for he is doing the quoting, not the author. He calls the statement a *statement*, an *assertion*, an *argument*, etc. He remembers that quotes do not speak, only persons.

For example, one quote states: "The Undersecretary rejected the budget proposals of the whole Council."	For example, an unidentified London *Times* reporter states that "The Undersecretary rejected the budget proposals of the whole Council."

The professional writer remembers that in conversation he must say "I quote" but in writing he indicates this act by quotation marks.

War Magazine says, and I quote, "Wretches strew the beaches in a lovely pattern."	*War Magazine* says, "Wretches strew the beaches in a lovely pattern."

If you respect your writing, learn the craft and learn the conventional systems of signaling meaning to the reader. But do not use these signals as a substitute for the order and clarity you must achieve with words. If you want the reader to become excited, you must write excitingly. You cannot force excitement by putting three exclamation marks at the end of your sentence! ! !

List of Sources

Page

1 Robert Morley, on the Jack Paar show NBC-TV, February 12, 1965.

1 Quoted in Clara M. Siggins, "Then It Got Buggles," *College Composition and Communication* (February, 1962), p. 56.

4 Friedrich Nietzsche, *Beyond Good and Evil* (Chicago, Regnery, Gateway Edition, 1955), p. 77.

5 John Donne, "Satire III," *Poetry of the English Renaissance* (New York, F. S. Crofts, 1929), p. 482.

5 Eudora Welty, *Delta Wedding* (New York, New American Library, Signet Edition, 1963), p. 220.

5 Eudora Welty, quoted by Reynolds Price, "A Kind of Valedictory," *The Archive,* Duke University (April, 1955), p. 2.

6 Peter Ernani, "What I'd Like to Be," *Portola Portals* (n.d.) submitted by Mrs. Nancy Wakefield.

8 Samuel Butler, *Works* (London, Jonathan Cape, 1923–26), XVIII, 210.

12 Wallace Stevens, "Adagia," *Opus Posthumous* (New York, Alfred A. Knopf, 1957), p. 158.

13 Alfred North Whitehead, quoted in *The Practical Cogitator,* edited by Charles P. Curtis, Jr., and Ferris Greenslet (Boston, Houghton Mifflin, 1953), p. 40.

14 E. M. Forster, *Aspects of the Novel* (New York, Harcourt, Brace, 1927), p. 197.

15 Henry Moore, "The Painter's Object," *The Creative Process,* edited by Brewster Ghiselin (New York, New American Library, Mentor Edition, 1955), p. 77.

16 Alfred Kazin, "The Language of Pundits," *Atlantic Monthly* (July, 1961), pp. 73–74.

16 Philip Booth, "First Lesson," *Letter from a Distant Land* (New York, Viking, 1957).

17 Wallace Stevens, "Adagia," *Opus Posthumous* (New York, Alfred A. Knopf, 1957), p. 162.

19 Anne Haven Morgan, *The Field Book of Ponds and Streams* (New York, G. P. Putnam's Sons, 1930), p. 199.

20 John Ciardi, "Work Habits of Writers," *On Writing, by Writers,* edited by William W. West (Boston, Ginn, 1966), p. 153.

21 Irma S. Rombauer and Marion Rombauer Becker, *The Joy of Cooking* (Indianapolis, Bobbs-Merrill, 1953), p. 451.

21 Joyce Macrorie, Trip Directions.

22 *Draftee's Confidential Guide,* pp. 9, 34–35.

24 Sidney Cox, *Indirections* (New York, Viking, Compass Books, 1962), p. 130.

25 William Hazlitt, "On the Familiar Style," *The Hazlitt Sampler* (New York, Fawcett World Library, 1961), p. 228.

Page

25 Benjamin Franklin, quoted in Carl Becker, *The Declaration of Independence* (New York, Alfred A. Knopf, Vintage Books, 1958), pp. 208–209.

27 Wallace Stevens, "Adagia," *Opus Posthumous* (New York, Alfred A. Knopf, 1957), p. 169.

31 Samuel Butler, *The Note-Books* (London, Jonathan Cape, 1926), p. 97.

32 Sir William Osler, "Teacher and Student," *Aequanimitas* (New York, Blakiston, 1932), p. 38.

35 Ray Bradbury, "Seeds of Three Stories," *On Writing, by Writers,* edited by William W. West (Boston, Ginn, 1966), p. 48.

37 John Ciardi, "Manner of Speaking," *Saturday Review* (July 2, 1966), p. 6.

38 P. W. Bridgman, *The Way Things Are* (New York, Viking, Compass Books, 1961), p. 213.

41 Eileen Crimmin, "Bernie Little and His Little Four-Seater," *Hot Boat* (Spring, 1966), p. 31.

44 Henry David Thoreau, *Walden and Other Writings* (New York, The Modern Library, 1937), p. 86.

46 Henry David Thoreau, *Ibid.,* p. 47.

47 Jack London, *People of the Abyss* (New York, Harcourt, Brace, 1946), p. 213.

48 Wallace Stevens, "Adagia," *Opus Posthumous* (New York, Alfred A. Knopf, 1957), p. 175.

49 Ralph Waldo Emerson, "Thoreau," *Lectures and Biographies* (Boston, Houghton Mifflin, 1893), p. 362.

49 James Thurber, "A New Natural History," *The Beast in Me and Other Animals* (New York, Harcourt, Brace, 1948), pp. 151–168.

50 Henry David Thoreau, *Walden and Other Writings* (New York, The Modern Library, 1937), p. 88.

51 Thomas Henry Huxley, To Charles Kingsley, September 23, 1860, in Leonard Huxley, *Life and Letters of Huxley* (New York, D. Appleton, 1901), I, 235.

52 Michihiko, Hachiya, *Hiroshima Diary* (Chapel Hill, University of North Carolina Press, 1955), pp. 11, 91–92.

55 Wallace Stevens, "Adagia," *Opus Posthumous* (New York, Alfred A. Knopf, 1957), p. 179.

58 Stuart Chase, "Writing Nonfiction," *On Writing, by Writers,* edited by William W. West (Boston, Ginn, 1966), p. 327.

62 Dr. Seuss, *Horton Hatches the Egg* (New York, Random House, 1940), n. p.

62 Thomas Paine, "The American Crisis," *The Complete Writings,* edited by Philip S. Foner (New York, The Citadel Press, 1945), p. 55.

62 William Shakespeare, *Macbeth* (New York, New American Library, 1963), IV, iii., p. 105.

65 Lilian Moore, *A Pickle for a Nickel* (New York, The Golden Press, 1961), p. 22.

67 Longchamps advertisement, *New York Times,* May 25, 1966, p. 29.

67 Ralph Waldo Emerson, "The American Scholar," *The Complete Essays and Other Writings,* edited by Brooks Atkinson (New York, The Modern Library, 1950), p. 47.

Page

68 James Baldwin, *The Fire Next Time* (New York, Dell, 1964), pp. 14–15.

68 N. H. and S. K. Mager, editors, *The Pocket Household Encyclopedia* (New York, Pocket Books, 1953), p. 168.

68 Irma S. Rombauer and Marion Rombauer Becker, *The Joy of Cooking* (Indianapolis, Bobbs-Merrill, 1953), p. 313.

68 Ralph Waldo Emerson, "Self-Reliance," *The Complete Essays and Other Writings,* edited by Brooks Atkinson (New York, The Modern Library, 1950), p. 152.

69 William Wordsworth, "The Prelude," *Complete Poetical Works* (Boston, Houghton Mifflin, 1904), p. 156.

69 Mark Twain, *Huckleberry Finn* (Boston, Houghton Mifflin, 1958), p. 42.

70 J. D. Salinger, *The Catcher in the Rye* (New York, New American Library, 1953), p. 144.

70 May Swenson, *To Mix with Time* (New York, Charles Scribner's Sons, 1963), pp. 86–87.

72 Sidney Cox, *Indirections* (New York, Viking, 1962), p. 6.

78 Truman Capote interviewed by Pati Hill, *Writers at Work: The Paris Review Interviews,* First Series (New York, Viking, 1964), pp. 294–295, 296–297.

80 Anton Chekhov, "My Life," and "In the Ravine," *Ward Six and Other Stories* (New York, New American Library, Signet Books, 1965), pp. 219, 339.

80 Reynolds Price, "The Warrior Princess Ozimba," in "A Story and Why," *Duke Alumni Register* (April, 1963), p. 33.

83 Samuel Butler, *The Note-Books* (London, Jonathan Cape, 1926), pp. 137–138.

84 George Bernard Shaw, "Who I Am, and What I Think," *Selected Non-Dramatic Writings,* edited by Dan H. Laurence (Boston, Houghton Mifflin, 1965), p. 449.

84 Samuel Butler, *The Note-Books* (London, Jonathan Cape, 1926), p. 106.

87 T. S. Eliot interviewed by Donald Hall, *Writers at Work: The Paris Review Interviews,* Second Series (New York, Viking, 1965), p. 96.

88 Marianne Moore interviewed by Donald Hall, *Ibid.,* p. 82.

89 Bernard Shaw, in *Ellen Terry and Bernard Shaw: A Correspondence,* edited by Christopher St John (New York, The Fountain Press, 1931), pp. 113–114.

97 Ralph Waldo Emerson, "Self-Reliance," *The Complete Essays and Other Writings,* edited by Brooks Atkinson (New York, The Modern Library, 1950), p. 165.

99 David Daiches, *A Study of Literature* (Ithaca, Cornell University Press, 1948), p. 3.

100 William Stafford, "Writing the Australian Crawl," *College Composition and Communication* (February, 1964), pp. 15, 12.

101 Ralph Waldo Emerson, "Nature," *The Complete Essays and Other Writings,* edited by Brooks Atkinson (New York, The Modern Library, 1950), p. 17.

112 Kenneth Clark, "The Value of Art in an Expanding World," *Hudson Review* (Spring, 1966), p. 23.

112 Samuel Butler, quoted in Henry Festing Jones, *Samuel Butler* (London, Macmillan, 1920), II, 294–295.

Page

114 Ezra Pound, *ABC of Reading* (New York. New Directions, 1960), p. 62.

116 James Thurber interviewed by George Plimpton and Max Steele, *Writers at Work: The Paris Review Interviews* (New York, Viking, 1959), p. 87.

117 Eudora Welty, "Must the Novelist Crusade?" *Atlantic Monthly* (October, 1965), p. 106.

119 Wallace Stevens, "Adagia," *Opus Posthumous* (New York, Alfred A. Knopf, 1957), p. 170.

120 W. Nelson Francis, "Pressure from Below," *College Composition and Communication* (October, 1964), pp. 147–148.

122 " 's' Vonderful," *The New Republic* (August 27, 1966), p. 7.

124 Henry David Thoreau, *Walden and Other Writings* (New York, The Modern Library, 1937), p. 288.

124 William Hazlitt, *The Spirit of the Age* (London, Oxford University Press, 1935), p. 13.

124 Anne Haven Morgan, *The Field Book of Ponds and Streams* (New York, G. P. Putnam's Sons, 1930), p. 388.

125 Sharon Butler, in "The Bicycle Spoke," *The Western Review,* Western Michigan University (January 24, 1966), p. 2.

125 E. E. Cummings, "XIV," *Poems, 1923–1954* (New York, Harcourt, Brace and World, 1954), p. 397.

126 Joseph Conrad, preface to *The Nigger of the "Narcissus"* in *Three Great Tales* (New York, Alfred A. Knopf, Vintage Books, n.d.), p. ix.

127 Lewis Carroll, *Through the Looking Glass* (New York, Random House, 1946), pp. 92–93.

127–128 *Ibid.,* p. 18.

128 Samuel Butler, *The Way of All Flesh* (New York, The Modern Library, 1950), p. 200.

128 Lewis Carroll, *Through the Looking Glass* (New York, Random House, 1946), pp. 64–65.

130 Ralph Waldo Emerson, "Nature," *The Complete Essays and Other Writings,* edited by Brooks Atkinson (New York, The Modern Library, 1950), p. 412.

130 A. A. Milne, "The End," *Now We Are Six* (New York, E. P. Dutton, 1955), p. 104.

131 George Herbert Mead, *Mind, Self, and Society* (Chicago, The University of Chicago Press, 1934), p. 151.

137 John Brown, quoted in *Incident at Harper's Ferry,* edited by Edward Stone (Englewood Cliffs, N. J., Prentice-Hall, 1956), p. 149.

139 Harold Lasswell, source unknown.

139 Henry David Thoreau, *A Week on the Concord and Merrimack Rivers* (New York, Holt, Rinehart, and Winston, 1963), p. 85.

140 Norman Mailer, *Presidential Papers* (New York, Bantam Books, 1964), p. 47.

141 James Joyce, *Ulysses* (New York, The Modern Library, 1946), p. 172.

142 George Herbert Mead, *Mind, Self, and Society* (Chicago, The University of Chicago Press, 1934), p. 147.

143 *Car and Driver* (September, 1966), p. 30.

144 Ezra Pound, *The ABC of Reading* (New York, New Directions, 1960), p. 60.

Page

145 Ben Jonson, *Timber, or Discoveries,* in *English Prose, 1600–1660,* edited by Victor Harris and Itrat Husain (New York, Holt, Rinehart and Winston, 1965), p. 352.

146 Kato Shuson, in *Anthology of Japanese Literature,* edited by Donald Keene (New York, Grove Press, 1955), p. 382.

147 Marianne Moore, interviewed by Donald Hall, *Writers at Work: The Paris Review Interviews,* Second Series (New York, Viking, 1963), p. 79.

148 McCandlish Phillips, "There's Never a Quiet Moment on W. 15th St.," *The New York Times* (May 14, 1966), p. 33.

151 Ring Lardner, source unknown.

151 Henry Vaughan, "The World," *Poetry of the English Renaissance, 1509–1660,* edited by J. William Hebel and Hoyt H. Hudson (New York, F. S. Crofts, 1938), p. 799.

152 Reynolds Price, *A Long and Happy Life* (New York, Avon Books, 1963), p. 120.

153 William Shakespeare, *Henry IV, Part 1* (New York, Washington Square Press, 1961), II, ii.

154 *Ibid.,* I, ii.

154 Henry David Thoreau, *Walden and Other Writings* (New York, The Modern Library, 1937), p. 123.

155 Lewis Carroll, *Through the Looking Glass* (New York, Random House, 1946), p. 29.

156 *The Heart of Emerson's Journals,* edited by Bliss Perry (Boston, Houghton Mifflin, 1926), p. 333.

157 Henry David Thoreau, *Journals* (Boston, Houghton Mifflin, 1906), IX, 158–160.

158 Samuel Butler, *The Note-Books* (London, Jonathan Cape, 1926), p. 97.

159 Dorothy Lambert, "What Is A Journal?" see p. v.

162 Samuel Butler, *The Note-Books* (London, Jonathan Cape, 1926), pp. 231–232.

166 Robert Louis Stevenson, "A College Magazine," *Works* (New York, Charles Scribner's Sons, 1903), vol. 13, pp. 211–215.

168 *Benjamin Franklin,* edited by Chester E. Jorgenson and Frank Luther Mott (New York, Hill and Wang, 1962), p. 14.

169 Henry David Thoreau, *A Week on the Concord and Merrimack Rivers,* edited by Walter Harding (New York, Holt, Rinehart and Winston, 1963), p. 106.

169 Henry David Thoreau, "Walking," *Walden and Other Writings* (New York, The Modern Library, 1937), p. 622.

171 Ben Jonson, *Timber, or Discoveries,* in *English Prose, 1600–1660,* edited by Victor Harris and Itrat Husain (New York, Holt, Rinehart and Winston, 1965), p. 330.

171 Mary McCarthy, "General Macbeth," in *Macbeth,* edited by Sylvan Barnet (New York, The New American Library, Signet Edition, 1963), p. 229.

171 John Holt, *New York Review of Books* (April 14, 1966), p. 8.

172 William Hazlitt, *The Spirit of the Age* (London, Oxford University Press, 1904), p. 124.

172 George Bernard Shaw, *The Quintessence of Ibsenism* (London, Constable, 1926), p. 40.

Page

174 A. A. Milne, *The House at Pooh Corner* (New York, E. P. Dutton, 1928), p. 96.

177 Lewis Carroll, *Alice in Wonderland* (New York, Random House, 1946), pp. 140–141.

179 Edmund Wilson, "It's Terrible! It's Ghastly! It Stinks!" *A Literary Chronicle: 1920–1950* (New York, Doubleday Anchor Books, 1952), p. 209.

180 Truman Capote, *In Cold Blood* (New York, The New American Library, Signet Edition, 1965), p. 113.

184 Ray Bradbury, "Seeds of Three Stories," *On Writing, by Writers,* edited by William W. West (Boston, Ginn, 1966), p. 49.

184 Lois Phillips Hudson, "When the Fields Are Fresh and Green," *Reapers of the Dust* (Boston, Little, Brown, 1964), pp. 87–97.

194 Sidney Cox, *Indirections* (New York, Viking, 1962), p. 132.

196 Oscar Wilde, *A Woman of No Importance,* quoted in *The Wit and Humor of Oscar Wilde,* edited by Alvin Redman (New York, Dover, 1952), p. 33.

197 James Agee, *A Death in the Family* (New York, McDowell Obolensky, 1957), p. 3.

198 Karl Shapiro and Robert Beum, *A Prosody Handbook* (New York, Harper & Row, 1965), pp. 14–15.

199 John Donne, "Devotion No. 17," *English Prose, 1600–1660,* edited by Victor Harris and Itrat Husain (New York, Holt, Rinehart and Winston, 1965), p. 274.

200 Ralph Waldo Emerson, "Self-Reliance," *The Complete Essays and Other Writings,* edited by Brooks Atkinson (New York, The Modern Library, 1950), p. 165.

203 Mark Twain, *Huckleberry Finn* (New York, Houghton Mifflin, 1958), p. 4.

204 William Carlos Williams, "The Dance," *The Collected Later Poems* (New York, New Directions, 1950), p. 11.

204 William Carlos Williams, "Poem," *The Collected Earlier Poems* (New York, New Directions, 1951), p. 340.

206 Wallace Stevens, "Adagia," *Opus Posthumous* (New York, Alfred A. Knopf, 1957), p. 176.

207 Sidney Cox, *Indirections* (New York, Viking, 1962), p. 31.

209 Gerhart Wiebe, "Mass Communications," in Eugene and Ruth Hartley, *Fundamentals of Social Psychology* (New York, Alfred A. Knopf, 1952), p. 179.

209 Ernest Hemingway interviewed by George Plimpton, *Writers at Work: The Paris Review Interviews* (New York, Viking, 1965), p. 235.

217 "TRB from Washington," *The New Republic* (July 30, 1966).

222 Pete Cooper, "Long Hair Warms the Head," *The Torch,* Rich Township High School Central Campus, Park Forest, Illinois (February 11, 1966), p. 3.

223 Sidney Cox, *Indirections* (New York, Viking, 1962), p. 131.

225 E. M. Forster, "What I Believe," in *Ten Contemporary Thinkers,* edited by Victor Amend and Leo Hendrick (New York, The Free Press, 1964), p. 101.

225 Archibald MacLeish, "The Conquest of America," *Ibid.,* p. 201.

Page

226 Lois Berg, "Old Creepy Death," *Western Review,* Western Michigan University (November 22, 1965), p. 2.

228 Mark Twain, *Huckleberry Finn* (New York, Houghton Mifflin, 1958), pp. 85–88.

233 Kathy Currier, "Triolet," *Aurora 66,* Portage Northern High School, Portage, Michigan, p. 23.

235 Horace, *The Art of Poetry* in *The Complete Works,* edited by Casper J. Kraemer, Jr. (New York, The Modern Library, 1936), p. 401.

236 Henry David Thoreau, *Walden and Other Writings* (New York, The Modern Library, 1937), pp. 84–85.

237 Julie Beach, "Driving's a Dilemma," *The Lakeview Crystal,* Lakeview High School, Battle Creek, Michigan (February 4, 1966), p. 4.

240 Horace, *The Art of Poetry* in *The Complete Works,* edited by Casper J. Kraemer, Jr. (New York, The Modern Library, 1936), p. 398.

241 Lewis Carroll, *Through the Looking Glass* (New York, Random House, 1946), pp. 143–144.

242 Walter Lippmann, *Public Opinion* (New York, Macmillan, 1922), p. 87.

243 Walter Lippmann, *Ibid.,* p. 16.

244 Paul Goodman, *Growing Up Absurd* (New York, Random House, 1960), pp. 19–20.

245 Walter Lippmann, *Public Opinion* (New York, Macmillan, 1922), pp. 89–91.

246 Henry David Thoreau, *Walden and Other Writings* (New York, The Modern Library, 1937), p. 97.

247 Gabor Peterdi, *Printmaking* (New York, Macmillan, 1959), p. xxii.

248 J. D. Salinger, *Catcher in the Rye* (New York, New American Library, 1953), p. 157.

250 William Hazlitt, *The Spirit of the Age* (London, Oxford University Press, 1904), pp. 130-131.

253 Archibald MacLeish, "Poetry and the Press," in *Thought and Statement,* edited by William G. Leary and James Steel Smith (New York, Harcourt, Brace, 1960), p. 481.

253 Mark Twain, "The Evidence in the Case," *Ibid.,* p. 373.

253 Walter Lippmann, "Stereotypes," *Ibid.,* p. 221.

253 Ivan Turgenev, "A Fire at Sea," *Ibid.,* p. 25.

253 E. M. Forster, "Anonymity, An Inquiry," *Ibid.,* pp. 440–441.

253 E. B. White, "Walden," *Ibid.,* p. 39.

254 Ezra Pound, *The ABC of Reading* (New York, New Directions, 1960), p. 64.

254 William Hazlitt, *The Spirit of the Age* (London, Oxford University Press, 1904), p. 76.

256 George Eliot, *Middlemarch* (New York. Houghton Mifflin, 1956), p. 52.

257 Reynolds Price, *A Long and Happy Life* (New York, Avon Books, 1960), p. 121.

258 Ben Jonson, *Timber, or Discoveries,* in *English Prose, 1600–1660,* edited by Victor Harris and Itrat Husain (New York, Holt, Rinehart, and Winston, 1965), p. 330.

index